The Stakeholding Society

The Stakeholding Society

Writings on Politics and Economics

Will Hutton

Edited by David Goldblatt

Polity Press

First published in 1999 by Polity Press
in association with Blackwell Publishers Ltd.

Editorial office:
Polity Press
65 Bridge Street
Cambridge CB2 1UR, UK

Marketing and production:
Blackwell Publishers Ltd
108 Cowley Road
Oxford OX4 1JF, UK

Published in the USA by
Blackwell Publishers Inc.
Commerce Place
350 Main Street
Malden, MA 02148, USA

ISBN 0-7456-2078-7
ISBN 0-7456-2079-5 (pbk)

A catalogue record for this book is available from the British Library and has been applied for from the Library of Congress.

Typeset in 10 on 12 pt Garamond
by Ace Filmsetting Ltd, Frome, Somerset
Printed in Great Britain by T.J. International, Padstow, Cornwall

This book is printed on acid-free paper.

Contents

Editor's Note

Editing this book initially appeared to be an enormous and complex task, for Will Hutton has written on an astonishing range of ideas, issues and debates. Yet in the end, selection and ordering proved to be relatively simple tasks.

The structure of this collection reflects the different, cumulative elements of Will Hutton's political project – the creation and advocacy of a radical political economy that could both intellectually challenge the neo-liberal consensus and provide the fountainhead for a coherent policy package of progressive economic, political and social reform. This project crystallized in the publication of *The State We're In*, but its genesis and development were a decade in the making. The selection of articles within each section of this book reflects, I hope, the core arguments that Will Hutton has developed, as well as allowing space for some of the other thoughts, detours and intellectual skirmishes there have been on the way. Articles have been arranged primarily in order of publication, but where thematic or intellectual connections could be more clearly illuminated by disregarding this editorial principle, I have taken the liberty of doing so.

Angela Burton has been endlessly helpful and unflappable. As ever, the Polity people have been a pleasure to work with. Thanks are due to Petra Moll, Lynn Dunlop, Sue Pope, Julia Harsant and the indefatigable David Held.

David Goldblatt

Acknowledgements

The author and publishers are grateful to the following for permission to use copyrighted material:

The *Guardian* and the *Observer*

'Back by Popular Demand' reprinted with permission from *The American Prospect*, 16 (Winter) © 1994 The American Prospect, PO Box 383080, Cambridge, MA 021138. All rights reserved.

'Reviving Bretton Woods' from *New Economy*, vol. 1, no. 4 (Winter 1994).

Every effort has been made to trace the copyright holders, but if any have been inadvertently overlooked, the publishers will be pleased to make the necessary arrangements at the first opportunity.

Introduction

The quest for the good society and economy is ceaseless. Yet at the end of the twentieth century there are some who genuinely believe that the argument is over. In their view there can only be one answer. We must look to individualist market capitalism, and our social organization must accommodate that economic system by being organized around market individualism as well. They understand that people of conscience want to intervene to alleviate what appears to be the brutalism and inequity associated with capitalism, but the temptation must be resisted before the greater truth: markets work, if only allowed time and freedom. It is attempts to intervene in markets that produces alarming results: unemployment, under-investment, social exclusion and inequality. Nothing must be allowed to get in the way of free decisions by free agents in free markets. The task of a free society, in a democracy, is to protect market individualism.

It is these propositions that I have spent my journalistic and intellectual life contesting. I accept that the price mechanism is the best means we have to allocate goods and resources, and that the signals of profit and loss are the most compelling means we can devise to drive both the level and composition of output in ways that correspond to real demands. But I cannot accept that individualistic market capitalism, as configured in contemporary Britain, is unimprovable. Nor can I accept that the under-investment and inequality it throws up are only avoidable by allowing the market to work yet more fiercely.

Moreover, these economic structures feed back into our social structures, and enfeeble individual well-being and social cohesion. Few living in today's Britain would claim they are living in a good society. It may offer great riches for the few and a remarkable array of choice for those on average incomes, but the fellowship and common purpose which allow life's risks and hazards to be better borne – and which in part define a good society – are under assault and diminishing. As a result I dispute that the principal role of democracy is to underwrite market freedoms. Rather, democracy provides the vehicle for the constant remodelling of economy and society so that it meets our needs. There are choices about how we organize capitalism, and we can and should make them.

There are many explanations on offer for the way our market economy and society has developed, and to seek to explain so complex a phenomenon in terms of one overriding element is plainly wrong. Yet no explanation is complete without some reference to the astonishing growth of inequality. The widening gap between the incomes of the rich and poor has had explosive effects across our entire society, whether it is undermining the conception of public education or balkanizing our culture. It is obvious that the disastrous and growing pockets of social exclusion are at heart about inequality; but no less menacing to social well-being is the establishment of an opted-out overclass, uncommitted and disconnected from the aspirations and moral judgements of their fellow citizens. At the limit this threatens the viability of our democratic institutions by corroding the common value system that underpins any democracy. Most importantly, these inequalities undermine a readiness to accept obligations to the whole. The new rich are vocal in the assertion of their rights, but largely silent over their own obligations to the society of which they are part. They excuse tax avoidance, and pride themselves that their incomes are so high that they need have no dependence on the 'state'. In doing so they make the public institutions, which embody conceptions of common purpose and public interest, necessarily second-rate and, worse, derided as unnecessary, inefficient and increasingly defunct.

My argument is that these social and political ills are umbilically linked to the economic structures, institutions and policies of British capitalism, and that the attempt to impose a model of an individualistic free market in every nook and cranny of British life has been at the core of our problems. This seems such an obvious truth that it is hardly worth saying, but over the last twenty years it has defined those who reject the new market fundamentalism as dangerous, leftist wild men. Why? Because it runs directly counter to the prevailing and entrenched wisdom that market systems based around the individual choices of individual market actors must be allowed to rule because the results can only be beneficial. If there are problems like unemployment or inequality, either we must understand them as transitional difficulties which the market itself will solve, or as the price we must pay for the greater good of a well-functioning market.

The election of a Labour government in 1997 has done little to stem the tide. Labour would like less inequality, better public provision of health and education, higher private and public investment. But in conservative times, like their counterparts in the United States, they are unable to achieve these aims; partly from fright, partly from lack of intellectual support and partly from the absence of political pressure openly to will the means. The currents that have carried Britain, and indeed the western world, to their present pass are still running strongly from the right. We are asked to make obeisance at the shrine of deregulation, liberalism, privatization, low taxes and the minimal state. New Labour still feels it has to genuflect before these gods if it is to earn legitimacy. It has yet to establish its own values as forces for good in their own right.

There is of course force in some of these conservative arguments. Much state enterprise is overstaffed and unresponsive to consumer needs. How much this is due to policy decisions to use the state sector as an employer of last resort, and the indifference to the consumer that accompanies most monopolies, and how much it is due to the fact of public ownership, should be matters for discussion and analysis. In today's world there is little interest in such exploration. The ideological injunction is that public is bad and private is good, with results stretching from the international consensus over economic management, of which Britain is part, to the unwillingness to champion any form of public enterprise, whether the air traffic control system or the Post Office.

It is these doctrines that the columns and articles assembled here have attacked over the last fifteen years. It was working for six years as a stockbroker in the 1970s that left me sceptical about the great international conversion to the perfectibility of markets that took place over the 1980s and 1990s. Nobody who works closely in the financial markets can fail to notice their preoccupation with the near-term; how market actors bet on market trends continuing, so that upward and downward price movements become overexaggerated; the lack of countervailing speculation; their very human enthusiasms and fads; how imperfect the information is upon which major decisions are made and how self-interested the players are. It is obvious that such a system oscillates wildly, imposing sometimes impossibly sudden and large costs of adjustment upon the economic and social organizations whose market valuations change so quickly. If you could, you would want to slow down the pace, build in some contra-cyclical components and set rules of market engagement in which some of these costs were imposed upon the market actors themselves. One could do all of this while continuing to recognize that markets are themselves great animators of economic progress. You can call such a philosophy Keynesian, social democratic or stakeholder – all labels I am happy to boast – but it is clearly at odds with the prevailing wisdom.

Yet even politicians sympathetic to these arguments are cautious about making the case. Their concern is that in the current climate, with a tax revolt that shows no sign of ending, suspicion over social security expenditure, distrust of government, together with the dominant power of footloose international business, it is difficult – if not impossible – to assemble a governing majority openly asserting the need for progressive taxation, higher spending on public goods, and new rules to restrain existing corporate freedoms. So successful has been the neo-conservative right that it has not only dominated the intellectual agenda, but it has also created powerful new economic and social forces and accompanying value systems that checkmate any attempt to launch a progressive politics. New Labour and the US Democrats are quintessential expressions of this new political economy. They are only able to hold the political centre by promising an end to 'tax and spend'. Middle-class voters can, they believe, only be persuaded to support a non-conservative party if it makes no challenge to their purse and places no inhibition on their economic and social freedom.

Thus the late 1990s present an intriguing political paradox. The right is in disarray. It no longer has an overriding enemy, either abroad in the form of communism, or at home in the form of social democratic corporatism, to unite it. It has won its key battles, but can find no answers to the current array of concerns that plainly worry the electorate but which are also consistent with the individualistic, pro-market ideology it has forged. The libertarian right is at odds with the One Nation right: they are both at a loss over how to marry market individualism and the conservation of the organic institutions of society hitherto a key element in conservative thought. Conservatism, pro tem, is a shattered credo.

But the left is also confronted with a conundrum. In the past it would have had internally coherent and ready-made programmes – however imperfect in practice – to address unemployment, inequality and falling social cohesion. They would have ranged from Keynesian demand-management and redistributive taxation to strengthening the welfare state and extending forms of public and social ownership. But now they face a dilemma. The Conservatives criticize such an approach because it is inflationary and weakens market incentives. This criticism is apparently borne out by experience; even the left would concede that by the 1970s such a programme was losing its effectiveness. The electoral constituency that supported it was weakening; the power of trade unions in manufacturing was dwindling before the rise of the service sector; and what union power remained was itself giving way to individualistic demands for local and customized pay-bargaining. A 'working class', with solid pro-socialist leanings, embedded in working-class organizations generating a comfortable electoral majority, which would support the old social democratic/socialist programme, was disappearing. Intellectual weakness, practical shortcomings and the fragmentation of their political base put the left everywhere on the defensive.

The Conservative programme has capitalized upon this defensiveness and made it impossible to recreate the old coalition. The privatization of utilities, the legal weakening of trade unions, and the rise of the service sector have meant that the great physical worksites employing tens of thousands of men, which were the great pillars of leftist solidarity, have disappeared and not been replaced. As importantly, the Conservatives have succeeded in creating a new public language in which choice and individual rights are seen as the overwhelmingly dominant values, rather than responsibility, mutuality of obligation and social duty. The left may now have gained power, but its old ideology and power base are emasculated. It faces a world hostile to its instinctive ethics. This collection of articles and essays represents my own efforts to analyse what is going on, and offers a way forward that is linked to the old liberal/social democratic consensus, yet is different from it. My values are those that informed my intellectual mentors – Keynes, Galbraith, Beveridge, Monnet and Berlin – but they need adaptation to new circumstances and challenges.

Part I, 'Enlivening the Dismal Science', collects articles attacking some of the core philosophical assumptions of orthodox economics, its depoliticized and abstract conception of markets, and their failure to measure in any meaningful sense real value and real worth. At the core of any potential opposition to the economic programme that has sprung from neo-liberal orthodoxy must be a reassessment of the meaning and enduring virtues of Keynes's work and his commitment to full employment and high output. The failures of deficit financing in the 1970s have unfortunately, and unfairly, tarnished Keynes's reputation. Part II, 'The Keynesian Revival', includes articles that seek to separate Keynes's own work and position from the policies executed in his name, but with little fidelity to his original vision. These articles continue to argue that the current orthodoxy of monetarist macroeconomics and 'free market' microeconomics is not enough: stimulating growth, investment, capacity and employment remains vital. As I have already argued, one of the main reasons for low levels of growth and investment in Britain is the peculiar institutions and values of our financial sector. Part III, 'London Babylon', includes pieces on the architecture of British financial power and interests, and the desperate need for better, more democratic, more open regulation. The key alternative to the finance-dominated economic value system of British capitalism is outlined in part IV, 'Ownership Matters'. The pieces here make the case for a stakeholding model of capitalism in Britain and includes articles that seek to defend this position from arguments of both left and right. I return to the fate of the stakeholder debate after the 1997 general election in the 'Afterword'. Two of the most problematic issues faced by anyone advocating a British model of stakeholding are international. On the one hand, how can a national model of capitalism survive an increasingly interconnected global economy, and what, in any case, is the meaning of British capitalism in the context of a single European market and EMU? In part V, 'Taming Mammon', the articles argue for a revival of the political will and courage needed for the reregulation of the international financial system, and the recognition that its effects are neither predictable nor benign. The 1997–8 economic crisis in the Far East bears this out more sharply than these pieces could envisage at the time. Part VI, 'European Dilemmas', collects articles on the key debates in Europe over the last decade. Closer to home, the enduring problems of social inequality, social exclusion and social fragmentation are addressed from two different angles. In part VII, 'The Political Economy of Penury', I have consistently argued that we are, as a nation, undertaxed and overgenerous to the wealthy, and that we all pay the price in terms of a fraying infrastructure and unsustainable deficits. This, combined with the transformation of Britain's labour markets, has I believe created profound splits and divisions in British society, whose fault lines do not correspond to those of an earlier era. In part VIII, 'An Age of Insecurity?', the pieces range across this new landscape of insecurity, fragmentation and concentrations of poverty and wealth. At least some of the elements of a proper response to this crisis are also discussed: for example a minimum wage, and investing in social capital. Another element of that response is to compare and contrast our own model of capitalism with those from abroad. While of course simple imitation of foreign models is unwise, there is much to be learnt in the process of comparison. In part IX, 'Lessons from Elsewhere', the articles cover the lessons to be learnt from East Asian success and failure, German economic stoicism and the ruthless dynamism of America. In part X, 'The State We're In', I address the uniqueness of British institutions – above all the political constitution and political culture of the United Kingdom. Finally in part XI, 'The Times they are Changing?', I have included some initial and provisional responses to the first year of New Labour as the difficult task of turning political power into a social and economic revival begins.

PART I
Enlivening the Dismal Science: The Limits to Economic Orthodoxy

New Economics Hits at Market Orthodoxy

A new economics is struggling to be born that promises to turn the world on its head. It will challenge the orthodoxies of Treasury and City; it will transcend the debate between interventionists and free marketeers; and it will rob the new right of its dominance of the economic and political agenda. With luck and a fair wind it could be the basis of economic regeneration and a renewed liberal consensus.

There are three interrelated themes that between them make free market truisms untenable, as one intellectual pioneer, Robert Lane of Yale University, describes it. They are: that economic man cannot be assumed to have perfect foresight; that the purpose of work is not to satisfy wants but is a basic source of human well-being; and that it is not true that as output expands, costs must necessarily at some stage rise. Put these ideas together and the intellectual foundation upon which the new right draws collapses; there is nothing left of the body of theory which gave us Thatcherism and the market revolution.

Typically, almost all the new thinking is going on in the US – and the conduits into British intellectual life are gummed up by a lethal combination of complacency and lack of curiosity. Yet it is this body of emerging theory, and the policy recommendations based on it, that is giving President Clinton an intellectual head of steam.

For the aim of the last generation of free market thinkers, notably Hayek and his followers, was less to build a robust view of what actually happens in a market economy than a model that could compete with Marxism. The aim was ideological and required all kinds of contortions to produce the desired result. As a source of inspiration in a battle of ideas which the West needed to win, it worked; but as a source of policy recommendations, millions have reason to curse the theory for the avoidable suffering exacted in its name.

For whether it is the scaling back of social security benefits to persuade rational economic men to search harder for work, or the removal of government support for high-technology industry, it has been the same body of theory standing behind the change. 'There is no alternative', gimlet-eyed trade, Treasury and social security ministers have intoned in turn. What they actually mean is that, given the implausible assumptions that govern their actions; no other course of action is open – a rather different statement.

The assumptions that drive the model are simple: that the purpose of economic activity is the maximization of money income; that all economic agents from workers to bankers are infinitely clever, capable of foreseeing all the contingencies and ramifications of what they do, and of choosing the best strategy to secure their ends; that each component of the economy necessarily experiences negative feedback – typically higher costs and prices as output expands – that prevents activity growing explosively and pulls the system to a point of balance. With these assumptions a free market will move to the best outcome for everyone – and foster individual freedom and responsibility, a property stressed by Hayek.

Thus if men and women work only to earn money then it follows that high social security benefits will deter them from gainful employment. If industry is subsidized then the natural forces that distribute resources between competing industries will be inhibited. Indeed if any obstacle, such as regulation, is placed in the way of infinitely clever economic actors arriving at necessarily the best outcomes then, necessarily, the world is worse off. It is this heartland of new right economic theory that is now being questioned more aggressively than ever before.

The most comprehensive assault is Robert Lane's new book,* which in time may rank with the classics of political economy – even if it is a mortal blow to the propagandists of conservative England. Lane marshals research to challenge the concept that work can be regarded, as market economists must, as a 'disutility'.

In the classic economic story, a worker surrenders leisure for work up to the point that the extra hour of pay exactly compensates for the utility lost through giving up leisure. The purpose of life is to consume, not produce; and to give up leisure is to surrender the chance of pleasurable consumption. Work is a disutility requiring compensation; the more people are paid, and the less they are taxed, the harder they will work. Production is conceived as a tiresome bore; the economic McCoy is consumption.

Not so, says Lane. Production and work are key sources of satisfaction and utility. Work fosters personal development, deepens skills, humanizes and structures lives; above all, it makes us cleverer and independent. The process of production is a source of profound satisfaction in its own right; and money income contributes very little to a sense of personal well-being.

In one astonishing chapter that will cause heart failure in the Institute of Economic Affairs and Adam Smith Institute, Lane even argues that money values obstruct rational market behaviour. Why? Because money is a symbol as well as a sender of economic messages. A growing body of research shows that money symbols trigger non-rational signals ranging from moral

---

* Robert Lane, *The Market Experience* (Cambridge: Cambridge University Press, 1993).

evil to shame. These symbols, says Lane, hinder rational judgement and undermine utility maximization in a market.

If even a fraction of Lane's insights are accepted as true, the new right's sneering attitude to 'producers', and the celebration of 'consumption' as the be-all and end-all of economic activity, will have to be qualified. The way will be open to consider the process of production as the source of human satisfaction; and how best to stimulate it.

Here too the new economics is making waves. Professor W. Brian Arthur describes in the *New Scientist* how he and colleagues at Stanford University and the Massachusetts Institute of Technology contest another part of the new right economic story – that economies are always driven to stable outcomes because at some point production costs rise.

A small example illustrates the point. In coal mining, expansion into harder-to-reach seams gets more expensive – so it becomes worthwhile not to mine more coal, but, say, to explore for oil. Consumers' willingness to pay for oil, technology, and the availability of the raw materials will dictate how much coal and oil should actually be produced. The system will find its way, unguided, to the best outcome.

But, says Arthur, costs in high technology industries do not always rise, as they must be assumed to do if a free market is to work. They fall. And once a product gets ahead of its rivals in price and quality, then it can get even further ahead. Technology is subject to increasing, not diminishing, returns. Industries can 'lock in' their competitive advantage which becomes impossible for new entrants to break; countries or regions which manage to establish an early lead can stay ahead – for example pharmaceuticals in Switzerland or consumer electronics in Japan. Free market economics disputes that this should happen, but it does. Industrial policy, in the sense of giving a particular industry a head start through favoured treatment, can thus make perfect sense; and industries can decline even if wages and prices are low. They cannot break into the virtuous circle.

Last but not least in the new economics' assault, there is the assumption of rational economic man who forms perfectly rational expectations. Nobody but the zealots ever believed in this; it is just that, until now, dropping the assumption and replacing it with the reality – that economic agents make mistakes, follow patterns and learn by trial and error – has produced results beyond the competence of mathematics and computer intelligence.

At the Santa Fe Institute, two Nobel prize winners are using super-computers to model a world in which 'adaptively intelligent man' replaces 'perfectly intelligent man'. The resulting economic models produce booms and busts, inflation and unemployment – all in a free market. Market models with more realistic assumptions produce unstable and irrational results.

But, it may be objected, if this new economics holds up it would mean that Britain has been the subject of an absurd fourteen-year experiment that could only work poorly; that if the lessons were applied worldwide there would be instability and recession; that there is a case for state intervention, a strong social security system, and vigorous support of production. But that can't be right, can it?

Guardian, 19 April 1993

Monetarist Mantra has Lost its Magic

Economics is said to be the new religion of the age. While belief in God is beset by doubts, economics has filled the breach, offering secular truths to anchor ourselves in a materialist world in flux.

The proposition that there is no long-run trade-off between inflation and growth has reached a status that Christian leaders would wish for the notion that Jesus saves. It is held universally by the world's capital markets, advisers of finance ministers and any professional economist who wants to be taken seriously by his or her peers.

Thus, any act of policy that serves to lift employment and growth in the near term but which risks increasing inflation is regarded as self-defeating. It means individual price signals get muddled by the instability of prices generally so that markets might depart from their otherwise guaranteed high efficiency. Price stability is the absolute precondition for economic good.

Yet, despite the obeisance to this new first law of economics, there is no agreed theory of how inflation is generated and therefore prevented. The monetarist conviction of the early 1980s – that there is a mechanical relationship between the rate of increase of some measure of the supply of money and the subsequent rise in prices – to which we owe the preoccupation with inflation, has collapsed before reality.

Between 1983 and 1988, for example, deposits in banks and building societies grew on average at 15 per cent per year while inflation averaged 5 per cent – and when inflation rose at the end of the decade nobody could disentangle cause from effect. Was this because of the the jump in world prices especially of commodities, or because of five years of excessive monetary growth? If it was money, why had it taken so long to impact upon prices? How important was the Lawson cutting of taxes at the top of the boom?

In the face of this uncertainty we are left with the monetarist proposition that there is no trade-off between inflation and growth, but without the theory to support how inflation is generated – or even, as we shall see, the incontrovertible theory that there is no trade-off. Policy-makers end up watching every potential source of inflation, as the Bank of England's admirably eclectic Inflation Report makes clear, because they are in the dark over which one might matter this time round. Yet, notwithstanding this ignorance, the country is hitched to a target of lowering underlying inflation to 1–4 per cent by the end of this parliament. If it were *Alice in Wonderland* we would laugh; but because these are grown men in suits we suspend our disbelief.

For, without a theory, any claim about the dynamics of inflation is beset by hazards. Even to argue that inflation is likely to occur when demand presses against the limits of industrial and commercial capacity cannot be taken as axiomatic. Inflation could be averted if excess demand were met from imports – or even if producers narrowed their margins.

But, more important still, there is no hard information about the current level of capacity in relation to demand. There are some, like UBS's Bill Martin, who, using CBI survey data, say that demand is already pressing against capacity limits and the inflationary 'battle of the mark-ups' will soon be upon us; others, like the *Guardian*'s Seven Wise Women, say that there is still a wide margin between demand and potential output. A government that was serious about inflation might act to improve the data upon which such key judgements are based – but not ours. In any case, because monetary policy acts with time-lags, the key assessment is not what is happening now but in two years' time when the effects of an interest rate rise start to bite. But to make that judgement we need to know not only today's starting point but also the underlying trend growth of capacity and the degree to which it might be over- or undershot by investment plans currently in the pipeline. Over this there is even more room for disagreement. For the optimists, Britain is undergoing a supply-side revolution: for the realists, the trend growth of capacity has weakened and is weakening further.

Nor can the time-lags with which interest rates affect the economy be taken as predictable. Banks and building societies ration the availability of credit according to the state of their balance sheets and their assessments of risk rather than lend mechanically at given rates of interest. Nor are their borrowers indifferent to the outlook for their incomes and job hopes. As their confidence fluctuates, so do their borrowing and savings – but forecasting by how much is again a matter of hunch. We are as uncertain about the determinants of spending as we are about the growth of capacity.

Once we drop monetarist simplicities and start to worry about the real economy, real capacity and real demand, and their impact on inflation, then necessarily we enter the world of trade-offs. Raising interest rates does not function like the immaculate conception in lowering inflation; it does so by lowering the growth of credit-financed consumption and investment and thereby lowering the growth of demand below capacity, so easing inflationary pressures.

But the very act of imposing a deferment or cancellation of investment plans on the economy to lower inflation in the present must necessarily lower the level and growth of capacity – and thereby the amount of demand that can be allowed in the future, and thus future monetary policy options. And if industrialists reckon that demand will be lower, they will lower their investment plans still further. In other words, by insisting that there is no trade-off between inflation and output, we risk being locked in a policy framework in which successive pre-emptive rises in interest rates trap the economy in a low-growth high-unemployment equilibrium – but where inflation is low.

The only way to resist this argument is to insist that investment in a market economy is not influenced by expectations of future demand. Rather, there are 'natural' levels of investment and unemployment which are determined by 'natural' market processes – and which inflation disturbs. The key to raising investment and growth is improving the efficiency of these market processes – which means price stability and attacking all forms of regulation and market obstruction, notably the welfare state and trade unions. When you are told there is no trade-off between inflation and growth, the speaker is looking to reduce your job security, your state pension and your child's chances of being taught in a class with fewer than 30 pupils. Beware.

OECD and UK inflation faithfully track one another, which is hardly surprising because, in an open economy like Britain's, rising export and import prices are going to cause the general price level to rise. Sometimes British inflation is higher and sometimes lower, but the trend is always the same.

Now suppose that world inflation rises in the next three years from 3 to 5 per cent, which it could if the US and Asian economies carry on booming. British policy-makers would be able to resist this trend only by throttling back activity, probably lifting unemployment back above three million. They would say they were laying the basis for future growth by emphasizing price stability; I would argue that losing investment and the chance of more capacity in the future is to trap the economy into low growth – and further constrain policy options.

In reality, the choice is the premium or discount British inflation bears in relation to world levels – and the greater the growth of industrial capacity, the more likely it is that demand will not press against capacity limits. Price stability is earned by raising investment levels and not imposed by ever-higher real interest rates – and to pledge yourself to an inflation target in an economy as open as ours is to limit much-needed flexibility in the prosecution of that aim. To move to a high-investment economy may involve transitionally higher inflation; but that is a route excluded by current policy. There are trade-offs, and economics should leave religion to priests.

Guardian, 12 September 1994

An End to the Rule of Fish Market Economics

For fifteen years the assumption has been that the market for jobs is like the market for dead fish. If the price is high, demand falls; if the price is low the demand rises. What is required is to make the labour market operate as freely as a fish market – find a 'market-clearing' wage for labour and unemployment will be solved.

This is a very simple thesis which for Conservative politicians has the happy merit of chiming with deeply held instincts. The great unwashed, who will organize themselves into trade unions to try to bargain for improved pay and conditions, are offending natural laws of economics – and this should be prevented in the interests of all. Union bashing and economic imperatives go hand in hand – a most felicitous combination.

This is certainly the view of the new Secretary of State at the Department of Employment, Michael Portillo. But he has two substantial problems. There is no more bashing of trade unions or lifting of labour market regulations to be done. Britain has no regulations and ranks bottom with the US in the international league table of labour standards, the OECD *Employment Outlook* informed us last week. Deregulation is virtually complete.

But secondly, and potentially more serious, there is a growing body of theory and evidence that the labour market does not operate like a fish market. Economists are coming to terms with the fact, as Nobel laureate Professor Robert Solow puts it, that the labour market is a social as much as an economic institution – and that interaction between human beings cannot be interpreted in the same way as the supply and demand for dead fish.* Whether Mr Portillo and his followers like it or not, ideas of fairness and morale imbue the labour market and turn on its head the way its operation should be modelled.

* R. Solow, *The Labour Market as a Social Institution* (Oxford: Blackwell, 1990).

For example, there is the perplexing refusal of employers to be as aggressive as they should about reducing wages in a recession, or about hiring workers from the vast pool of unemployed at the low wages for which rationally they should work. As the Bank of England plaintively put it in the February Inflation Report, 'wages are still strikingly un-responsive to changes in unemployment' – despite the labour market reforms. Quite so.

In Britain the reaction is to redouble the efforts to remove all forms of labour market protection and incite employers to be even more hawkish in their hiring and wage-setting policy. But some of the world's best economists are beginning to wonder why better employers consider it rational not to behave as free market economics predicts. Perhaps it is employers who are rational and free market economics that is irrational.

For when you start to question employers about why they behave as they do, as Harvard's Truman Bewley has done in Connecticut, new right economists get some discomforting replies. Firms do not slash wages in recessions because they fear there would be a calamitous drop in morale; they do not hire unemployed workers at lower rates than the existing pay scale because of the disruption and sense of injustice that results. And when they try to implant systems of performance-related pay, closely tying wages to productivity, they find perversely that the consequent drop in morale leads to worse performance.

In fact, the paradox, as the Institute for Manpower Studies reported in its study on performance-related pay earlier this year, was that such incentives worked best where workers trusted that they were fair and just. There needed to be relations of trust with immediate superiors who made the judgements of performance, and workers themselves needed to be involved in the design of the system. But of course those are the circumstances, with strong bonds of trust and high motivation, where performance-related pay is not needed. People, exasperatingly, refuse to obey the laws applying to the fish market.

All this has prompted two British economists, David Blanchflower and Andrew Oswald, to examine the data in twelve countries showing the actual relation between wages and unemployment – and what they have discovered will cause Mr Portillo and the free market acolytes at the Department of Employment heart failure.* Free market theory would predict that low wages would be correlated with low local unemployment; and high wages with high local unemployment.

But Blanchflower and Oswald have found precisely the opposite. In twelve countries the same law holds – the higher the wages, the lower local unemployment and the lower the wages, the higher local unemployment. This is

* D. Blanchflower and A. Oswald, *The Wage Curve* (Cambridge, Mass.: MIT Press, 1994).

not a conclusion that can be squared with free market textbook theories of how a competitive labour market should work.

None of the chain of causations supposed by the text-books work in practice. Somebody with precisely the same skills will earn more in a city or region with high employment than somebody with the same skills in an area of high unemployment. Whether in trade union dominated Germany, the deregulated US or the police state of South Korea, there was no measurable competitive effect: the unemployed in the adjacent area of high unemployment did not bid down the wages of those in work in areas of low unemployment. There was no tendency – as the market theorists would predict – to equivalence of wages or employment whatsoever.

Indeed, as unemployment rises, so wages fall marginally in all twelve countries – but this does not lead to the jobs market correcting itself and moving back towards higher employment. It is simply a new equilibrium in which both unemployment is higher and wages lower. Wages do not operate as a market-clearing device at all in any national, regional or local labour market, regulated or non-unionized. It is one of the most devastating findings of contemporary economics.

The way to visualize the labour market, say Blanchflower and Oswald, is not as the interaction of the supply and demand for labour – for there is no labour supply curve as free market economists suppose. Rather, there is an employed labour force and a stock of unemployed who have little or no impact in determining the clearing price of labour in any kind of labour market that exists in the real world. Moreover, as Robert Solow argues, it is perfectly rational for any individual unemployed person not to bid down the price of wages – because when they get a job they will be poorer as a result. The rational option is to get the fair or just wage that prevails for the mass of those in employment. It is those ideas of fairness again – people just won't behave like dead fish.

Indeed, the more you attempt to run the labour market as a market in a commodity like any other, the more destructive the results. Blanchflower and Oswald have no simple explanation for the relationship they have uncovered, but all the theories they advance are united by some form of human agreement that raises the value of work above the market-clearing level and so decommoditizes the wage bargain.

It might be that when times are hard, workers who have jobs put in more effort, thus warranting a higher wage than the market-clearing wage (the so-called efficiency wage); it might be that employers choose to reward their existing labour force highly because they have known skills, and retraining and monitoring the performance of new workers is expensive. But these are human bargains in which morale, motivation and productivity have been achieved independently of the wider jobs market and so underline Solow's point that this is a social institution.

More important still, the key to making the labour market efficient is to respect people's desire for fairness. In Switzerland local workforces react to economic downturns by sharing out the short-time work and parcelling out wage reductions equally – but only on the promise that they will be reversed equally when times improve. But this is not the result of an atomized deregulated labour market; it is constructed around legally binding consultative relations, unions on boards and strong relations of trust. Exactly the system that the government has spent fifteen years dismantling, and when represented in the European social chapter is regarded as the work of the devil.

Yet the new thinking will out. It is seeping into the OECD, which invoked collective bargaining, unions and workplace consultation as a means of promoting labour market efficiency for precisely these reasons – and which, if internal politics allow, is poised to give a critical assessment of the way the deregulated UK labour market works. It would be nice to think that Mr Portillo will read both Solow's book and the Blanchflower and Oswald paper – it would take no more than a morning – and reconsider his position.

After all, each economy is capitalist, driven by the profit motive, so that a change of policy could hardly be represented as a sell-out to socialism. But British government is not about the application of sensible economics; it is the hysterical application of ideology – and none more hysterical than the effusions from the Department of Employment and its new Secretary of State.

Guardian, 25 July 1994

Equality is the Casualty of an Unhealthy Market

Was it only thirty years ago that the British health service was 'the envy of the world'? As the 1990s wear on the sobriquet is less and less deserving. It may be cheap – but an NHS founded around the principle of fairness to all is being steadily sacrificed before the distrust in everything public and the ideological imperative to mimic a market.

In real terms, says the government, health spending has never been higher, but that depends on what you mean by real. The important question is whether the proportion of national output devoted to real health demands has risen – and to that the answer is emphatically no. Despite an ageing population that makes ever-greater demands upon the NHS's resources, Britain spends less as a proportion of GDP on health than it did in the mid-seventies.

For the NHS is nothing if not cheap, now as in the past. A centralized and publicly controlled system of health care has kept a tight control over the volume of health spending; and the gate-keeper to access to the expensive hospital system has been the cheaper general practitioner service. But above all the NHS has been a monopoly buyer of everything from drugs to doctors; there was no capacity to bid up prices because nobody had the same market power. Over the 1980s NHS pay has never lagged less than 10 per cent behind private pay and sometimes the gap has loomed even larger.

The system did have problems. The consultants had a vested interest in long waiting lists, thus encouraging patients to jump the queue by paying. It was undermanaged, with hospitals having little interest in relating costs to health outcomes and even less incentive to improve areas like outpatient and casualty treatment that might be very important to their patients but less so to them. And the quality of treatment varied substantially from region to region.

But against this the service was animated by a proud tradition of disinterested public service. Although Britain spends less on health than any other countries in the OECD except Turkey and Greece, the indicators of national health were in the middle of the international league table. On balance the British had a good deal.

But for the Conservative Party that was not good enough. Claims that the NHS was efficient were necessarily bogus; as a state-run monopoly it had to be inefficient. Real efficiency required the disciplines of a market, the incentive of profit and the involvement of the private sector.

This was pure cant. Wherever the private sector has been involved in health provision there has been an explosion in cost and a decline in efficiency. In the US, for example, fee-based health services are three times more expensive than the collectively organized health maintenance plans (mini national health services) but deliver no better health. Even within Britain the rate of increase in private health insurance premiums has grown very much faster than state-financed health expenditure.

If you want to contain health spending, promote efficiency and keep people healthy, you keep market principle and profit motive well away from your organization. Because for all of us there is nothing more important than our personal health. If they have the means and the opportunity, everybody is prepared to pay whatever is needed to attempt to get successful treatment; and consultants, while they may know the average chances of success, cannot know whether these will apply in particular cases. Neither side has any interest in saving money.

But with no prior experimentation the health service suffered the famous split between providers and purchasers doing business in an internal national health market, at the same time enlarging the incentives for private provision. District health authorities and some GPs with large enough practices who opt to hold part of their budgets individually buy health services from hospitals and GPs. Hospitals themselves are encouraged to become self-governing commercial organizations – trusts.

In this brave new world purchasers specify what they want from providers, and haggle over the price. It may be taxpayers' money, but purchasers are empowered to direct it to those providers who give the best deal; and both parties to the bargain can use savings as they will – to invest, to provide more services or just as sheer profit. For hospitals and GPs alike, trade-offs between cost and quality of service are intruding into the calculus of health care.

The tragedy is that these trade-offs, which must exist in any health system and were not clearly recognized before, have had to be carried into the health service by a market mechanism; and market mechanisms are blind to equity, the very foundation of the NHS. Inequality of income for example, an effect of the market in the wider economy, can be defended in terms of incentives even if it is a thin defence; inequality of access to health cannot even claim that. Simply, it is damnable.

The reforms have not been accompanied by any more resources except in the run-up to the last election, and in real health terms resources are set to fall over the next three years. For 'choice' has not meant that the public can elect to divert more resources to its health; the government remains firmly in control with the aim of tax cuts dominating everything. In short, purchasers and providers will be competing for an ever-smaller share of the cake.

The fundholding GPs will thus become ever more important to the hospitals competing to get their contracts. The good point is that hospitals are having to meet fundholding GPs' concerns, from outpatients' waiting times to the quality of medical advice. The bad point is that those GPs who have smaller practices or who do not want to be in the invidious position of trading off cost and treatment are being progressively disadvantaged.

There is growing evidence throughout the country that hospitals, especially the trusts, are being compelled by the reforms' logic to put fundholders' patients first. One memorandum from the Nuffield in Oxford at the end of September, for example, unequivocally states that its outpatients must be restricted to referrals from fundholders or private payers until the beginning of the next financial year. A two-tier health service is appearing before our eyes.

Hospitals simply have to respect the contracts they have made with fundholders if they want to 'keep the business'; and with falling real resources that must displace non-fundholders' treatment. Nor is it merely a problem of transition. If and when all hospitals are trusts and all GPs fundholders, then necessarily there will be differing prices, terms and conditions attached to each contract. Your health care will depend on the entrepreneurial quality of your doctor and hospital.

The theory is that the search for maximum financial savings will deliver the public interest as in all markets; but Keynesians have less sanguine views of markets. In any case there is no back-up health regulator to guarantee the public interest or even provision of information. Instead we must take it on trust from these quangos run by Conservative Party placemen or their sympathizers. Formerly public information is now 'confidential'. And the web of contracts and passing of funds has necessarily led to an explosion of administration and accounting, with the number of NHS managers jumping by 25 per cent in 1992 against virtually no growth in medical staff. The NHS has been undermanaged but do any new 'efficiencies' compensate for the new layers of accountants? We do not know.

Yet with patchy and unmeasured gains in efficiency – mostly achieved by casualizing and cheapening the workforce – we have certain losses of equity. A patient of a fundholder adept at working the system will do better than a non-fundholder; and patients of fundholders will fare better or worse depending upon their doctor's commitment to make financial savings or the time of the financial year. Equally, those who live in a district where purchasers buy well will do better than those who do not. And, with fundholders encouraged to buy privately, taxpayers' money will be used to subsidize the expansion of private health facilities where priority will always be given to those who pay.

So welcome to today's NHS. The collapse of a free national eye and dental service points the way ahead. Health, a public good, is becoming a personal lottery with gains in individual choice only for those who can pay. But it's an internal market and the top rate of tax remains 40 per cent; so that's all right – isn't it?

Guardian, 10 January 1994

Priceless Assets Amount to Folly

The Sea Empress spilt 70,000 tonnes of oil in the sea around Milford Haven, but that act of environmental destruction will have boosted growth in GDP.

Cleaning up the mess, salvaging the ship and assembling reports on what went wrong will generate a marketable and thus measurable increase in output; destruction of the environment, by contrast, will not lower GDP. Why? It's not included in the measure.

It is but the latest event to dramatize the growing debate about whether a measure that incorporates such judgements makes sense any more. The brutal elegance of GDP – gross domestic product – is that it simply counts the purchases of goods and services by households and the government, and of plant and machinery by firms. Non-market transactions – like the costs of an oil spill to ecology – are not reckoned.

But it is not merely environmental degradation that goes unmeasured. No non-market transaction – whether it is child-rearing or devaluation of the skills of the unemployed – is included. GDP measures the rate of change of essentially business activity; the sustainability of that activity – whether in terms of the natural, economic and social habitat – is not captured by the measure, nor intended to be.

Nor, in more conventional economic terms, is there any national balance sheet measuring the stock of the nation's physical and intellectual capital – annual depreciation or appreciation of which can be charged or credited to GDP. We are in part flying blind in measuring what we really care about – and even in having the information to manage the growth of the activity that GDP does measure. The statistical inadequacies are beginning to be economically and politically important.

The criticism extends far beyond the environment. Development economists, for example, want measures that indicate the importance of improving literacy or succouring family structures.

Above all, there is a recognition that GDP growth of itself does not promote well-being. Suicide rates for young men, for example, are climbing as their unemployment rate rises. If GDP rose by 3 per cent per annum over the next five years, while that suicide rate doubled, how much richer would Britain be at the end of the period?

But the sharpest criticism is that orthodox measures of GDP offer only an indifferent guide to policy – as witnessed by the debate over interest rates. In a rational world you would want some hard evidence about the width of the gap between actual and potential GDP, the 'output gap', and therefore how much demand can be boosted without pressing against those constraints.

But with the current measure of GDP, and without a national balance sheet of the economy's capital stock, the Treasury has little more idea of potential productive capacity at any given moment and the dynamics of its relation with future demand than it had before the era of national accounts. Chancellor Kenneth Clarke's decision to lower interest rates last week was a seat-of-the-pants judgement supported by a well-informed guess about the direction of the economy and reinforced by his electoral hopes; nothing more or less.

In the same way, Michael Heseltine's forthcoming campaign (sadly, backed by the Civil Service) to persuade us that the economy can grow much faster despite the pitifully poor levels of investment, because business can squeeze more from its stock of assets, is also a finger-in-the-wind judgement. He has no reliable evidence to prove his case; but equally there is none to prove him wrong.

A properly constructed national balance sheet would go some way to close the information gap. For example, while GDP measures the depreciation of plant and machinery, there is no accompanying measure of its quality or any assessment of investment in intangibles, like the skills of the workforce, that might raise the economy's potential as Mr Heseltine wants to argue.

Nor, crucially, is labour treated like capital so that the waste of skills that results from carrying a growing stock of unemployed and economically inactive people is measured. Instead, economists are forced to estimate the growth of underlying capacity and then judge how much above or below that trend existing GDP is. It is as though ships' captains measured the sea's depth not by radar but by throwing out a plumb-line at the stern and hoping that the front is not going aground. The radar could be available in improved statistics; all we have to do is to get them.

As a series of essays in the the Institute for Public Policy Research's quarterly review, *New Economy*, highlights, this is not easy. The moment you leave the tried and tested area of measuring what is traded, you have to make judgements about what is important and the weight you attach to it – without a market benchmark.

For example, it is easy to agree that growth should be environmentally sustainable. Thus, if in any year oil and gas depletion exceeds the rate of new discoveries, then the economy, in economic terms, has dis-saved. Measurable increases in air and water pollution are also environmentally degrading. But what weight do you attach to varying forms of pollution? How do you adjust for the discovery that a chemical – like methyl bromide, the active agent in pesticides – is eroding the ozone layer?

Giles Atkinson and David Pearce from the Centre for Social and Economic Research on the Global Environment have threaded their way through the minefield to develop the idea of 'genuine saving', in which conventional measures of saving are adjusted by the degree to which a country is replacing the natural resources it consumes every year. The conclusion is surprising: the British were overconsuming net environmental resources until the 1987 fall in the oil price meant that the value of running down North Sea oil fell away. On the other hand, the production of methyl bromide has increased, but that could not be factored into the computation – at least until the toll on the ozone layer is quantified.

The same difficulties confront Randi Hawkins, Jo Webb and Dan Corry when they construct a 'new economy well-being index'. The aim is to build a statistically robust means of comparing well-being over time – incorporating the level and growth of real income per head, inequality, the level and growth of unemployment, inflation and base rates into a composite index. Inclusion of each is eminently justifiable, but the issue is what weight to apply to each component.

The three show how, if all seven components are equally weighted, there has been a gentle downward slide in well-being since the 1960s. But if they weight unemployment more, on the grounds that it is the single most important cause of unhappiness, then the decline in well-being is more marked. If interest rates were weighted more heavily, the fall-away would be much less.

This only goes to show, GDP defenders argue, how futile and unobjective the process is – and how one should stick to market measures. But they, too, represent a value judgement in deciding not to bother about measuring environmental degradation, personal well-being or true yardsticks of national wealth. Indeed, the advantage of bringing the debate into the open is that it starts to make explicit what the goals in economic policy should be.

The discussion in Britain is only a pale reflection of what is happening internationally in response to the same concerns. The World Bank has developed a 'new wealth accounting system' including four kinds of assets as the real wealth of nations – natural capital, produced assets, human resources and social capital. The Clinton administration has published a measure of 'green GDP', while the new 'system of national accounts' developed by the OECD, EU, IMF and World Bank has protocols for integrating social and environmental statistics into national accounts.

The standardization of national accounts will oblige even the British government to move in this direction. This does not mean GDP will be discarded – it is too important for that. But if we want better decisions on economic management, and measures that reflect our true concerns, we need better measures. And we need them soon.

Guardian, 11 March 1996

Wealth or Happiness may be in Store

Are you happy? Do you expect to get any happier? You might think economics allowed such questions to intrude into its deliberations: after all, the pursuit of happiness is central to the economic project. No such luck.

Economics does not want to worry about what makes human beings happy. That might compromise its attempt to be a value-free science. Instead, it offers a set of guidelines about how happiness might be attempted but makes no judgement about what happiness itself might be. As long as we know what we like and can organize a pecking order of such preferences, it is the exercise of free choices that will make us happy – and economically efficient – says economics.

By dodging the happiness question, by insisting that we only have to choose, economics disables itself in two ways. It surrenders itself to being captured by the right – and it imposes upon itself a wholly artificial construction about how human beings behave. In short, economics becomes an ideology whose predictions about the real world are frequently wrong.

But, for the new right the proof that choice is the key to happiness is a godsend which it has seized upon with enthusiasm. The privacy of choice and its individual nature were attractive enough, but if choice meant economic efficiency the circle was squared. It was not for nothing that Professor Milton Friedman entitled his proselytizing book *Free to Choose*, and born-again Conservatives everywhere hammered on about the morality and efficiency of choice. Markets were deregulated and public activity privatized to allow us to make those efficient and happiness-making choices.

But, fifteen years on, there are growing doubts about the results. Choosing has not led to either happiness or economic welfare, and the more reflective economists have begun to wonder whether economics' famous dodge works. What if individuals do not possess the mental equipment to be rational about why and what they choose? Maybe economists have to wonder what it is that makes us happy after all; and at the Happiness Conference at the London School of Economics last week, some of the best and brightest in the profession gathered to ponder whether that might be the case – and what would be the consequences. It was a revelatory experience.

What would Michael Portillo, the high priest of choice, make of the results of Daniel Kahneman's exhaustive tests at the University of Princeton about whether the human memory and the psychology of choice are consistent with rational economic behaviour in markets? He showed that even in controlled situations individuals make choices which are persistently and painfully wrong, and which require the intervention of a paternalist figure to correct.

Mr Portillo and his ilk had better hope that Mr Kahneman is mistaken, for the case of tax cuts and deregulated markets depends upon our ability to organize rational choices so that basically the choosers get things right. But Mr Kahneman shows that because our memories are so distorted by the peak experience of any episode – whether good or bad – and what we felt like when the experience stopped, there are even doubts about whether we can be rational about what we have liked or disliked.

Our memory of a painful hospital operation, for example, is dictated wholly by how we felt at the end of the operation – and what the worst feeling of pain was during the course of it. The operation's duration has virtually no impact on our recollection. Thus, our memory will rank a short and relatively painless operation which ends on a painful note as worse than an operation which ends on a painless note – even if it lasted longer and was overall more painful. As Mr Kahneman concludes, most of us are simply incapable of maintaining the coherence and consistency in our choices that allows us to be conceived of as being able to maximize outcomes – which is rather a serious blow to economics.

But even if we exclude areas that depend on the rationality of our memories, we cannot be relied upon to choose to maximize our outcomes. Economics demands that our happiness equals our capacity to maximize profits; so that if, for example, we were given £20 and offered two options – split it 50/50 or keep £18 and give away £2, economics predicts that, as profit maximizers, most of us would opt to keep the £18.

But when Mr Kahneman does the experiment, he finds that three-quarters of respondents choose to split the money 50/50 – a completely irrational response in terms of profit maximization. This happens even under conditions of complete anonymity so that the respondent does not know with whom they are sharing; or who is offering the choice. A large number of us choose to be happy not by doing down our fellow men and women but by being altruistic and fair-minded. Horrors!

What this means, of course, is that many of the predictions of economic theory relying on maximization of outcomes and willingness to put one's own interests first fall apart – and so they do. Professor Truman Bewley of Yale, one of the US's leading econometricians, frustrated by the incapacity of economics to predict actual outcomes in the real world, interviewed 183 managers and people professionally involved in the jobs market in an attempt to understand its real dynamics.

Labour market economics relies heavily on economics' assumptions about

choice and rationality. In particular, it predicts that employers' first preference is to lower wages in recessions rather than lay off workers; that unemployment is essentially a matter of choice, and that the unemployed worker
who chooses to lower his or her wages will quickly be hired; and that well-
qualified workers get hired more quickly than poorly qualified workers.
But Professor Bewley's work challenges the received wisdom. He finds these
predictions are wholly wrong – and do not succeed in forecasting what
firms and workers actually do.

Labour market theory insists that firms bend every muscle to make workers' wages exactly equal to the incremental value of their output – so that
firms produce up to that point where the last unit of output equals wages.
Unions, social habits, inefficiency and monopoly power may get in the
way, but good firms know that is what they should be trying to do. Above
all, wages should be flexible.

But as Professor Bewley notes, wages are not flexible – even in hire-and-
fire, non-union America. Piece rates, the classic free-market wage contract,
are surprisingly stable throughout the economic cycle – and in recessions
firms will lay off workers rather than reduce everyone's wages. At the same
time, employers are wary about taking on unemployed workers who have
dropped their wage below what their skill level commands. The 'flexible'
job-seeker is less likely to get work than the one who is inflexible. Labour
market economists fail to describe what is going on.

Employers find that workers have a conception of fairness which they
simply have to respect to preserve their firms as ongoing social organizations. Cutting wages is not seen as 'fair'; nor is it possible to pay a worker
either above or below what is deemed to be fair inside the internal pay
hierarchy without others insisting on parity or deploring the unfairness.
Taking on a group of unemployed people at below the firm's going wage
rate – to 'price them into jobs' – proves to be impossible.

And if firms disregard these injunctions, even the most capitalist find
themselves encountering problems of low morale and staff disaffection,
causing low productivity, that require the decision is reversed – or at least
never repeated. When Henry Ford invented his $5-a-day rate on the new
lines at Ford, he never changed the rate in recessions; and it was that which
won him the productivity gains. Workers could trust the rate and thus gave
of their best. Professor Bewley captures why Ford's strategy worked – and
why employers today are reluctant to lower wages and change piece rates;
but economists are necessarily perplexed.

One of the saddest by-products of the new right revolution is that, under the barrage of propaganda, some employers are beginning to believe
that respecting fairness and creating trust is economically irrational – and
are trying to make wages flexible, as the economists recommend. But, as
the recent debate over why performance-related pay produces less good

performance shows, the initiatives are not raising productivity. The new right's world does not work.

Human beings, economists and managers alike are discovering, value fairness. As social animals we like esteem and being ranked highly in our firms' pecking orders. We need to be able to trust the social networks in which we are embedded; and unless we can trust them we perform less well. We are not happy simply choosing and maximizing our individual preferences – which is just as well, given that so many of our choices must be mistaken.

In the meantime, we must live with the world economics is inventing: nasty, brutish and unproductive. But economics can no longer take refuge in the fiction that the route to happiness is choice; it must confront reality. In that, maybe – just maybe – lies hope.

Guardian, 8 November 1993

PART II
The Keynesian Revival: New Arguments for Growth and Employment

Back by Popular Demand

Is Keynes staging a comeback? The recent experiment in free market economics whose falsities Keynes exposed has not proved notably successful. As our economies have become more marketized, growth has slowed and unemployment has risen. The search is on for a theory and policy that might produce better results. But if Keynes is being rediscovered, please God let it be the real Keynes – not the bastardized version that betrayed his revolution and allowed the barbarians back.

Many self-described Keynesians, as well as his critics, understand only the distorted version of Keynes: the doctrine that governments can spend and borrow their way to full employment. Critics typically concede that this approach worked passably well for a short time in the 1950s, but like a drug, they say, its efficacy diminished until finally it collapsed in inflation and excessive union power. Defenders – 'neo-Keynesians' – insist the old verities stand, and some recommend government pump-priming almost indiscriminately.

Yet this debate is sterile and misleading and offers only a caricature of the man and his ideas. Keynes was more than the advocate of actively managing the overall level of demand in the economy by government borrowing, although that is part of the story. He also offered a revolution in the way the capitalist economy should be conceptualized, and that should be the inspiration for revisiting his ideas.

Let's begin at the beginning: Keynes's assault on the intellectual tradition in economics that free markets, if left to their own devices, must necessarily deliver the best results. Keynes saw as a fiction the settled world imagined by the so-called classical economists in which supply and demand can always be reckoned to balance or tend to balance. In the Keynesian universe, the market is unstable and inefficient; it is in a permanent process of experimentation in which malfunction and waste is systemic. It can alternate between boom and bust; it can get trapped in perversely low output. The capitalist system, left to its own devices, does not work.

As the British economic historian Robert Skidelsky shows brilliantly in the just published second volume of his three-part biography, *The Economist as Saviour*, Keynes resisted attempts to over-mathematize his insights – the 'grey, fuzzy, woolly monster' inside his head. A vision of how the economy functioned was the heart of his message, and the real economy that Keynes understood so well was anything but mechanically precise.

The key to his difference with the classical school is an understanding of how the existence of money transforms the way we should conceive buying and selling as a system for organizing the economy. Free market economics imagines exchange in a Robinson Crusoe world of hunter-gatherers who must necessarily barter what they have today because otherwise it would perish. Thus on the day when all the perishable produce is brought to market, either it is exchanged for other goods or, because the terms of exchange are not attractive enough, left in the possession of the original holder. The process cannot fail to produce a stable outcome. Obviously, at the end of trading, everyone has exactly the fish, fruit or whatever that they want because otherwise they would have traded it. Everybody is perfectly happy, and the system is perfectly efficient. But introduce money and everything changes.

Suddenly marketplace agents – entrepreneurs, consumers, and savers – have the capacity to make bets about the future through saving or borrowing, which the free market's hunter-gatherers do not; and the future is uncertain. Instead of trading perishable goods, market agents hold money. They can withhold their buying power because they think they might get a better bargain tomorrow; or they can borrow and spend today because they think the opposite. The market starts to be driven by expectations of the future, and producers have to decide whether the changing pattern of demand for their product is real or just the reflection of a series of bets that will unwind themselves.

Since Keynes's death, neoclassical economics has cannibalized Keynes's vision, attempting to reconcile the unreconcilable in order to save the classical paradigm. Although the 'neoclassical synthesis' (classical economics plus emasculated Keynes) concedes the need for management of aggregate demand at the macroeconomic level, the rest of the model is resolutely pre-Keynesian. Modern neoclassical economics is no more than a vast intellectual game to prove the rules that apply to hunter-gatherers also apply in a complex industrial economy. Robinson Crusoe and General Motors play the same game.

Central to this exercise is an assumption of economic rationality: market agents, whoever they are, can be trusted to do no more than always want to maximize their advantage; prices contain all the information they could ever want to know; and even though the future is uncertain they make bets that, on average, reflect a mathematical calculus of the chances of success – even though they do not know this is what they are doing. The famous analogy is with the flight of a ball. The catcher does not know the physics of aerodynamics but can still successfully catch a ball.

But Keynes all his life distrusted the notion of mathematical probability applied to economics. He insisted that the future is not reducible to a series of outcomes to which economic agents can attach calculable probabilities.

The future is not like a ball in flight because the catcher is blind; he or she can only make guesses about where the ball might land because the flight cannot be seen. It is in the future.

For Keynes, the future is simply incalculable, and that is what gives the money-exchange economy its unstable character. That is why inflation, unemployment and booms and busts exist. Once the snowball of expectations, hopes and fears is loosed and is fuelled by excessive saving or borrowing, the unregulated market system cannot deliver any pattern of prices that can check the subsequent swings in economic activity until they have run their course.

Indeed this may take not just years but decades, for economies can get locked in a pattern of behaviour that prices alone can do nothing about. Classical economists – like their new right descendants today – argue that unemployment, for example, is essentially voluntary. If unemployed workers lower the price of their labour sufficiently, they must eventually price themselves into work; not to do so means unemployed workers are choosing to stay jobless. Essentially, the firm and the worker behave like hunter-gatherers over worktime: the worker wants to sell it and the firm to buy it, and if they haggle freely, there must ultimately be a price – the wage – that will allow the worker to sell his time.

But according to Keynes, this bargain does not realistically capture what happens in an economy with money and uncertainty. If the firm hires a worker, it encounters a certain rise in its costs, with no compensating certainty that the extra output the worker produces can be sold. Thus, even if the wage is very low, it may still not be worthwhile hiring the additional worker – unless all firms could be told that if they hired workers simultaneously, those workers' wages would provide the demand that justified the increased production. But that is what they do not know, and in the absence of a benevolent angel telling them, they act prudently and hire nobody. Unemployment, in short, can be involuntary.

Keynes was not describing the special circumstances of the 1920s and 1930s, as his critics patronizingly claim, when analysing involuntary unemployment and so-called 'wage inflexibility'. He was making a statement about how the price mechanism works at all times. The hunter-gatherer model cannot be bolted on to the modern money-exchange economy by some sleight of hand about rational economic behaviour; with money and uncertainty, the motion of the capitalist economy is fundamentally different. There are credit booms and persistent unemployment, and they characterize our times as much as they did his.

If money destabilizes the economy, the counterpart of that destabilization will be in financial flows. If there is too much hoarding, then there will be oversupply of liquidity; if there is too much spending, there will be an excessive build-up of debt.

Stabilizing a market economy, therefore, requires that governments have influence over financial flows, domestically and internationally.

This is the unifying theme in all of Keynes's work. In his *Treatise of Money*, he is preoccupied with how the central bank can manipulate financial flows by altering bond sales and interest rates to change the overall price level. In the *General Theory*, his target is the larger one of mobilizing idle funds for investment by manipulating business expectations about future returns. If the government can assure private businesses that demand will be rising in the future, they can be more confident about borrowing for investment and the idle finance can be utilized after all. Low interest rates cannot do this by themselves; there needs to be the promise of demand in the future.

Keynes famously turns the free market chain of causation on its head; it is not higher saving that leads to higher investment and thus higher income, but higher investment that produces higher income and thus higher saving. In a depressed economy, increasing saving in order to increase investment will boomerang. Higher private or government saving will only depress demand, leading businesses to anticipate fewer customers and hence to invest less. Moreover, investment has a snowball effect on income and output, the so-called multiplier.

This is a much-forgotten element in Keynesian thinking, because again his proposition rests upon the view that the market economy systematically malfunctions. For a classical economist, the economy is always at some best point of balance – the famous 'equilibrium' – so that if there is unemployment it is because it has been chosen by prospective workers who refuse to work for prevailing wages. Resources are allocated the way they are because that is how market agents want it, and external government stimulus will only upset that balance. As a result, either there will be no effect or it will be self-defeating. Government borrowing will push up interest rates, choking off private investment by the exact degree government investment has risen. The two effects cancel each other out. (Curiously, in the years since Keynes's death, the 'neoclassical' synthesis has become less and less Keynesian; today many self-described neo-Keynesians commend budget balance and expect the economy to return to a natural, and hence optimal, presumed equilibrium path.)

Keynes, in contrast, pointed to the dynamic consequences of investment, both government and private. Investment purchased the 'lumpy' part of national output – the machines and factories that had long lives and that raised future productive capacity. In the process of raising capacity, investment so lifted employment and demand in the present that the process became self-justifying. When, for example, investment created jobs in the construction or machine tool industries, that created demand; and that created more investment. As output grew, so savings grew – but after investment. There were no 'crowding-out' effects of public deficits displacing private investment, because the whole system was in a state of permanent movement.

Thus the aim of policy is to find ways of acting upon the financial system – the true commanding heights of a market economy – so that the real economy functions efficiently. Monetary and fiscal policy, and active direction and control of the financial markets, are a continuum. The Keynes who designed an international financial system in 1944 is the same Keynes who ten years earlier wanted Roosevelt to borrow to pay for public works and who inveighed against Britain's deflationary return to the gold standard in 1926. The means might be interest rate manipulation, changing taxes and spending, or even directing private lending; but the end game was influencing financial flows and acting upon expectations.

What is so refreshing about Keynes is his belief that the best form of economic policy is attack – and his willingness to find the theoretical justification for initiatives to boost growth and employment that turned the free market orthodoxies upside down. This required, as it does today, colossal self-confidence, for the guardians of the orthodox view occupy the very pinnacles of the social and economic pyramid.

For all of Keynes's optimism that capitalism could be fixed, there is a political conundrum at the heart of the Keynesian project. Capitalism may need to be managed and regulated to give its best; but that implies that the business and financial elite give up some of their autonomy of action – the very autonomy that their economic power and personal inclination demands should remain unimpaired. In addition, policies that produce more output and stability of employment benefit the labour interest – and so again directly constrain business power. From the elite's point of view, it may actually be preferable to run the economy more unstably and inefficiently if the alternative is any reduction in its autonomy of action. In effect there is a trade-off. Although there is a business gain, it is uncertain and qualified by the certain loss of autonomy. An abiding attraction of laissez-faire is that it demands no such trade-off; rather it celebrates the current balance of economic power and requires the state to leave the business cycle alone.

Thus Keynesianism works best in those states that have democratic constitutions capable of best expressing a general or common interest over time, as well as institutions that mobilize wage-earners to participate coherently in politics. There needs to be some combination of constitutional machinery that permits clear-cut executive action while respecting democratic disciplines, together with strong mass parties that can dynamize the system if Keynesian policies are to succeed; but few constitutions possess such qualities. Britain in the immediate postwar period, Sweden from the 1940s to the 1980s, and the United States around the New Deal threw up circumstances that permitted successful Keynesianism. But interest group politics and weak parties in the United States, and the demise of the Labour Party in Britain, undercut the capacity of both countries' political arrangements to express common interests. The vacuum was filled by the new right. These political exigencies have forced Keynes's interpreters to water down the Keynesian message in an attempt to rebuild support for at least a watered-down Keynesian programme; half a loaf is better than no loaf at all.

Professor Skidelsky, for example, wants to rescue his hero from the stigma of being a liberal and to show that Keynes was as attached to sound money and free enterprise as any good conservative. But in so doing Keynes's more conservative interpreters are in danger of betraying Keynes's central insight. Keynes, a lifelong mocker of the conservative establishment in Britain and the United States, would not be falling in line today with proponents of price stability, deregulation and balanced budgets as the precursor of growth; rather, they would be the objects of his coruscating scorn.

Those who counsel deficit reduction and tight monetary targets before the demands of the productive part of the economy would have been parodied as suffering from Freudian anal retention – in effect arguing that to do anything so disturbs the markets' natural processes that we must do nothing. The defenders of the Reagan and Thatcher economic miracles would be exposed for what they are: self-interested promoters of the rentier financial interest who like tight money and high financial yields and hence argue that the hollowing-out of the British and US industrial sectors benefited everybody.

A Keynesian response today would have a number of strands ranging from implementing public works programmes to recapitalizing chronically enfeebled banks. But his starting point would be an acknowledgement of the febrile condition of the national and international finance system. Global financial deregulation has established a new financial regime that not only has begun to exert a permanent veto over individual states' expansionary economic policies but also is acting as a wedge for dismantling all forms of market regulation. The destabilizing build-up of private debt in the United States, Japan, Britain and the Nordic countries in the 1980s, for example, was prompted everywhere by the new deregulated offshore markets forcing the dismantling of national systems of financial regulation. The consequent credit booms left a debt overhang that is inhibiting a balanced and sustained recovery; and there is no certainty that once recovery gets under way the same forces will not reassert themselves – and the boom–bust cycle will repeat itself.

So Keynes would be increasingly interested in the interrelationship between domestic policy options and the new international financial system –

because that is the new deregulated locus of the unstable, inefficient market system. He would be exploring ways of stabilizing and reducing the vast movement of short-term capital that, because of the capacity to move so quickly and in such size, terrorizes governments into economic minimalism and public inactivity; turnover taxes in the foreign exchange markets and new tougher requirements on international banks' capital adequacy ratios so biasing them to behave more cautiously would interest him.

But he would go further. Capital flows from currency to currency in the expectation of capital profits, and with a system of floating exchange rates the possibility for making such profits is embedded in the system. Floating exchange rates are central to the system's functioning, because they facilitate capital movement; it is no accident that the explosion of capital movement has accompanied floating exchange rates. Thus if countries could find a way of re-establishing a means of pegging their currencies and adjusting parities to diminish the expectation of speculative profits and losses, that would reinforce the bias to stability – and give states a greater chance of running expansionary economic policies.

And for a man who lived through the financial consequences of 1929, the parallels with the world capital markets in 1993 would seem eerie. In the late 1920s buying on margin helped fuel a stock market boom, providing the collateral for the banks to lend more against not only rising stock market prices but real estate values. When prices fell the whole system unravelled, leaving banks with such capital losses that their capacity to lend was mortally impaired – the proximate cause of the US depression.

Today the markets in financial derivatives, instruments that allow investors to bet on future financial prices by investing just a fraction of the value of the underlying asset – *de facto* margin trading – have proliferated wildly on a global scale that makes 1920s Wall Street margin trading look like child's play. Now, as then, the great international banks are accepting risks they scarcely understand by underwriting financial derivatives and buoying up stock markets and capital values; but if prices cracked, the knock-on impact on bank balance sheets and their capacity to lend would be as severe as in the early 1930s.

The idea is that individual investors can use the derivative markets to gain protection against risk, but as Keynes would surely point out, by definition there can be no protection for the system as a whole. Keynes would be lobbying hard for proper supervision and regulation of a market that has gone mad. Banks do not know what risks they are running, and if the markets ever move unexpectedly, one bank will find itself with colossal exposure for which it is uncovered. It will renege on its obligations, and the system will crack. Keynes would be ridiculing bankers' protestations about the system's soundness for what they are: self-interested bleating.

Keynes's continual concern was the real economy – of employment, investment and output. He would be increasingly disturbed at the intensity of international competition and the way countries find themselves having to make astonishing economic adjustments in a matter of months and years. Although he was a convinced free trader, he would insist that the system can be kept open and liberal only if states can regain the possibility of pursuing full-employment policies to counteract the resulting dislocations. Free trade, as he argued during the Bretton Woods negotiations establishing the postwar financial order, the International Monetary Fund and World Bank, requires regulated international finance to allow expansionary domestic economic policies. Nor is free trade an absolute imperative. If the dislocation is too intense, then free trade too may need to be regulated.

With unemployment in the industrialized West standing at 36 million and rising – and with inflation at a thirty-year low – there is little doubt that Keynes would now be urging economic expansion led by governments. In economic management as in war, offence is the best means of attack. As a believer in the multiplier, he would urge debt-financed public works programmes, scorning the paranoia about budget deficits. He would again and again stress the difference between current and capital government spending, mocking the classical economists' preference to pay to keep men and women on unemployment benefits. He would call for government accounts everywhere to be organized into current and capital components, thus highlighting scope for borrowing more, given the lack of debt in relation to government assets. And taxes, he would urge, should be lifted only once the economy was growing – and be targeted on the incomes of the well-off.

To the American right he would endlessly and patiently explain the economic benefit of state and federal debt. Highways, bridges and education, for example, have yields that cannot be captured through the price mechanism and thus cannot be left to private initiative. A new road, for example, improves journey times not only for those who use it but for those who use the old roads from which traffic has been diverted. Real estate values improve along the road. Business turnover rises. The only economic agent that can capture the benefit is the state through taxes and reduced social security spending; it is thus the state that must finance the construction of the road – and if the returns are demonstrable there is no reason why the money should not be borrowed. Indeed, the spending on the road will snowball around the economy – the multiplier.

Nor would he allow fear of inflation to stymie his expansionary recommendations. Although aware of the destructive impact of inflation on democratic societies, he would have mocked the fear that inflation of 3 or 4 per cent presaged hyperinflation and the end of democracy. Indeed, he would be the first to see that a rise in the price level would have the advantage of reducing the real debt overhang and restoring the viability of the banking system – and he would have drawn a distinction between a once-and-for-all increase in the price level and inflation.

Indeed, given the centrality of the financial flows in his thinking, he would be anxious to get the banking system back on its feet. He would be championing government-led schemes for retiring mortgage debt from distressed borrowers. Initiatives to recapitalize the banking system so that it could undertake long-term lending would pour from his pen – while the case for taxing the over-rich, redistributing to the poor to boost consumption, would seem overwhelming.

The operation of the financial system on investment, particularly in Britain and the United States, would be a major preoccupation. Keynes was always critical about the stock market principle of buying and selling enterprise freely from day to day – as if the farmer can sell in the morning when it is raining and buy back in the afternoon when the sun is shining. The explosion of turnover in the capital markets would profoundly trouble him. Wall Street is becoming increasingly disengaged with the enterprises that it finances, and wealth creation is more and more a question of short-term financial engineering and paper entrepreneurship.

Indeed, the hollowing out of the US economy has less to do with low-cost international competition than with the incessant demand for dividends from the institutional holders of most of the nation's equity. Under permanent pressure to beat the average performance indices, pension funds, insurance companies and mutual funds have begun to regard dividends not as the return for risk – but as an income stream that should be as secure as interest payments on risk-free debt. As a result, company managements are compelled to make current assets work harder to deliver the required dividend stream, while using cash flow to support future investment risks the disapproval of the dividend-hungry institutions. Required real rates of return in the United States are spectacularly high in comparison with Japan and Germany; but that is the price managements must pay to persuade uncommitted and footloose institutions not to sell their shares. Wall Street has become the prime cause of US deindustrialization.

After the end of the Cold War, Keynes would feel the necessity for magnanimity by the western victors. The condition of the former Soviet Union and eastern Europe would alarm him immensely, with unemployment and despair potentially fuelling ugly political movements with an arsenal of nuclear weapons at hand. Turning around these depressed economies would not only alleviate a security threat, it would create an expanding market for western goods. He would be ceaselessly travelling the West's capitals trying to drum up support for a Marshall Aid plan for the former communist world. Defence spending in the West should be slashed and the money spent instead on supporting the growth of Russian capitalism – and he would be careful to support the social market variant of western capitalism rather than its pitiless Anglo-Saxon strain.

And Keynes being Keynes, he would have access to Clinton, Hosokawa and Yeltsin. His books and pamphlets would be selling worldwide, and at home he would be busy sponsoring new drama and dance. The spirit of optimism and action he craved could not take place in a cultural vacuum; it needed counterparts in the world of art and architecture. Confidence about the future and the capacity of the commonweal to act in the public good is an attitude of mind; it needs buttressing from every quarter.

But we do not have such a man, nor is one on the horizon. Yet the least we can do is to understand what he stood for and why. Part of his effectiveness was that he was able to terrorize the Anglo-Saxon establishment with the prospect of communism if the capitalist economy failed. But that terror has gone.

Instead, Keynesians have now to point not to the prospect of a communist revolution but rather to the slow and pervasive decay of western society brought about by running economies with millions of jobless and semi-economically active people. The collapse of employment for unskilled men is a major cause of US violence; and as expression through work becomes remoter for millions throughout the West, so they turn to nationalism and religious fundamentalism. Protection and confrontation start to characterize international relations, and who can know where that will lead?

But the gains from public initiative are diffuse while the costs are certain and concentrated; and in any case the linkages between economic failure, social distress and political calamity, while obvious, cannot be proven. For the moment the classical economists and their political allies continue to dictate the agenda. They have failed this century before with disastrous consequences; they will fail again. We need a Keynes. Without him, we need to revisit the extraordinary power of his ideas.

The American Prospect, 16 (Winter 1994)

Who's Whistling the Best Tunes Now?

The two great traditions in economic thought – Keynesian and laissez-faire – have fought themselves to a standstill. The so-called neo-classical counter-revolution that gained ascendancy over the past twenty years has at last run its course but, although the new Keynesians have arrested its intellectual advance, they have yet to turn their advantage into winning the policy debate. These are in-between times.

The right's setback is remarkable, especially as sheer momentum still allows it to set the political agenda and thus give the apparent impression that it is intellectually dominant. But this is more because of the vigour of the 1970s attack of the new wave of new right economists, almost entirely from the US, insisting that western capitalist economies had to return to first free market principles if they were to break the log jam of stagflation.

Vigour in argument has not been matched by subsequent economic performance – hence the growing vulnerability to counter-attack. In the US, for example, the long-run growth rate is unchanged, while the business cycle seems as unstable as it ever was. In Britain, the growth rate may have improved relative to our European peers, but it has still fallen absolutely.

Britain's deficiency in manufacturing productivity has partly closed, but that has brought no accompanying improvement in the growth of manufacturing output. And, if inflation has declined, so it has worldwide, with the British rate improving only marginally against the average. This is a pretty chequered record, and the right's intellectual case needs even more careful scrutiny.

The counter-revolutionaries' attack in the 1970s was two-pronged. Governments, they argued, should drop any attempt actively to manage the level of demand in the economy through fiscal policy (changing the gap between government spending and revenues) or monetary policy (changing interest rates and the liquidity in the financial system). All they should do is make sure the amount of money in circulation grew constantly to ensure minimal or no inflation.

Microeconomic policy should be focused solely on ensuring that market incentives were as pure as possible. In the US, in particular, a group of so-called 'supply-siders' insisted that taxation was the major economic distortion blighting western economies.

Behind these claims – highly congenial to conservatives everywhere – lay some fancy new economic theory. Discretionary macroeconomic policy of the type Keynes favoured was necessarily self-defeating, argued University of Chicago Professors Milton Friedman and Robert Lucas over the 1970s. If governments tried to offset the effect of a recession or boom, then, paradoxically, the impact would be to make the next swing in the economic cycle more, not less, unstable. Stagflation arose because of government attempts at economic management, along with high taxes and union power.

Professor Lucas's theory of rational expectations argued, in essence, that, as long as markets work freely, economic agents never make other than short-term mistakes in understanding what is going on around them.

A recession, for example, is caused not by deep-set market failure but by the short-run phenomenon that firms and workers do not drop their prices quickly enough to price themselves back into activity. They can't be sure in the initial stages of the downturn whether they need to lower their prices; but once they realize they face a recession they soon realize what they have to do, and the economy self-regulates itself back to normal. The best economic policy in response is patience.

The Bank of England or the Treasury cannot be substantially wiser than the many firms which make up the economy, so they will act only when everyone else is recognizing what is going on, and thus boost an economy that is already recovering, causing it to overshoot if policy has any real effect, said the new right.

There is also the notion that the only good direction for taxation is down. This just about held up when inflation and interest rates were in double figures in the 1970s, so that, as Harvard's Professor Martin Feldstein showed, taxation of the high nominal interest rates paid to savers without adjusting for inflation meant that the real return on savings after inflation went negative – depressing the incentives to save and so hurting saving and investment levels.

It is obviously true that very high marginal rates of tax are deterrents to effort. But once inflation falls to low levels and high marginal tax rates are reduced, the tax-cutting supply-siders are left with little substantive proof for their claims.

As MIT's Professor Paul Krugman argues, even the great homes of free market economics like the University of Chicago never endorsed the wilder supply-siders' case. Today there is no US economist of the stature of Martin Feldstein pushing the idea that tax cuts paid for themselves by the boost to economic activity, and the case is made by right-wing ideologues rather than economists.

The same is increasingly true of the critique of Keynesian demand management. American New Keynesians have made a substantial dent in the idea that rational expectations mean the entire conception is impossible. Professors George Akerlof at MIT and Greg Mankiw of Harvard have developed the intriguing idea that it is rational for economic agents not to be completely rational. Most of us proceed not by exhaustively gathering every piece of information so that the market bounces back to normal as we realize our mistakes, they say, but by making rough guesses.

A restaurateur doesn't change his prices every day. And taxpayers don't think, when the government borrows money for a large road-building programme, that it will have to raise taxes some time in the future to pay off the debt, so they had better save now to be ready for the extra taxation. It might be 'rational', but nobody in the real world behaves like that.

But if individuals are rational in being nearly rational, then Friedman's and Lucas's proof that demand management is self-defeating fails. Economies, as Keynes said, can get locked into disequilibriums for long periods because individuals and firms are just unable to find the array of prices that allows the economy to return by itself to the path of rising output and full employment. Prices are not reliable enough in a nearly rational world to co-ordinate economic activity except in the very long run, and by then we are dead.

We need the government to act to break the impasse; and the economy does respond to deflationary and expansionary stimuli.

There is growing acceptance that the quality of human capital, public infrastructure and trust relations within firms are key determinants of growth. Economists arguing for capitalism and careless about inequality and income distribution are increasingly hard to find, even on the free market right.

But, on the left, there are few who advocate old-fashioned government pump-priming and intervention. The new Keynesian ideas advocate government acting more subtly, building up human and physical capital, moderating inequality. While accepting that demand management remains a powerful tool, it is best used sparingly.

It is fashionable to argue that the right still has all the best tunes. Wrong. Its case is evaporating. A new range of ideas is emerging that will underpin a new politics. The only question is how long it will take to get there.

Guardian, 29 January 1996

Follow Spitfire, Not Concorde

The deeper Britain gets trapped in its low-skills, low-tech, low-wage equilibrium, the more hysterical the praise for so-called economic recovery and the quasi-Thatcherite policies that generated it. The creation of 185,000 part-time jobs over the past nine months – which serviced the recent rise in consumption while 124,000 full-time jobs disappeared – is hailed as a master-stroke of employment generation by a world-beating economy. But it is nothing of the sort.

Companies that can win market share at home and abroad have to do more than invest in labour-saving devices and shed workers. They have to innovate. The increased productivity of which the government boasts is nothing but degenerate, sweat-shop capitalism; if it were not, there would be signs of increased spending on research and development, of an upsurge in patenting, of a new interest in science and technology. Instead there is lassitude and decline.

R&D spending is a pretty good proxy of business vitality. In the early

1970s, Britain's R&D spending as a proportion of GDP was second only to the US; now it has sunk well down the league table. Indeed, through the 1980s the decline accelerated from relative to absolute.

According to Gavin Cameron of Nuffield College, manufacturing R&D, measured as a percentage of value added, has actually declined, while other major industrialized countries' spending has increased. With one or two exceptions, like pharmaceuticals, the picture is ghastly; and in low-tech areas such as paper and textiles Britain has virtually given up R&D altogether. Competition can only be through low wages.

Government spending on R&D has consistently fallen as a proportion of GDP since 1979, with attempts being made to divert the dwindling sum to applied research with provable commercial uses. This way, runs the argument, Britain will get a bigger bang for its buck – and avoid another Concorde.

The trouble is that there is little resemblance between the model of innovation in the Conservative ministerial head and reality. In the model, the innovations produced by white-coated, other-worldly scientists in laboratories need to be carried into the marketplace by go-getting low-taxed entrepreneurs. Bring the two together, light the blue touch paper and hey presto. Innovation is a 'supply side'-driven phenomenon, best left to the markets.

Yet at a conference organized by the Institute for Fiscal Studies and supported by the Economic and Social Research Council, it was painfully obvious that innovation was a much more complex phenomenon. There needs to be rising demand, so that businesses have some prospect of making profits from the innovations in which they invest; companies need to be equipped with cultures, and skilled personnel capable of taking research into development and production; there need to be financial institutions ready to value R&D and finance it; and government spending and tax incentives are imperative to raise R&D levels. Had the Treasury secretary, Michael Portillo, been at the conference he would have seen it as a prime exponent of the 'New British Disease'; for the rest of us it was an outbreak of applied intelligence and common sense.

Above all it was clear that science and research are public goods. Even companies find that, however much they may want to exploit their findings privately, one of the best incentives to researchers is not the promise of high incomes (although that helps), but the undertaking that research will be published. There is a scientific community animated by the search for knowledge in its own right. If companies want scientific collaboration and respect they have to concede to its priorities.

As Keith Pavitt from the Science Policy Research Unit at Sussex University made clear, the notion that R&D is an individual activity, undertaken by individual scientists whose results are exploited by individual entrepreneurs, is moonshine. Increasingly, research is a team effort, the success of which depends on the exchange of ideas within the team and beyond. One of the purposes of companies publishing research is that it signals that the research team is a member of that community and governed by its mores.

It is to support a public good that government involvement, in particular government finance, is imperative. Science ranks with law and order or defence as deserving public support. Indeed, Bronwyn Hall, a leading US economist, from Berkeley, declared that the social rates of return to R&D in industry and agriculture are demonstrably far above private rates of return – that a new invention had huge benefits beyond the gains capturable by an individual company.

This, she said, was why there was a case for subsidy. Yes, subsidy, to raise the private rate of return to the social level. The US government had introduced an incremental tax credit for new R&D, so as not to subsidize R&D that would have taken place anyway. There had been $1 billion (£670 million) a year spent over the past decade in tax credits, and R&D had been lifted by $2 billion a year. Even allowing for some reclassification of company spending to claim the credit, the policy palpably worked.

But in Britain no such intelligence rules. The science budget is shaved, tax credits are dismissed as subsidy, the private sector is told to go it alone. This policy not only misunderstands the dynamics of the whole exercise, it misinterprets recent British economic history.

It is a commonplace that the British economy has been in relative decline for more than a century, but what is less remarked upon is that had Britain stayed wedded to its textile, coal and heavy engineering economy of the late 1920s the decline would have been even more marked. Yet from the early 1930s to the early 1950s there was a transformation in the country's economic base.

This was led by technology, and in particular, by state support of science, which reached a peak during and immediately after the war. The right-wing story told by Correlli Barnett in *The Audit of War* – of Britain's anti-scientific, welfare-oriented, liberal elite, personified by Labour, spending a fortune on a welfare state and neglecting science and technology – is bunk. For a brief period, in fact, the imperative of war and then the commitment to full employment forced the British to recover the *élan* of the Industrial Revolution. By 1950 Britain had established, by tight regulation of finances, and state support, an extraordinary array of high-technology industries which had not existed in 1930.

The story of the past forty years has been of the squandering of this inheritance through the insistence that a free financial system and reduction of state support are the elixirs that drive innovation. No surprise that in the 1980s, when the biases in the British system were celebrated as strengths, the run-down accelerated.

Even in the postwar period, innovation was more of a demand-driven phenomenon than the supply-side creature of the right's imagination. Professor Paul Geroski of the London Business School showed that, when demand rose during the postwar period, businesses dipped into the stock of innovations and developed them for the market, but when demand fell so did the rate of innovation. To lift the economy on to a higher growth and innovation path requires finding ways to lift and sustain increases in demand.

Which means that if Britain wants to get into that virtuous circle, policy will have to be recast. There will need to be a sustained increase in demand. There will have to be increased state spending on science. There will have to be tax credits to make R&D cheaper. There will have to be a redesigned financial system that supports long-term investment. And there will have to be a recognition that the state has a powerful role. The model is not Concorde but the Spitfire, radar, synthetic rubber, the computer and the jet engine.

None of this is set to happen. Instead of looking to raise growth potential, the government is determined to cut spending to adjust down to the low-growth, low-skills equilibrium – which, unaided and unreformed, is all the private sector can deliver. The lesson from our history, from international comparison and from economic research is that this policy is self-defeating. But that will not change a thing.

Guardian, 17 January 1994

Trade with a Tangible Return to Well-Being

There are more than a million men and women of working age in Britain who have been officially unemployed for over a year. As their numbers are swollen by people losing incapacity benefit with the new tougher tests, Britain will rank only below Italy among leading industrialized countries as having the highest proportion of long-term unemployed.

This dubious honour comes despite having the least regulated labour market, the least generous levels of income support and one of the most developed economic recoveries. Notwithstanding the daily drumbeat of insistence that Britain must lower its social costs, cut its social security spending and resist all forms of regulation to capitalize upon its 'success', the brutal facts tell otherwise. Far from the system working, it continues to malfunction.

To be out of work for more than a year, especially for the young, is desolate beyond most people's imagination. Some take to their beds for most of the day; most withdraw from social life altogether. They get locked in a rhythm of idleness which stretches endlessly before them. They are the forgotten, and a standing condemnation of the supposedly moral community in which we live.

The economics of the new right is not too good at explaining why this is happening or how to respond. The basic concept is that the labour market reflects a balance between incentives to search for work and incentives to hire, and if long-term unemployment is high, that suggests only that the incentives are gummed up by some extraneous influence – unions, regulations, social security payments – so the market has not delivered as it 'naturally' should. Moreover, any government-induced boost to economic activity is prohibited. That will only drive unemployment below its 'natural' rate, and so create self-feeding inflation.

The dispute with this view is not to contest that incentives drive economic activity (which they must), but that it refuses to acknowledge that the market itself patterns incentives into a destructive process which results from the 'natural' operation of the price mechanism. For instance, the long-term unemployed are less attractive to hire than the recently unemployed – they have more redundant skills and have lost the culture of work, and so necessarily the longer they are out of work, the more rebuffs they have had and the more demoralized they become. Thus the market, if allowed to work freely, gives jobs to those who have lost work most recently and those who are in most need are least likely to receive job offers. This bias is real, whatever the Conservative hate-objects, such as benefit or unionization levels. The most socially necessary result is the one that the 'invisible hand' is least likely to produce or alone can capture.

There can be no effective intervention other than to change the real incentive pattern – that is, the long-term unemployed must be compelled to look harder for jobs and to accept very low wages to reflect their lack of employability. The market's harsh judgement of their worth is the only real solution.

But there is an alternative. Suppose you recognize the Keynesian truth that markets work as traps, of which long-term unemployment is a classic example. Then there has to be intervention to change markets' 'natural' pattern of incentives and re-empower the long-term unemployed.

Interestingly, an entrepreneurial company in Glasgow is exploiting this market failure successfully. The Wise Group, specializing in the training and employment of the long-term jobless, is now one of Glasgow's forty largest employers. It bids for public contracts in environmental and infrastructure improvement, which it undertakes solely by hiring the long-term unemployed to whom it pays low but market rates of pay. After two months' training and ten months' work, its workers move on, mostly to be hired by other contractors who know they are hiring trained, motivated workers. In economic terms, the group has enabled the long-term unemployed to escape the market's rationing system.

Every year, around 2.5 per cent of Glasgow's 18,000 long-term unemployed pass through its books. The jobs they do would not exist but for the Wise Group, nor would their new-found employability. Equally, the group challenges the Malthusian view that an economy has only a fixed stock of jobs, so that if the population rises, unemployment results. Moreover, the improvements to Glasgow's housing stock, pavements, spare land and parks is reflected in the city's well-being, as I witnessed on the infamous Easterhouse estate. This is win-win stuff indeed.

But it is social entrepreneurship that has succeeded in the face of profoundly adverse odds, and it does not come cheaply. The Wise Group reckons each job it creates costs £15,000. The City of Glasgow, one of the group's important customers, could not justify that alone; but because its contribution is matched by other public authorities, like the European Commission, it calculates that it gets a good deal. The Wise Group is a kind of juggling act, offering each partner more than it could achieve on its own.

For fighting long-term unemployment is expensive, and needs more than a simple subsidy to employers. A quarter, sometimes more, of each Wise Group cohort has to be dropped during the year because it requires more help than the organization can provide. There has to be intense support to find work, and occasionally only half of its leavers successfully move on, although typically the results are better.

On the other hand, the advantages, in terms of saved benefit payments, extra taxes, improved infrastructure, better training and above all the higher level of social well-being more than pay back the initial costs, although it can take years. If we want more Wise Groups, we have to find ways of allowing all those benefits to be captured – which implies substantial reforms to the whole of public finance.

For example, doing 'a Wise Group' with 100,000 nationally would cost £1.5 billion – on the face of it insupportable. But suppose the programme could reclaim the cost of the income support that would have been paid to the long-term unemployed for a year: that would reduce the cost by some £300 million. And there is also the value of the pure infrastructure work, worth around a third of each tender, that would have to and should be undertaken anyway; that's worth another £500 million. The net cost in year one is £700 million.

If every worker in the second year gets a job at average pay, the Exchequer will gain £8,000 per person in extra income tax and saved income support – some £800 million for 100,000 workers, so the programme pays for itself over two years. But each worker won't get a job at average pay, so the savings will be less, and may require a third or even fourth year before the scheme becomes self-financing.

If on top each worker could transfer their £65 income support as an incentive to their new employer for the first six months of employment, as Richard Layard proposes in a forthcoming pamphlet for the Employment Policy Institute, the effectiveness of the programme would be yet higher, even if the pay-back periods were longer.

Public bodies would need to have a more imaginative accounting system to allow them to increase capital spending by £500 million; alternatively it could be financed by a special utilities tax, as shadow Chancellor Gordon Brown proposes. Getting the initial infrastructure of Wise Groups in place would take a couple of years, but over a ten-year period, there is little doubt long-term unemployment could be lowered by at least 500,000 towards the OECD average – and that it would be self-financing. It would also allow the economy to be run at higher levels of demand, generating spill-over effects for all – that will be the best way of entrenching the employment gains. This is win-win economics, requiring nothing but political will and a proper understanding of the market process. Let's do it.

Guardian, 25 September 1995

PART III

London Babylon:
The City, Finance and
the British Economy

Money before Machines

This year the fruits should start to show as Britain enters the fourth year of recovery. The relentless assaults by companies on their workforces, led by the privatized utilities, ought to ease and the fear of job insecurity should recede. Investment should start to accelerate and a sense of economic improvement begin to permeate. The question is: will it?

Enter the City of London. To most people it means little more than the television images of young men and women buying and selling furiously in vast dealing rooms. Yet this is not just a technocratic and slightly eccentric game. This is a seat of economic, political and social power built up over centuries – and some of the answers to 1995's big economic questions lie here.

It is the City's demands for high returns, for example, that lie behind the ceaseless rounds of rationalizations and downsizing from Britain's privatized utilities – with 66,000 more lost jobs predicted in the next five years. And it is the City above all that shapes the character and level of British investment. Unless it changes unexpectedly, 1995, inevitably with its own twists and turns, will just be another year of more of the same.

In its own terms the City is an astonishing success story. Here Britain remains pre-eminent in international markets. The size of its financial markets and the variety of financial assets it trades are breathtaking. Moreover it has succeeded in holding on to its position despite the loss of Empire and run-down of the British economy. Even its curious medieval rituals – the Lord Mayor's parades, sheriffs attending judges at the Old Bailey, the incorporation of ancient liveried trading companies – survive with their lustre undimmed into the last decade of the twentieth century.

But by another yardstick the City has failed. It was Winston Churchill who observed in the 1920s that in Britain finance is too proud and industry too humble, ventilating a complaint that had been rumbling since the 1860s. It remains no less valid seventy years later. British companies, with their footloose shareholders hungry for ever higher dividends and their arm's-length bankers who keep them on a short lease with short-term loans on onerous terms, are at a permanent disadvantage in an increasingly cut-throat international marketplace.

Hire-and-fire labour practices and low social overheads, of which the British government boasts, are not the key to industrial success – rather it is patient, committed, long-term finance. Without this, investment is always constrained and companies can never develop the financial muscle to build new products and take on their overseas competitors. But Britain has lacked and still lacks such finance; and the City, the heart of the financial system, is the reason why.

There are a growing number of industrial and even financial voices who believe that Britain has paid too high a price for the City's success. Former ICI chairman Sir John Harvey-Jones certainly thinks so – as does Ivor Yates, former deputy chief executive of British Aerospace, one of the country's largest manufacturing companies. And some bankers, like the Frenchman Hervé de Carmoy, who ran Midland Bank International in the 1980s, share the view that there is a systemic unwillingness to mobilize large amounts of committed finance to support British manufacturing.

But these are voices crying in the wilderness. Within the City itself there is intense resentment at such criticism – and its leading representatives are anxious instead to present British finance as an undersold success story. More foreign exchange is traded here than in any other financial centre. More international lending and sale of international bonds is undertaken here than anywhere else. Its stock market and insurance market are the largest in Europe. And so the superlatives carry on.

The common thread is that these are all markets. In the same way that London boasts famous markets for fruit, fish and meat, so it now possesses the world's most formidable array of financial markets. Therein lies the explanation for both its successes and its failures. Well-run financial markets where all the parties can trust each other to settle their debts are an essential lubricant to financial activity – providing those who part with their money to invest in a company or lend to a government the reassurance that with a market they can get their money back when they want it.

But at the same time markets keep the users and providers of finance apart. They are anonymous; they foster lack of commitment by both parties; they actively promote the restless search for the highest return in the immediate future; they are impatient of failure and setbacks. If London has built its financial pre-eminence on its markets, it is the excessive reliance on them and their associated culture that has cost British industry so dear.

City people and the Bank of England alike regard London's market-based way of doing things as pretty near to unimprovable – and as it is something that the British are pretty good at, the system should be protected and admired rather than criticized. There is, after all, a happy congruence between the values and bearing of the British upper middle class and the trust that is imperative to making financial markets work. Despite the Names crash at Lloyd's and the scandal over the sale of pensions, the famous aphorism that a London financier's 'word is his bond' lives on – and remains a worldwide magnet.

But as Anthony Sampson, long-time chronicler of British affairs, observes, if you want people to trust you it is best to appear impressive –

hence the City's fondness for dining rooms that appear to have been trans-
posed from stately homes and even more so for the kind of chap that emerges
from a good family, public school and Oxbridge, which still provides nearly
half of all City top jobs.

Yet the City is not an English gentleman's preserve; its doors have always
been open to outsiders prepared to sign up to its mores and demonstrate
financial acumen. A Rothschild or a Warburg, just as today a Mallenkrodt
(the outgoing chairman of the merchant bank Schroders) or a Yassokovitch,
have mixed and mix alongside a Buxton, Baring or Lloyd. Whatever their
background, all come to share the bearing, attitudes and manners of the
English upper class.

For despite the talk of the rise of East End barrow boys in City markets,
the route to the top remains, as Sampson argues, the same as it has always
been. Its denizens may no longer call their butlers for the three Bs – bowler,
brolly and briefcase – before they come to work, but here is the place where
fortunes are made and a place in society secured. The income from spending one day occupying a senior job in a City firm is rarely less than £250,000
a year and usually very much more.

But such salaries are intimately linked with the City's market-based organization. Every transaction in a market commands a commission or fee,
so the busier the markets the more transactions and the higher the commissions. Moreover there are no huge investments in machines, factories or
large blue-collar workforces; if a City firm employs more than 5,000 it is
large. It is a recipe for high profits and salaries.

This brokerage, dealing and exchanging – restlessly searching for the
highest return at home or abroad – combined within a culture of trust built
up by English gentlemanliness, has defined the City since its foundation.
Professor Anthony Hopkins argues that the value system which has per-
vaded British business life produces a business culture he dubs 'gentlemanly
capitalism'. The Industrial Revolution happened completely independently
of the City of London, which had existed for the preceding two centuries,
he argues. Britain's industrialization was financed in the first instance by
local people backing and lending to local entrepreneurs, and latterly by
local banks. The City was not involved in the mobilization of industrial
finance. Its job was not to back British industry but to finance international trade; to lend and invest profitably abroad inside and outside the
Empire; and to raise loans for the government.

Throughout this century the criticisms have kept on coming – but to no
avail. The Macmillan report in 1931 damned the lack of bank support for
Britain's small and medium-sized firms – the equivalent of the *Mittelstand,*
the family-owned companies forming the backbone of German industry.
Also criticized was the failure of the City to mobilize support for giant
combines. In 1960 Prime Minister Harold Macmillan (no relation to the

report!) deplored the insistence of the City in arguing that its job was to make money for its shareholders, refusing any wider public role: 'if capitalist society as a whole were still to take that view', he wrote, 'we should be very near to the crash.' Successive Labour initiatives followed, including the Industrial Reorganization Corporation and the National Enterprise Board. But all suffered the same fate as their nineteenth-century predecessors – ignored, abolished or withered on the vine for want of support.

Geoffrey Chandler was director of the National Economic Development Office in the early 1980s. Its job was to bring industry, unions, government and the City together but he recalls that one of the most fruitless exchanges was between representatives of industry and the City. Industry wanted patient, cheap, long-term financial backing and complained that investment was suffering for want of it; the City institutions would retort that there was no shortage of finance for bankable investment propositions. In a free market anything worthwhile would get finance and if the cost was high the City had to protect itself against the vagaries of inflation. It was a dialogue of the deaf.

Yet the British market-based system indisputably raises the cost of British finance. Rosemary Radcliffe, chief economist at accountants Coopers and Lybrand, calculates that British companies have had to make 17 or 18 per cent return on their investments over the last few years to satisfy the demands of their bankers and shareholders; Japanese companies have had to make 10 per cent and German and French companies between 13 and 14 per cent. The differences may seem small but, as Harvey-Jones insists, it is upon such margins that the success and failure of whole industries depend.

The stories of firms and industries that have suffered are legion – and although the particulars may differ there is always a financial explanation at bottom. It might be the disappearance of the country's last indigenous fork-lift truck manufacturer, Lancer-Boss, into German hands because it was unable to organize the same long-term debt from British sources as its international competitors. The car industry is a more complicated story, but Michael Edwardes, former chairman of British Leyland, recalls the endemic under-investment and short-termism of the company when he took over in 1977; there had been no external pressure from the multiplicity of shareholders to raise investment levels – rather the preoccupation had been to maintain and raise dividends. And Joel Joffe, a now retired senior figure from the insurance industry, believes that City pressure on insurance companies to grow and deliver high dividend growth has been a prime factor in the creation of commission-driven salesforces that have led to so many wrong pension and insurance products being sold to so many people. And so on, and so on.

The heart of the problem is, as Professor Colin Mayer at Oxford says, a systematic failure of the financial system to commit to British companies – providing them with neither a stable, long-term ownership base nor with cheap long-term debt. Instead British finance is always near the exit door, ready to bail out by calling in its short-term loans or selling its shares – just as a highly market-based system provides. There is much scoffing of other financial models, like Germany's, in the Square Mile; but Germany remains committed to its companies and provides them the long-term backing they need. Britain's investment, three years into a recovery, is still languishing; Germany's, less than a year into recovery, is up by more than 15 per cent from an already higher base. Surely that proves something.

It is not difficult to propose changes to the tax and legal systems together with reform of institutions that could change the way the City operates. But that has been said for more than 100 years without making any impact.

Pen Kent, a director of the Bank of England, concedes that the returns the City has demanded have been onerous but blames Britain's roller-coaster inflationary economy and says things are now changing as inflation subsides. Banks are offering less short-term overdraft finance and, with low inflation, shareholders will accept lower growth in dividends. Moreover, he says, Britain's market-based financial system is the way of the future.

It is hard to share such optimism. Britain's financial structures and attitudes predate the inflationary 1970s and 1980s. They are the product of 300 years of history and are recognizably the same today with the same fundamental attitudes. These are brokers and traders; not men and women who believe it is their business to help construct a stronger British economy.

Moreover this is where Britain's social and economic elite is situated; it controls the commanding heights of the economy, and challenging its view without the support of a formidable coalition is – as successive reformers have found – impossible. But as the industrial base weakens, so the ability to build any such coalition wanes.

Anthony Sampson believes only a national crisis will shake the City's role, and as that is improbable nothing will change. It is hard to gainsay him. Yet if there is no change Britain's wider economic run-down will continue, ultimately entrapping the City too. Here perhaps there are grounds for hope – but after 300 years who would bet on it?

Guardian, 3 January 1995

Why Rover was Driven out of UK Hands

Richard Arkwright had to rely on the support of a local publican to get finance for the spinning jenny; 100 years later John Kemp Starley and William Sutton relied on their own savings to begin the manufacture of penny-farthings that was to become the Rover group. Nor are things much different now.

The advantage of being first to industrialize, Empire and the intervention of the state in two world wars gave British manufacturing some shelter from its ruthlessly anti-industrial financial system, but fifty years of peace and progressive deregulation and it is exposed as never before. The sale of Rover abroad is one more milestone in the process of destruction.

This is not to surrender to Portillo-like xenophobia. Given where Rover stood in the international car pecking order after the British capital market had damaged the domestic car industry, and given the pressures on British Aerospace at the mercies of the same system, Rover's future could only lie in collaboration with a foreign company. The issue is the industrial terms of such a deal.

For fifteen years Rover had built a relationship with Honda – using Honda engineering and production expertise to drive up-market. If your production base is 300,000–400,000 cars a year, you simply have to operate in the higher-price segment of the market to have any hopes of profitability.

At bottom, Honda's strategy suited Rover and Britain. For, as Andrew Mair describes, the Japanese company is dedicated to an idea of global localization of production.* Honda's refusal to take its stake above 48 per cent of Rover was part of that strategy.

The Japanese might regard shareholdings as tokens of long-term commitment, but they reckoned without the ingrained fecklessness of British finance. BAe's choice was to sell 28 per cent more equity to Honda to raise another £167 million or to sell the complete company to BMW for £800 million.

BMW's key models might compete head to head with the British, so rationalization in favour of Munich is inevitable; to retain no equity meant complete loss of control and forgoing any share of future benefits – but that did not trouble BAe or its chairman, John Cahill.

* A. Mair, *Honda's Global Local Corporation* (New York: St Martin's Press, 1993).

A man who can only step into the country for ninety days a year for tax reasons could hardly make his own priorities clearer. Long-term industrial thinking or the country's welfare can go to hell: the object is to get the share price up.

In any case, Mr Cahill is a creation of the British system. BAe needs to reconstruct its balance sheet after some grave strategic mistakes, and it operates in a capital market that notoriously places a high premium on the security of dividend flows and immediate profit prospects.

Its multiplicity of shareholders, following late-Victorian trust law, keep at a distance, exercising their control over the management of the company through the laughable formula of the annual meeting – or, more simply, by selling their shares. BAe cannot afford a chairman who plans industrially; his world is necessarily beset by the constraints of short-term bankers and footloose shareholders. If there was not a Cahill he would have to be invented.

Defenders of British finance insist that short-termism keeps management on its toes. British Aerospace's record suggests otherwise. The company has had to arrive at a crisis before attempts were made to instil proper financial controls; and beforehand it indulged in such wayward acts as buying a property company at the top of the last boom.

This bought short-term stock market favour but it was yet another disastrous misjudgement. BAe had bought itself a few more months of stock market peace, yet months of peace are no substitute for the capacity to mobilize sizeable sums of cheap long-term money to support industrial investment.

The clusters and networks of firms competing and collaborating in innovation and investment are progressively thinned out as one company uses its stock market quotation to buy others out.

The British motor industry is a textbook example of the strategic inhibition placed upon companies by the priorities of the stock market. There was no reason after the war why Jaguar/Daimler, Austin/Morris, Standard/Triumph and Rover could not have grown into British variants of BMW, Volkswagen and Daimler-Benz. That they never did is largely due to the capital markets.

Up-front finance for model development was offered only on onerous terms, insisting that funds were generated for each new wave of investment by efficiency savings from consolidation and merger – never ensuring that this took place on the ground where myriads of factories remained unrationalized. Instead, the concern was with balance-sheet magnitudes. Why dirty your hands in a factory?

The capital markets never rewarded building market share or technological pre-eminence; the concern was always for dividends and immediate profits. And if the unions can be fairly accused of obsessive concern with increasing wages and job demarcations, who, given the fecklessness of the companies' owners, can blame them for their preoccupation?

Coventry and Birmingham, classic industrial districts, were damaged. Unparalleled engineering skills were devalued, and innovation systematically underfunded. After the banks refused BL's request for funds in 1973 – Lloyds and Midland had only acquiesced in similar demands in the 1930s because of the strategic necessities in the run-up to the war – the die was cast. Nationalization, decline and dismemberment lay in store.

This capital market remains firmly in place. Already there is talk of 'consolidating' BAe and GEC; instead of each company using external finance and its existing business as a platform for growth and innovation, the injunction is to merge into one. In which case, one can predict with complete confidence that aerospace will follow the car industry into decline and junior partnership in some foreign enterprise. BAe and Rolls-Royce – RIP.

Yet this destruction is the natural operation of the system. Companies, as Jonathan Charkham writes in his superb overview of the leading industrialized countries' financial systems, are not 'desiccated profit-making machines.' 'The commitment to colleague, product company and society which is to be found in the greatest companies is not wholly compatible with the financial view of purpose. Profit is necessary but not sufficient', he says.*

BAe, run by a tax exile, could hardly be governed other than wholly for short-term profit. Nor, as Mr Charkham comments, are there any counterbalances. Non-executive directors can hardly be expected to be monitors, advisers and decision-makers – and the board's structural weaknesses are compounded by an entire system.

The way we fund our pensions, the system of corporate governance, the lack of interest by the banks, the centralization in London, the lack of shareholder commitment, self-regulation of the City, the values of our business elite, the role of accountants all hang together, as they always have.

Behind them lies a network of social institutions and values that create our business and financial elite. Educated apart, housed apart, socially apart, they consider themselves to be superior but offer no reciprocal loyalty to country, company or community. It is no accident that the role model is an opted-out tax exile or that Britain no longer possesses a car manufacturer. This is what British civilization and its institutions necessarily deliver.

Guardian, 7 February 1994

* J. Charkham, *Keeping Good Company* (Oxford: Oxford University Press, 1993).

A City without Controls has Resulted in a Capital Market out of Control

The global capital market is a fact of life, we are told. The genie cannot be put back in the bottle and governments and firms worldwide must submit themselves to the judgement of the capital markets' Nick Leesons. Their freedom to trade in whatever financial instrument they choose and to move money across whatever frontier they want is God-given, absolute and cannot be challenged.

The City, more reliant than any other financial centre on turnover in the capital markets, is the most vigorous exponent of this credo – and one of the most important creators of the new world. Only if financial markets have their freedom and if public intervention is minimal can finance prosper; and it is only if finance prospers that the economy can prosper – or so goes the syllogism. Barings – the most significant bank collapse for more than a century – is the signal that at last the game is up.

It has always been a self-serving and partisan doctrine – and largely illusory. The City has not just been the citadel of free financial markets; it has been the prime beneficiary of the most determined industrial policy sustained continuously by the British state in any branch of economic activity. Law, taxation, regulation and economic policy have been bent to suit its needs.

The importance of the Barings collapse is that it exposes everything from the mystic belief in minimal regulation to the celebration of the global capital market as shams – self-defeating for the City and increasingly risky for the world at large. More important, the state-backed free market has not been able to save an important British bank at its moment of trial – the losses were just too big for either the banks or the government to bear.

The trade-off used to be that the City could live with minimal regulation because when things went wrong it would pick up the pieces, with the Bank of England at the helm; now that it cannot, there will have to be a tightening of regulation to prevent such losses occurring again.

This has already been happening in the City's dealings with the public – notably over pensions and other savings products – but now that will extend to the banking and derivatives markets. Indeed, not only the regulations but also who polices them and how will be called into question, beginning with the very instrument that the government has chosen to investigate the affair, the report from the Board of Banking Supervision.

This is not an independent body, but a Bank of England-run board chaired by the Governor of the Bank of England, Eddie George. Neither the Treasury, still thanking its lucky stars that the Bingham report into BCCI did not force a ministerial resignation, nor the Bank wants to let another independent judge loose in a case which it is now obvious will highlight yet another chapter of missed warning signals, slack regulation and poor internal controls.

As the evidence mounts that Barings knew what was happening, shipping hundreds of millions of pounds out to its Singapore operation in the weeks leading up to the crash, and that auditors were warning of poor internal controls as early as 1992, this will not wash. The Japanese, Germans, Americans and, not least, Singapore – all losers from the fall-out – want a proper, independent investigation, such as they would perform; and although Mr George is respected for his integrity on the international circuit, nobody considers that he should be judge and jury in his own case. Labour will find that it has important allies in its call for an independent investigation.

But this is just the tip of an iceberg – symptomatic of the clubby way the City is run and its anxiety to close ranks to keep the old order alive. Minimal regulation has been seen as a key source of competitive advantage for too long for an event like Barings to shake the belief.

While a few sops will have to be offered to assuage domestic and international opinion – like calling for watertight separation of dealers and their back offices – the Bank and City want to keep the deregulatory show on the road. They are programmed that way.

As Ewan Green of Reading University has shown, the Bank and Treasury have been relaxing controls to favour the City's international interests over industry since the 1950s. In internal memos after the war, the Treasury was keenly aware that, as physical controls were scrapped, interest rates would necessarily shoulder more of the burden of containing credit growth, with deleterious effects on manufacturing. But the City had to be restored to its former glory, and with it the economic activity that benefited Britain's upper middle class and their skills – accountancy, law, banking and trading.

From a tax regime which allows foreign nationals to pay minimal tax and national insurance to a Bank of England that welcomes all and asks few questions, as its approach to BCCI revealed, the thrust of policy has been the same: light regulation, highly liquid markets and the capacity to maximize individual rewards have been regarded as the magic elixir.

When an individual bank gets into trouble, the Bank and Treasury will be there to rescue the unfortunate. It might be directly through organizing a financial lifeboat; or indirectly by extending the Jubilee Line, despite it offering the lowest return of any transport investment in London, so that the bankers to Canary Wharf have a bankable asset. This has been the state-backed free market.

Barings' collapse has to be seen through this prism. Andrew Buxton, chairman of Barclays and scion of an old City family, was regarded by one banker as 'brilliant', reported the FT on Friday, at the weekend crisis meeting. 'This is the future of the banking industry', he told some reluctant contributors to the financial lifeboat that was being assembled, 'and you are going to contribute.'

Despite the brave faces after the whole effort failed, Mr Buxton was right. One bank chairman tells me that the City's reputation is now irredeemably compromised. 'My word is my bond' has been exploded as cant. The crisis at Lloyd's only adds to the sense that at bottom London is no longer rich enough to weather its own financial misdemeanours. The US investment bank Morgan Stanley drew back from buying the merchant bank S. G. Warburg, which had signalled in its readiness to merge that trying to be a British global investment bank was beyond its resources. In the backwash from Barings, British banks find new question marks about them – and that is reflected in their credit standing and status.

The signs of City weakness are all around. It needs to be richer – but to be richer it has to have a bigger industrial base. That needs to be nurtured with patient money and could take twenty years to grow; but that is too long a time scale for a City of London that needs its profits now – to keep its shareholders happy and to compete with rivals. The reason why all British banks rely more and more on income from market-making and trading in the derivatives markets, along with fees and commissions from investment banking, is that that is where the immediate profits are. But they are of low quality – and run the permanent risk of turning into embarrassing losses.

The terms of the game are changing. Minimal regulation in London is not a source of competitive strength if it generates such doubts about the integrity of the City that British-based financial institutions are seen as unreliable business partners. As countries outside the UK recognize, it is essential to have regulated financial markets and financial institutions whose activities are closely monitored. What is more, those countries are prepared to act.

In the US, there were Congressional hearings as early as Tuesday to assess whether a Barings-type collapse could happen there. Simex, the Singapore-based futures exchange where Barings was operating, announced within forty-eight hours that henceforth it would be mandatory for a member's dealing and settlement arms to be separated. Japan recently tightened margin requirements for trading in its futures markets. In Germany and the US, regulatory agencies independent of the central bank and financial markets are re-examining their rules.

The global markets are powerful; but the terms on which they trade are set by governments. Barings is a call for action – and the City and Bank will find themselves competed into change. No more casual regulation. No more can the Bank of England combine regulatory and monetary duties. No more indifference to the industrial hinterland. No more reliance on dealing profits to sustain British finance. The City may try to ignore the warnings – but if it does there will be more Barings, and yet more dominance by foreign banks. It's the end of an era – thank God.

Guardian, 6 March 1995

Jobs and Growth Mean Regulation

What a disaster financial deregulation has been. The legacy of debt, financial instability and depression will be with us for years, and all so that we could turn our houses into personal banks and temporarily improve the fortunes of the financial services 'industry'.

Unless governments find the will to undertake a wholesale financial re-organization or concede the alternative solution and allow inflation to take off again, not only Britain but also the countries that followed us into the mire, ranging from Norway to Australia, face years of depressed activity as their economies retrench before the débâcle.

For Keynesians the worst of it is that the passage of events has been so predictable; we have had to stand by watching the policy-making establishment, aided and abetted by the financial sector, make a series of avoidable policy mistakes.

For the essence of the Keynesian account of economic instability is that the banking system plays a central role in generating the economic cycle; overexpanding credit in times of economic optimism beyond the level of savings and so providing the means to justify excessively high expectations of profitable investment but only temporarily. The system runs away with itself and economic dénouement ensues as surely as night follows day.

Equally, deregulated financial markets and institutions have only a limited number of ways out of the situation in which they find themselves, for problems in the financial sector necessarily become generalized. As banks cut back their lending and borrowers their demand for credit, the entire economy suffers.

Unless the rules of the game are changed, market mechanisms provide the only ways by which the financial system can claw its way back to some semblance of normality.

1   A return to inflation, so reducing the value of debt in real terms and, by increasing borrowers' money incomes, providing them with the wherewithal to meet their current financial claims and accept new ones.
2   A prolonged depression in which banks effectively stop new lending and rebuild their balance sheets and borrowers, both personal and corporate, use any buoyancy in their income to reduce debt.
3   The financial system attempts to solve its problems itself, with weak institutions surrendering control to stronger ones through merger and takeover, reconstituting themselves into stronger entities capable of new lending and using their strengthened market power to increase their margins.

One extra avenue is for banks to parcel up their loans to be bought by other organizations and subsequently bought and sold in the debt markets. This 'securitization' of the banks' debt relieves their balance sheets of old loans, thus allowing them to extend new ones.

In practice this third 'solution' takes place in parallel with either of the first two but exacerbates the basic trends in the system. The widening of margins in the financial sector must necessarily prolong depressed economic activity; while the offloading of debts via securitization is but one more 'free market' adaptation by the financial system which underlines its propensity, if unregulated, to generate instability and inflation.

By displacing the consequences of its own bad lending decisions on to other economic actors it can preserve its own viability, but only to retain the capacity to make further mistakes.

For, as an excellent new book by Bank of England adviser Eric Davis argues, one of the properties of a competitive deregulated financial system is to make systematic misjudgements about how much debt the wider system can bear.* This is not because of managerial imprudence or incompetence, as suggested by Lord Lawson, who still seems to believe that this can be the only reason why financial deregulation had such 'unanticipated' results, but because of the necessary behavioural consequences of banks operating in a more competitive industrial structure.

Mr Davis homes in on the central fact of the banking relationship – the 'asymmetry of information' between borrower and lender. No bank can

* E. Davis, *Debt, Financial Instability and Systemic Risk* (Oxford: Clarendon Press, 1992).

ever be as well informed about the prospects for the repayment of any loan as the borrower nor would it be reasonable to expect a bank to acquire as much information about its thousands of its clients as they themselves possess (although Davis concedes that this control function is better performed by banks in Japan and parts of Europe than those in Anglo-Saxon countries).

Equally, a bank, which makes a small profit on lots of loans, is in a position where one bad loan can offset the profits on all the others.

Neither is the bank any better equipped to foretell an uncertain future than its customers, so banks are structurally compelled to offload as much risk as they can. What else would be rational?

Mr Davis seems to suggest that whenever the opportunity has come to reduce their risks and cover for their inability to control information banks have seized it, either the chance to lend to sovereign governments in the less developed world who apparently would never go bankrupt or the chance to develop a market for mortgage loans whose borrowers would accept that interest rates would go up and down with short-term interest rates generally, so that the banks could add their own margin secure that interest revenues always matched costs.

In both cases, of course, the banks ran riot. There was too much Third World lending; and too much property lending, for the system provides no means for telling individual banks that what may be sensible for one may not be sensible for all.

Mr Davis describes the bankers' dilemma: condemned by asymmetric information and uncertainty to be cautious but ready if any block to lending seems to be removed to respond over-zealously because the industry as a whole has no ex-ante system of preventing systemic mistakes.

The book's insight is to demonstrate that financial deregulation must inevitably compound this dilemma and deliver yet more instability. In what Mr Davis calls an 'industrial approach' to financial instability he argues that when rules governing banking behaviour are relaxed, so allowing new entrants or products into the business, the rational market response is to generate lending that would not otherwise have taken place.

The key is that to gain business the new entrants have to relax the terms on which they lend and invent new financial products, and existing banks must follow suit. New entrants in effect are redefining lending possibilities and notions of risk in the same way that, say, sovereign lending seemed to redefine balance-sheet options; and as a result bank lending shoots up in aggregate.

The theory has a universal application in financial markets. Whether it was the collapse of the Swedish commercial paper market or the problems of Australia's Pyramid Building Society, Mr Davis traces a similar evolution: deregulation, new market entrants, relaxation of credit terms,

excessive debt growth, unsustainable asset prices, reduced bank capital-
ization, tightening of credit terms, the collapse of liquidity among some
participants, financial retrenchment and then a wider economic deterior-
ation.

It is a compelling argument and therefore Mr Davis can hardly be
optimistic about what is going to happen in Britain. The excuse for all this
was that financial deregulation would necessarily promote economic
efficiency; but competition to lend money is not like competition in other
product markets. Excessive production of cars or Barbie dolls does not impart
instability to the whole system in the same way that excessive production
or reduction of credit does; money has generalized properties and the terms
of its supply need to be highly stable.

This opens the way to the fourth avenue for recovery: financial reregulation and reorganization. We need to build up the banks' core capital,
insist that they exercise their 'control function' better, have in place
systems to warn them when they are lending too little or too much, and
develop policy instruments that can prod them into more rational behaviour.

But because financial instruments are now so diffuse the counter-attack
must be root and branch, involving not merely tightening the rules over
how money is lent, but how it and banks travel between countries.

So what is it to be: financial freedom or regulation, jobs and growth?
How that choice is made will determine the 1990s.

Guardian, 28 December 1992

The Sad Story of British Biotech

'When the capital development of a country becomes a by-product of the
activities of a casino', wrote Keynes in the *General Theory*, 'the job is likely
to be ill-done.' He should have lived to watch the practice of British investment in 1998 and the naïve terms of the debate about why it has the
character it does.

He would have mocked the seminars currently conducted by Gordon
Brown debating low British productivity as exercises in avoiding the central issue; his mordant pen would have savaged the refusal of British savants
and economists to describe the world as it is.

And if he had wanted evidence for his case, none better would have
presented itself than the sad story of British Biotech, whose chief executive,

Keith McCullagh, resigned this week. This was the company whose entrepreneurial zeal would generate new anti-cancer drugs and which the stock market propelled to a value of billions, despite it not yet having made any profits. It was the living rebuttal of critics such as Will Hutton who argued mistakenly that the financial system was short-termist, anti-investment and anti-scientific.

But now it is mired in scandal, accused of falsifying information about the prospects for its drugs, and fighting for its commercial life. The development of the next generation of British drugs and drug companies is the by-product of a capital market more casino-like than any Keynes knew. To describe the job as ill-done is the mildest of understatements.

For the stock explanations offered by the apologists of the status quo cannot explain the rise and fall of British Biotech. It is not boom-bust economics, inflation, strong trade unions or excessive product regulation that menace this once proud and ambitious company. It is the cancerous contagion of the British financial community and the murderous incentives it generates – to investors to regard companies as gambling chips, to directors to misinform about their prospects and to research departments to attempt to compress a task of years into months.

In this witch's brew, good people do things they know they should not, hoping that the means will justify the end. But in Britain, the only end is to be clever enough to buy at the bottom and sell before the house of cards collapses. The losers are the national economy, and worse, the growing sense that British capitalism is the preserve of a bunch of hucksters.

McCullagh, a former vet, had a noble commercial dream. He believed he could build a new Glaxo Wellcome, using the vast financial resources of the British stock market to back the proven inventiveness of British research science, in particular in gene technology.

The difficulty, of course, is that although the profits on successful drugs are staggeringly high, the processes by which they are developed, clinically tested and finally given regulatory approval are time-consuming, exhaustive and very expensive. For every successful drug, there are hundreds of failures.

The British drug industry, as Oxford University Business School director John Kay points out, was not built on the short-term priorities of the stock market; it was built by the pharmaceutical division of ICI in the fifties and sixties, which openly declared itself more interested in long-term profits than short-term share-holder value (a statement it could not make today).

Glaxo's current world-beating anti-ulcer drugs are direct spin-offs from that effort. McCullagh was vainglorious and self-confident enough to believe he could do what no one else had managed. At first, it worked well. The company began in 1986 and by 1992 had a track record of research sufficient to persuade the Stock Exchange authorities to allow the loss-maker to win a share quotation.

The company seemed to have two drugs – Marimastat for cancer and Zacutex for acute pancreatitis – that together would generate sales of £1 billion a year by 2004/5. Most of that would be pure profit. The City, which boasts not one single scientist in any investment bank capable of fully understanding the complexity of the drugs, went ape at the prospect. British Biotech's share price soared, allowing it to raise hundreds of millions by issuing new shares, which it ploughed into developing the drugs.

But McCullagh found himself in a fix. To sustain the share price and the capacity to raise finance, there had to be good news – and the very best gloss put on any bad news. He did not have the succour of a long-term majority shareholder or trade investor who would insulate the company from the short-term vicissitudes of any drug research programme; he had a collection of go-go, short-term performance-orientated unit trusts as his shareholders.

All wanted to ride the upward movement of the share price, but all knew that to secure the good investment performance they would sell at the first hint of trouble and try to dump the now depreciating shares on some greater fool.

British Biotech, and its chief executive, found themselves under increasing pressure to be economical with the truth. Warnings from regulators and setbacks in the research programme alike could not be openly acknowledged; the flagship drug Zacutex had to be kept alive at all costs. Worse, it seems the directors, including McCullagh, coolly disposed of £1.35 million of their own shares just weeks before clinical trials of the drug were suspended.

Both the US Securities and Exchange Commission and Food and Drug Administration are now investigating the company; a real threat rather than the limp-wristed efforts of their British counterparts. As the crisis mounted, McCullagh's position became untenable; last week he stood down.

British Biotech still has cash and scientific resource, but its future is clear. It will be sold to a large drug company and its research team dissipated. If Britain wants to harness its scientific know-how, which is world-class, it will need to reorganize its financial system and structure of corporate governance. There is a task force on the financing of high-tech industry to monitor these issues, and you might hope it had the wit to make such recommendations. But there is one problem. Its chairman until a fortnight ago, appointed by an awestruck Tony Blair, was McCullagh.

The truth is that no powerful voice in Britain's commercial, financial and political establishment is prepared to confront the truth. The arguments are known; the facts are clear. But New Labour is terrified that it would damage its pro-business credentials by even daring to offer the mutest of criticism. It was true when Keynes was alive; it's true today. Until Britain addresses its financial casino, it will never develop a critical mass of self-standing, world-class, high-tech companies.

Observer, 24 May 1998

PART IV

Ownership Matters: Short-Termism, Stakeholding and Corporate Governance

Raising the Stakes

The reaction to the idea of the stakeholder economy and society, which Tony Blair first unveiled in his Singapore speech ten days ago, has been extraordinary. Ministers do not miss an opportunity to attack the notion; reams of newspaper copy and video-tape have been expended on exploring what it could mean. The political and journalistic establishments are united in their judgement. Stakeholding, whatever its ambiguities, could have legs as New Labour's big idea.

But for all the ministerial protestations that Mr Blair has made his first mistake by putting some 'red water' between him and the Conservative Party, the inexperienced team at Central Office have played into the Labour leader's hand.

By insisting that no media interview or parliamentary intervention should be complete without some challenge to the idea, they have disobeyed the first law of politics. Setting the agenda is half the political battle; and by the middle of week two, stakeholding has become the agenda.

The Conservative calculation is that it was more dangerous to allow Mr Blair a free run in developing what might be a very attractive political idea that could pull together a potent coalition of the centre and moderate left of British politics. After all a number of leading British companies, including BT, BP and Marks and Spencer, call themselves stakeholder companies and can hardly dissociate themselves from the idea – while the level-headed element in the union movement are actively campaigning for the unions to abandon their long-standing opposition. Pull these wings together, and here is a very powerful new political coalition united by an overarching political concept.

Hence the urgency, from the Conservative vantage point, of defining stakeholding in negative terms before Mr Blair could define it so that it sounds attractive. The business community and the Tory voters whom John Redwood describes as the lost five million had better beware; this means a return to the bad old days of British corporatism, red tape, tax-and-spend governments – and bringing back trade union militancy.

With equal urgency Mr Blair has been resisting such attacks. It is about empowerment, he says, quality education and training for all; the creation of a moral community at work as much as in welfare state, and of 'treating workers as partners rather than factors of production' (as he said in his interview with David Frost). Above all it is about giving individuals a stake.

Yet for all its occasional lapses into a language of platitudinous generality, this is a political exchange of fundamental importance which both sides regard as essential to win. Cynics inside the Labour Party and in abundance beyond in the media like to prove their independence and powers of professional scepticism by scoffing at stakeholding; to display enthusiasm, interest or understanding is to depart from the unwritten code. All politicians are knaves and propagandists; all their ideas are confused, inadequate or boil down to the same old left/right divide in the end.

Yet stakeholding is a genuine departure; it attempts to offer a set of guiding principles that could organize a reformist political programme in five chief areas: the workplace, the welfare state, the firm and the City, the constitution, and economic policy more generally. This is not socialism in the twentieth century, Scargillite tradition of trying to build a socialist Jerusalem by planning and public ownership; but it is not the orthodox advocacy of free market capitalism championed by the Conservative right. It is an explicit statement of the values and principles that have underpinned the century-long attempt to build a just society and moral community that is congruent with private property, the pursuit of the profit motive and decentralized decision-making in markets – the famous third or middle way. There are ambiguities and difficulties; but as a system of ideas it deserves to be taken seriously.

The unifying idea is inclusion: the individual is a member, a citizen and a potential partner. But inclusion is not a one-way street; it places reciprocal obligations on the individual as well as rights – and in every domain and in every social class. These rights and obligations can be organized in a voluntary code; or they may be codified into law. The institutions that grow out of these relationships foster relations of trust and commitment; they tend to be high-investing, attentive to human capital and highly creative. OK, you may be thinking, but what does it mean in practice?

Start with the workplace. A worker in Britain is legally a disposable commodity, a view backed by a body of economic theory, company and employment law which insists that no further privileges can be afforded. In stakeholder theory, building on the knowledge that most firms are reluctant to treat their workers as commodities, and pay them above the market-clearing wage to gain their commitment and loyalty, workers are seen as members of the firm – committed and enabled to upgrade their skills, and encouraged through trusts or share ownership to own all or part of the firm.

They deserve representation, consultation and prior notification of major events – a round of redundancies or new investment alike. This does not mean 1970s-style union power, which Conservative ministers accuse me of advocating in my book *The State We're In*; nor does it mean German collective bargaining. It means constructing trust relations with groups of workers, which are best gained if the workers themselves can be formally grouped and represented and if firms accept that such is their responsibility as firms.

This is where workplace relations overlap with the new thinking on corporate governance. There is a crisis in accountability in British firms, with pension fund and insurance company owners having rock-hard proprietorial rights to secure a flow of dividends and to sell their shares as they choose – but with no accompanying obligations when times get hard or when directors over-reward themselves. Shares are not an expression of a relationship, as many small shareholders still regard them; they are chips in a fast-moving casino in which the game is, as Keynes put it, to pass the depreciating half-penny to the next man and cash in yourself.

This, as Keynesian theory shows, paradoxically deters investment by maximizing uncertainty – but stakeholder theory adds a new twist. By giving most British companies an insecure ownership platform because their shares are casino chips in the British game of takeover, they can't construct long-term trust relationships at the workplace. Managers have other gods to please. But owning a company carries reciprocal obligations – to participate in decision-making and to stand by it in times of crisis.

Ownership thus re-enters the political debate; not in the old public/private typology – but by insisting that private ownership has responsibilities, and championing a wide diversity of means to achieve that end. Public ownership is but one of a spectrum of possibilities that range from a new legal definition of the public company, through profit-sharing, employee stock ownership plans, mutuals and friendly societies, to worker co-operatives.

Then there is welfare. Here inclusion and membership imply a universal welfare state, financed by progressive taxation, in which every individual has a stake. It implies a solid state pension as the first building block in the pension system; a non-tiered National Health Service free at the point of use; and an inclusive national education system in which the long tail of education underachievement is firmly tackled and the opted-out middle class are reincorporated – rejuvenating the comprehensive principle by tackling its weaknesses. But private delivery systems, organized themselves along stakeholder principles, are more than admissible; as are public/private partnerships with a public sector that itself has been revitalized by reform.

Here again the same principle applies. Citizenship is an expression of political inclusion, and decentralization of government along with more accountability a means of permitting local citizens some leverage over decision-making and power.

A stakeholder economy and society is mirrored by a stakeholder polity; directors of quangos have to be elected – local authorities are accorded more autonomy of action. Public institutions gain more constitutional independence; in a stakeholder polity, the BBC and the Bank of England alike would suffer less political interference over their proper spheres – notably appointments.

But the ultimate stake for most adults is a job. Stakeholder institutions must be buttressed by full employment policies – implying that the full battery of economic instruments be deployed to stimulate demand, investment and growth. Training and education are thus part of a wider effort to include all in the world of work.

In some of these areas, notably over training and political reform, Tony Blair has assumed a clearly discernible position with hardening commitments; in others his position is more minimalist and cautious – notably over corporate governance, City/industry relations and the regulation of the labour market. Over the welfare state he can sound the most ambiguous note, but the outline of a consistent position is apparent. In economic policy he preaches fiscal rectitude and financial orthodoxy, necessary for any left politician given today's viciously anti-inflation financial markets – but there are important markers about combating long-term unemployment, and even adopting a medium-term growth target. In short, in all the five key areas he ventures something towards the stakeholder conception; he has, willy-nilly, made an important political declaration of intent – with which the right, centre and left of his party can properly engage – along with the centre ground of British politics.

But Blair's position is not a return to 1970s corporatism; any more than the chapter in *The State We're In* dealing with stakeholder capitalism, waved by Conservative MPs in the House of Commons as proof positive that this is the stakeholding aim. They will be hard put to find any line in justification. There are none; indeed stakeholding has arisen out of a determination never to revisit the failures of British corporatism.

There is no reference in the entire lineage of the stakeholding idea. Not in J. K. Galbraith's *New Industrial State*. Nor in George Goyda's *The Just Enterprise*, which first set out stakeholder principles in detail, or in Professor John Kay's *The Foundations of Corporate Success*, where the ideas are developed still further. Indeed David Marquand, in *The Unprincipled Society*, one of the inspirations behind the concept, offers a devastating criticism of postwar British corporatism. There is no trace in the Royal Society of Arts *Tomorrow's Company* report, which sets out a voluntary code for the stakeholder company, while Frank Field's *Making Welfare Work* is overtly an effort to establish a non-corporatist but universal welfare state.

There are difficulties to be solved. Stakeholding simultaneously endorses the market economy while attempting to achieve some proper balance between capital and labour. It does involve a challenge to powerful vested interests. It emphasizes inclusion above equality. It involves a remaking of the British system in which the current winners will protest loudly. Blair's speech is a first move; the larger question is not its political and economic importance – it's whether he and his party can hold and extend the ground they have won, or whether before the controversy they will judge it expedient to beat a tactical retreat.

Guardian, 17 January 1996

Time for Labour to Put some Spine into its Stakeholding Idea

Changes of government and changes in ideas go hand in hand. The outgoing administration loses internal coherence as it battles to marry incoming ideas with its outdated programme and rusting ideological anchors. The opposition gains in confidence and coherence.

We saw it happening in the late 1970s with the rise in monetarism. In the mid-1990s it could be happening again with stakeholding.

For it was not the Thatcherites who launched British-style monetarism as they entered office in 1979. It was the Labour Chancellor, Denis Healey, who, after the 1976 IMF crisis, began focusing policy on lowering the public-sector borrowing requirement, targeting money supply growth and lifting exchange and credit controls. The intellectual climate had been changing for three years before Mrs Thatcher took office. This, as much as her political prowess, laid the foundations of her success.

Historians will make similar remarks about the years up to 1996–7. British business and the unions have themselves begun the move towards stakeholding as a principle of company relations. It was the *Tomorrow's Company* inquiry, published by the Royal Society of Arts in 1995 and backed by leading British companies, that first set out the merits of organizing a company as an inclusive social entity, to maximize creativity and trust. The job of a board is not to act exclusively as the agents of the shareholders, the report said; it is to act more as the long-term trustees of the business, furthering its productive capacity, reputation and the skills of its workforce and suppliers.

Furthermore, Sir Adrian Cadbury (over the constitution of company boards) and Sir Richard Greenbury (over executive pay) have chaired committees that developed voluntary codes which, whatever their compromises and shortcomings, begin to uphold elements of the stakeholding notion. Long-term corporate success is a more subtle business than simply maximizing shareholder value. There is a wider public interest to be protected.

Best if it is voluntary – but most know that legislation will ultimately be needed.

Which is a process that has been started by the Conservatives. Although Messrs Major, Mawhinney, Heseltine et al. react with horror over the danger of introducing legislation into company–investor–employee relations – which should all be voluntary according to Conservative theory – in practice their government has led the way in passing such laws.

The most closely regulated institution is the trade union. With nine Employment Acts, successive ministers have taken the law into industrial relations and this voluntarily established economic institution. But the pressure of events has also forced ministers to extend the arm of the law into the regulation of the City, privatized utilities, pensions and even the heartland of capitalism – the firm.

The 1986 Financial Services Act established the basis for semi-statutory regulation of the City. The 1995 Pensions Act extended the law into the management and trusteeship of pension funds, while the 1985 Companies Act first qualified the absolute sovereign rights of shareholders. In the event of a liquidation, shareholders no longer have an exclusive claim to any residual assets. Directors, says the Act, have instead a legal duty to strike a balance between workers' interests and any others who have a reasonable claim. Here is a first tentative expression of stakeholding.

The trade union movement has also been rethinking itself. In the 1970s the TUC castigated the idea of stakeholding and worker participation because if workers were treated as members of firms, then staff associations and the like would have the right to sit on company boards – undermining trade unions' claim to be the sole legitimate representatives of the workforce. Worse, unions would be made party to managerial decisions and thus inhibited in their capacity to negotiate high wages. If twenty-five years ago a general secretary of the TUC had come out in favour of stakeholding, as John Monks did last week, the movement would have regarded him as a class traitor.

It is this movement of opinion that helps to explain why the stakeholding idea has taken off in the manner it has.

Most senior British businessmen and financiers know that the Conservative initiatives have been incomplete. There cannot be another Maxwell or failed trial. And mega-bids like that of Granada for Forte may enrich City institutions but their wider effect is baleful. The question is whether the necessary reforms will be introduced by a government that does not believe in what it is doing, or one that does.

Take the basic constitution of the British firm. John Kay and Aubrey Silbertson argue in a recent article in the National Institute of Economic and Social Research's *Quarterly Review* that it is closely analogous to the former authoritarian regimes of eastern Europe. It is run by a self-perpetuating elite. Voting at annual meetings is fixed in a manner that outdoes a Brezhnev or Honecker. Secrecy in the management of affairs is paramount. Accounts are not trustworthy. Hostile bids mirror military takeovers as a means of changing top personnel.

The owners of the majority of most companies' shares, the pension funds and insurance companies, do not take their proprietorial responsibilities seriously. Fewer than 30 per cent of them vote. They want, above all, the right to receive growing dividends. They accept no reciprocal obligations.

The conspiracy of interest between management, anxious to retain their East European privileges, and institutional fund managers, jealous of their right to play with shares like so many chips at the casino, is at the heart of the malaise in British corporate life. The name of the game is to achieve high immediate financial returns, constraining investment and displacing risk on to workforces. Creativity, long-termism and trust are conspicuous by their absence.

Stakeholding can advance partially through more effort in education and training, and partially through better bridges from welfare to work. But there have to be parallel initiatives in corporate governance. Kay and Silbertson recommend that directors' terms of office should be limited to four years, that they should be paid accordingly, and selected by independent non-executive directors. This, they say, will break the self-perpetuating oligarchy of most British firms. Managers will be more predisposed to act as trustees of the business than as the shareholders' agents. The effect will radiate through the firm.

This could be negotiated initially as a voluntary code, but ultimately it would have to backed by legislation. New Labour should not be frightened of putting some spine into its ideas – and following the path the Conservatives have blazed.

Guardian, 22 January 1996

Stake that Claim

The snap reaction of the left to the idea of the stakeholder economy and society is that it is little more than Thatcherism in drag, just another way of talking about popular capitalism or the enterprise culture. The right is no more forgiving. The dynamics of capitalism are immutable and brook no reform. Tony Blair will find that championing stakeholding is no easy ride; he has entered the political battle of ideas with a vengeance.

But the stock criticisms are wrong. Like it or hate it, stakeholding does represent a different political economy of capitalism with profound implications for economic, social and political organization. It stresses that workers should be seen as members of firms rather than locked into an antagonistic confrontation between capital and labour. In this world view, firms are social organizations embedded in a complex skein of rights and moral obligations, and if they are reduced to commodities bought and sold on the stock market, that undermines the trust and reciprocity of obligation on which long-termism and productivity thrive.

Too much fracturing and tiering of society in the quest for simple economic efficiencies is ultimately socially unsustainable – and that spills over into the sustainability of economic growth. Social citizenship and economic membership are interdependent – but this links up with political citizenship. An active participative democracy goes hand in hand with underpinning social cohesion and promoting stakeholder firms.

These are no platitudes. A different vocabulary opens up – social inclusion, membership, trust, co-operation, long-termism, equality of opportunity, participation, active citizenship, rights and obligations – in sharp contrast to the right's language of opting out, privatization, the primacy of individual choice, maximization of shareholder value and the 'burden' of welfare and social costs. Behind the vocabulary lies a different value system, a different view of what makes a successful market economy tick – and a dramatically different approach to economic and social policy.

Corporate law, the organization of pensions, systems of training, company decision-making, the behaviour of the Stock Exchange and the role of education are markedly different in a stakeholder world. The international evidence, as Blair said in Singapore, is that this approach delivers social cohesion and economic growth; the two feed off each other. By pinning his colours to the stakeholder mast, Blair has taken a decisive political step. New Labour has now enlisted a substantial and novel body of ideas: it stands in sharp opposition to the laissez-faire, financially driven model of capitalism promoted by the right.

This may have been good enough to beat its ideological rival, communism, and even good enough to take on and beat British collectivism – but as a model for the good society or efficient economy it falls far short of any decent yardstick. It is characterized by endemic short-termism, economic volatility and social divisiveness – and, when married to the top-down centralized nature of British government, has delivered a society in which civic duty and public service have become progressively emasculated.

It was exactly against this kind of laissez-faire capitalism that the stakeholder idea was first developed – by the American left during the sixties. The word derived from the way US settlers staked their claim in virgin territory. Business strategists in the late fifties and early sixties used it to rethink the idea of a company as a network of reciprocal *claims* between shareholders, employees, bankers, suppliers and managers. Large industrial organizations were bureaucracies which arbitrated between these rival claims – a necessary function in any industrial economy, market capitalist or market socialist.

But it was when J. K. Galbraith picked up the idea in *The New Industrial State*, published in 1967, aided and abetted by Robin Marris, author of *The Theory of Managerial Capitalism*, that the idea first gained economic and political currency. During the seventies, American corporate raiders complained that companies were cynically appealing to stakeholder interests to obstruct takeovers and limit shareholders' rights (a complaint they still make). But as no US politician has attempted to organize the ideas into a legislative programme, stakeholding has not progressed much beyond encouraging worker share ownership through Employee Stock Ownership Plans.

In Germany, the social market ideas developed by left theorists in opposition to fascism and communism had similar roots – they thought of the firm as a social organization with long-term stakeholders, which operated in highly competitive markets. The welfare state was seen as a protective social instrument to promote social inclusion, and allow capitalism its much-needed flexibility to build up and run down industries without worrying about the social consequences. The political purpose was the same as Galbraith's: to secure the fecundity of capitalism whilst humanizing it – and defending it from authoritarianism of the left and right.

In Britain the whole debate has never taken off before. The postwar settlement was a compromise, allowing the left to achieve its social goals through raising public spending and extending public ownership, but leaving the right to protect City freedoms and the ancient notion that the firm represented no more than the shareholders' interests. The case for stakeholding was left to fringe groups campaigning for worker participation and co-operatives. But with the instruments of Old Labour collapsing, and the right building on the laissez-faire model, the most promising avenue for the left is stakeholding.

The TUC has recognized this for some time, and General Secretary John Monks has established a task force to suggest legislative proposals and ways the unions might profit. The Dahrendorf Commission on Wealth Creation and Social Cohesion came out firmly in favour of stakeholding last summer. Tony Blair has been tantalizingly slow to adopt it publicly but the Singapore speech is a watershed.

It establishes authentically left credentials, blindsides his opponents and has a reforming sting. Witness just one passage. 'It is surely time', he said, 'to assess how we shift the emphasis in corporate ethos – from the company being a mere vehicle for the capital market to be traded, bought and sold as a commodity – towards a vision of the company as a community or part-nership in which each employee has a stake, and where the company's responsibilities are more clearly delineated.'

Michael Portillo immediately attacked this as a straight copy of long-standing Conservative policy – but it is difficult to recall a Conservative politician ever indicting the operation of stock market capitalism for *commoditizing* companies and workers, or proposing a clear delineation of corporate rights and obligations. Isn't the Conservative idea to promote deregulation and to regard stock market freedoms as sacred?

But Blair's advocacy of what he calls the Stakeholder Welfare System may arouse more concern. There is a clear accent on social cohesion and the necessity to recast the welfare state so that it ceases to offer an obstacle to training or self-employment; and it is equally attractive to open up col-lective means of self-insurance to allow individuals to produce pensions or sickness benefit above the basic levels. The danger, though, is also clear: Singapore-type provident funds could be progressively used to replace ex-isting welfare structures, with their accompanying need for a distributive tax system.

Yet in sum the commitment to a stakeholder economy and society is a key moment – a way of binding the centre and left together in common cause while providing the ideological impetus for important economic and social return. Blair went to Australia this Christmas with no advisers and a suitcase of books. On this evidence he should go again.

Guardian, 9 January 1996

Only Working Together will Save the Economy

Written with John Kay

Begin at the beginning. Any economy or society will aim to be as good at wealth creation as it can. But that's where the problems start. The simple injunction to be less 'socialist' and more 'capitalist' – the cry of the age – is not helpful as a guide to action. Capitalist economies vary hugely in their vitality, and not just to the extent to which they have caught the 'socialist' virus. The task is to unmask the subtleties at work, and then apply them as we can.

For the not so 'new right', the motley crew of libertarian philosophers, market-oriented economists and radical-right politicians who supplied the backdrop to Thatcher and Reagan, there is no such job; they have found the philosopher's stone already. Economic wealth has its origins in the capacity of individuals to trade in markets. Governments should advance a market structure across every nook and cranny of economic and social life so that individuals can get on with creating 'wealth'. Thus we will arrive at the good economy and society.

Seventeen years on, it is obvious that the experiment in individualism has not kept its promises. Yes, the new right re-established the virtues of competition, but it has no more solved the problem of successful wealth creation than the philosophies that preceded it. Whether it is the widening gap between rich and poor, the way strategic thinking in our companies has become dominated by 'the deal' or the dilapidated public infrastructure, new right thinking is at a dead end. Today, it is impossible to believe that high taxation and excessive regulation are Britain's major economic problems – whatever partial truth that once represented.

There is no appetite to return to the old order. 'Stakeholding', which we both advocate, is our language to recast the way to think about wealth creation. We argue that wealth is created by people working together in teams and organizations – and these can work only if the motivation recognizes basic human priorities. It is wrong to think of businesses as no more than a network of individuals where success hangs on the degree of inspirational leadership – and where each individual's sole preoccupation is how much he or she can take out of the company.

Moreover, a business – whether a corner shop or multinational – is doing something unique. It holds a franchise in the widest sense of that term, and it discharges that franchise through a network of co-operative working relationships cemented by trust and a desire to sustain a good reputation. None of this takes place in a vacuum. The financial demands that owners make upon the business, the rules governing what happens if the firm goes bust, and the legal obligations to employees, set parameters to how people build such vital relationships. Wealth creation in stakeholder terms depends upon building institutions, systems and values that allow co-operative relationships to flourish within capitalism rather than trying to remove them because they are seen as inconsistent.

But if this is true, it also raises fundamental questions about the nature of private property. You cannot own morale; you cannot buy and sell trust; you cannot wish into being commitment from those who make the business franchise what it is. Owners cannot exercise their property rights without recognizing that they have obligations to whatever working community they purportedly 'own'; they certainly cannot behave as if they were autonomous masters of all they survey.

The right to be a member of a functioning economic community is among the most important of individual rights. The key stakeholder value is inclusion, rather than the equality sought by the old left or the individual autonomy of the new right.

The heart of the matter is that markets are rooted in a social context; that the values that govern our behaviour must necessarily extend across all our actions. We do not want to be understood as arguing on the one hand for capitalism and on the other for separate ways of tempering its brutality, in which people are aggressive individualists in business but suddenly become altruists when they consider the less well-off or their own families. This humane variant of individualism, the doctrine whose latest exponents were Charles Leadbetter and Geoff Mulgan on these pages last week, demands a dichotomy of values that no one can sustain. People's behaviour is of a piece; the idea that we are 'caring' at home and 'hard-nosed' at work is wrong. Selfish behaviour in any sphere corrodes all our social values.

But worse, what lies behind this attempt to construct 'capitalism with a human face' is a poor description of how markets work. It offers no challenge to the perverse idea that property confers rights and no obligations; Leadbetter and Mulgan want to spread such 'obligationless' property rights more widely. But the mad machine will carry on regardless. Firms will still try to maximize shareholder value by displacing risk on to individuals (with the costs, in due course, falling on the taxpayer) and entrenching the segmentation of society. The engine of short-termism will be unreformed.

Leadbetter and Mulgan use BMW's acquisition of Rover to support their case. It is lack of education and high-quality skills, they say, that hamper the success of BMW's investment – and so, in part, they are. But they do not analyse why our system persistently delivers poor education and training, or why the long-termist BMW can even consider doubling investment above the level where it stood under British ownership. They tinker at the edges rather than address the fundamental points.

In fact, Rover's experience under British ownership eloquently makes our case. Britain combines an efficient stock market with its system of absolute shareholder property rights; as a result, financial institutions have no incentive to commit to the companies they own – they can buy and sell their shares too easily. Hostile takeover is the culmination of this trend. British business is yoked into maximizing shareholder value for these uncommitted owners.

The best British companies know that serving their customers well and caring for employees is essential to their long-term health – but even they are compelled to claim that their objective is increasing shareholder value, and find that there are heavy penalties for not raising dividends and the share price as much as possible. This intrudes into the warp and woof of company decision-making, so that financial criteria outweigh all others –

The seven principles of stakeholding

1 Open economies and democratic societies are the basis for wealth creation.

Decentralization of economic and political decision-making is more effective than the imposition of wisdom from the centre. Market organization, allowing the stimulus of competition, is the route to innovation and efficiency. This exactly parallels the stimulus to good and responsive government which comes from a free press, an open political system and government rotation between parties.

2 We must all be included in the workings of the economy and society.

The good society is founded on the right and associated obligation of individuals to be part of that society in which they live. Thus people who want to work and are able to do so have a right to a job because working and earning are central elements in economic and social life. To work is to be. Clearly firms rise and fall, taking on or shedding workers as they succeed or fail. But workers should be treated as members of firms and where possible offered a share in their rising prosperity.

But those who opt out of the right to work – secured by guaranteeing access to training and work even if in a different part of the country after a clearly defined period – have no strong claims on the rest of us. The claim to benefit must be conditional on acceptance of those obligations.

3 Ownership confers obligations – including paying tax.

To owe and to own have a common Middle English origin. It is only in contemporary British and American usage that owning is understood to come without any accompanying *owing* of obligations. It is a separation we do not acknowledge.

Those who own shares in companies or assets of social and environmental significance cannot act as if they were in a social vacuum.

Nor can the wealthy exercise the rewards of riches without accepting the obligation to pay proportionately higher taxes for the wider good.

4 The good economy is one where you do the right thing without being policed.

The rules of the economic game we seek to introduce are much better operated by people and firms themselves than by elaborate rule-books. For example, it would be better if Britain's financial institutions understood that it is their responsibility and not the regulator's to ensure that the products they sell are suitable for those who buy. Equally public utilities must recognize that the public expects a fair share of the efficiency savings they make.

But we understand that the reward system in markets often persuades firms to behave in ways that are irrational for the wider economy – deal-making, undertraining or exploiting monopoly. This requires both a regulatory response and an understanding that there is no long-term commercial virtue in profit-making in these ways.

5 Businesses are social institutions, not creatures of the stock market.

A company is a social organization. We need a renewed stress on developing the strengths of the organic business – and to design a constitution for British companies in which owners' obligations are more clearly defined. This will involve important changes to the rules governing takeovers, the composition of company boards, insolvency, banking law and accounting practice.

6 Good businesses are bound to make healthy profits but they must share their prosperity.

Successful firms are unique institutions with strong business franchises. If they are going to sustain their position they must share the rewards equitably between all their stakeholders – workers, customers and suppliers – rather than proclaim their sole aim is to increase shareholder value.

7 Successful market economies rely on a host of intermediate organizations.

There is a whole network of institutions that lie between the state and the individual – ranging from voluntary organizations and hospitals to quangos and firms. The insistence that our choice is either the state or the individual wholly neglects this institutional infrastructure and the importance of the social capital they generate. Rather the aim must be to nurture and sustain them.

with the time horizons for making profits shortening and an expected rate of profitability so high that investment is confined to betting on the prospect of large gains from buying or selling assets.

BMW bought Rover from British Aerospace, whose commitment to the business was demonstrated when it bought and sold the company in five years as part of a wider frenzy of inept deal-making that nearly brought the internationally renowned company to its knees. BMW, meanwhile, has had a stability, continuity and commitment of ownership that most British businesses can only envy.

Nothing Leadbetter and Mulgan suggest would change this dynamic of swapping and trading of assets rather than building them up. Moreover, their policy gizmos are dangerous. In their desire to individualize the way the welfare system is organized, they are undercutting the value system that admits social responsibilities. Already it is hard enough to mobilize resources for education; but to intensify the decline of the public sphere leads to a political armageddon in which individuals simultaneously assert their right to individual welfare and to lower taxation. Society will break.

What all this ignores is the role that trust, co-operation and commitment have played in creating successful capitalism. That does not mean we want to build yesterday's Japan into tomorrow's Britain, but we do want to change the context and architecture in which the British do business – and this will be no less applicable in the high-tech future so faddishly celebrated by Demos.

Indeed, it is because we emphasize the social context of markets that we are keenly aware that each country's model of capitalism is specific to it and constantly evolving. We could not transplant the economic and social systems of Japan and Germany even if we wanted to – but that does not mean we cannot influence and refine what we do in Britain. We can and we must.

Observer, 13 October 1996

Tony and the Tories: This is what we Mean

Written with Frank Field, John Kay, David Marquand and John Gray

Any civilized community should be justly concerned to create as much wealth as it can, to ensure that income and wealth are fairly shared and that centres of private and public power are properly accountable. The aim must be to build a free, moral, socially cohesive society based on universal membership, social inclusion and organized around the market economy. This is what we mean by the stakeholder economy and society.

If these are the ends, what are the means? According to the Conservative theorists of the new right who have dominated public debate for two decades, the route to the good society is the ubiquitous insertion of the market principle into every economic and social transaction. The only important or valid form of economic relationship is one in which one person buys what another sells. If all prosecute their individual interest in some form of market, they argue, then naturally and spontaneously we will arrive at the best outcome for economy and society alike. The freedom of the individual to choose is thus raised to the status of the highest economic, social and moral principle to which all others are secondary.

The state is portrayed as coercive and sinister, though by a malign paradox it has only been by exploiting concentrated state power, wielded with unprecedented assertiveness, that the obstacles to economic individualism created over a century have been quashed. Laissez-faire economics combine with extreme liberal individualism and High Tory authoritarianism into the cocktail that makes up the political project of the new right.

We repudiate this economic individualism and its associated political philosophy absolutely. Above all, we believe it to be a gross misunderstanding of what really drives a market economy and wealth creation. It is true that competition and rivalry are essential to economic progress, markets produce winners and losers, and there is no economic system on earth that can spare loss-making firms from the pain of restructuring and redundancy. Profit is essential to a market economy and so is the freedom to trade.

But successful capitalism, as well as the good society, require much more. By insisting that individualism and private property are the alpha and omega of capitalism the new right set in train tensions and forces that paradoxically menace the very system they claim to cherish. Capitalism is too subtle and complex to be entrusted to them.

The market system is more than the sum of its parts. All markets are social and political as well as economic. They are made to work by *real* people embedded in a *real* culture, interacting in *real* institutions. What may seem rational for the individual firm – to downsize its workforce, to economize on new investment, to poach trained workers from other firms – is irrational for the entire system. When everyone pursues a short-term boost to profitability there is a weakening in the sustainable pattern of demand that threatens long-term profitability; when everyone relies on poaching to secure a trained labour force, the level of training falls away.

The claim that the market is self-regulating and no more is needed is false. The market reinforces adverse trends because the best bet for any individual is that what has happened in the immediate past is likely to repeat itself in the immediate future. The overvalued exchange rate becomes more overvalued; the sink school becomes more of a sink school as parents send their children elsewhere. Unless we respond collectively as well as individually, markets over-reinforce failure and success. The paradox is that capitalism does have the capacity to regulate itself – but only if it allows full expression to values which are absent from the new right philosophy. Firms depend upon more than buying cheap and selling dear and trying to do each other down in a constantly changing network of spot-market relationships. They need the flexibility that market relations allow but they also need relationships of *commitment* which may not produce immediate economic pay-offs. A willingness to create trust and to co-operate – instincts which new right theorists either ignore or dismiss as 'socialist' and 'statist' – is fundamental to the capacity of firms to produce and the ability of the economy and society to function without extensive state regulation.

But these instincts and values need to be carefully husbanded and sustained – precisely what has not happened over the past seventeen years. Social consensus has been mocked. Owners of enterprise are less and less committed to their firms. Contracting has been extended into education, health, even the criminal justice system. The notion of shared responsibilities – in firms, in communities, in welfare – has been denigrated. Public goods – everything from the capacity to watch top-class rugby and football on television to our library system – have been diminished.

This has been done in the name of economic efficiency and the good society, but the diminution of commitment, trust and co-operation that has resulted has brought inefficiency and the bad society. Personal insecurity has increased. Income differentials have widened. The bonds holding the community together have been sundered. Long-term investment in machines and people has been discouraged. The business class has become preoccupied with deal-making rather than business-building.

The results are all around and obvious. The heroes of the Thatcher years are not those who built businesses by adding value but those who bought cheap and sold dear. The individualist society is creating substantial costs in its own terms. As market transactions multiply unbounded by trust relations, so the reliance on expensive auditing grows – most famously in the management costs of the new market-based National Health Service. 'Opting out', and the growing gap between rich and poor, fuel social disaffection and crime – among white-collar workers and the socially excluded alike. As honest relations become suborned by contract relations, so more and more people seek justice in the courts. Litigation is growing explosively. The social security bill grows relentlessly as incomes for the bottom 20 per cent fall and economic inactivity rises.

The right's response, like Druids with sacrificial victims, is to redouble its efforts at blood-letting. The welfare state should be reduced. Legal aid curbed. Law and order made tougher. Market relations carried still further. Taxation reduced. This, they claim, will ultimately deliver a self-regulating, robust market economy and self-reliant society.

Our view is the opposite. More of the same will produce still more of the same. The country needs to strike out in a different direction. But our critique of the current system does not imply that we advocate a return to 1970s corporatism or east European collectivism. Nor does it mean that we wish mechanistically to transplant the so-called Rhineland model of capitalism to British soil. We can and should learn from the Rhenish experience, but it should be adapted to British needs. To be against excessive individualism is to believe there is more to economic life than market relations rather than to argue for old models of collectivism and corporatism. The familiar contours of economic and political discourse no longer serve.

The task instead is to construct a new form of capitalism. The necessity is to rebuild the intermediate institutions between the individual and state so that they incorporate what we describe as stakeholder values, while simultaneously reforming state structures so that they are more open, accountable and responsive to the balance of public opinion. They too need to be freed from the market imperialism of the past twenty years.

But many of these intermediate institutions – of which the most economically important is the firm – will be privately owned in a capitalist society. Thus, any attempt to reconfigure the dynamics of British capitalism must challenge the new right notion that private property confers absolute rights and minimal or no obligations.

We assert the alternative proposition that property ownership confers obligations to match rights – and that a prime task for any democratic system is to allow the electorate to express choices about what the balance of rights and obligations should be. Only thus is there any chance legitimately to make choices about the kind of capitalism in which we live. This is not coercive of private interests as the right alleges; rather it is the operation of the democratic principle and the recognition that ownership does not take place in a social and moral vacuum.

The assertion of rights and obligations also means that there can be no neutrality about the distribution of income; put bluntly, the rich have the obligation to pay progressively more tax than the poor. Equally the most viable form of welfare – whether of pensions or of health – is one that is based on an insurance system of which everyone is a member. This does not mean that the state must perform the insurance role; indeed by subcontracting the task to intermediate institutions – insurance companies and friendly societies – there is a means of tailor-making individual welfare needs within a universal system.

All of this requires public initiative, at the very least to construct the legal architecture and tax structure within which stakeholder ideas can be expressed. But this needs to be clearly distinguished from the corporatist world of incomes policies, tripartite planning and extending public ownership. To build a framework which defines the rules of the game is a different political and economic project from directing the movement of each player on the pitch. Our critics wish to characterize us as arguing for the latter – but that is not our aim nor intellectual case.

However, it is true that an important focus for reform is the way the stock market, ownership structures and corporate governance interlock. The relations between the owners of British business – largely the great insurance companies and pension funds – and managers encourage endemic short-termism and undermine the role of directors as trustees and custodians of the underlying business. If British companies are to raise investment levels and engage less in deal-making and more in organically growing the business, the rewards from takeover need to be greatly reduced – and the rewards to those shareholders who stand by and engage with their companies greatly increased. New means need to be found of encouraging more committed, long-term and responsible ownership – otherwise the endless rounds of downsizing and delayering that are generating such high levels of job insecurity promise to continue.

But if the government is to intervene, it needs to be cleverer, lighter on its feet, more transparent and accountable. Interwoven with our ideas for revising the social contract and remodelling the British firm is thus a parallel commitment to reform the institutions of the British state – from the Treasury to local government. The programme should be seen as an interlinked whole.

This is the direction in which we believe Britain should now go. It is a programme to construct a more dynamic capitalism as much as a more socially cohesive society – and we observe that whether it is Norway and Switzerland in Europe or Hong Kong and Japan in Asia, economic success goes hand in hand with strong institutions that foster co-operation and trust. Mr Blair and the Labour Party say they should not be interpreted as either new right or old left, and advocate stakeholding. We agree that is the right course. But the programme so far championed falls far short of what is required. The risk is not in doing too much. Rather it lies in doing too little.

Observer, 7 July 1996

Healing Community Requires Reform rather than Rhetoric

It is a commonplace that the democratic process worldwide is in difficulties. It is another commonplace that the old certainties of the postwar labour market – the forty-hour week, tenured employment and the predictable career – are being shattered.

What is less commonplace is to regard the two as indissolubly linked. Could it be that the operation of contemporary capitalism is placing liberal democracy in danger?

The right denies any connection – to do otherwise would be to betray the whole right-wing project. Thus, as Michael Portillo proclaims, the growing crisis of political legitimacy is the result of a collapse of deference, due to a liberal enemy within corroding respect for still fundamentally sound institutions.

If the public sector is decaying, the right says that is essentially about accounting and lack of resources – as the market fills the breach so there will be a moral rebirth accompanying the individualization of what used to be collective responsibilities. As for job insecurity, this is no more than a hangover of the attitudes produced by the second recession within ten years, but will dissolve as the fruits of success become apparent. If there are problems, modern Conservatism has the answer.

The left is in more of a state of flux – but again there is a tendency, ranging from the old Labour right to the old conventional left, to regard the problems as discrete. The root of the political malaise is that there have been four successive Conservative parliaments. A Labour government will restore health to the political process through the act of winning; redistributive taxation will give extra resources to revitalize the public sector; stronger trade unions, a minimum wage and employment protection will rebalance power and ease job insecurity, a process reinforced by a more deliberately expansionary economic policy. The current malaise is but temporary.

The new right and old left can find enough evidence to allow each passionate adherents – but, as the American cultural historian Christopher Lasch argues in a powerful if disjointed new book, ultimately neither gets at the roots of the issue.*

A Labour government, for example, would certainly improve matters – but it could not absolve the profound tensions between capitalism and democracy. Democracy, after all, is a much bigger idea than simply allowing different parties to govern; and current capitalism requires more than different tax and spending policies for its menace to be lifted.

Citing the great fathers of the democratic tradition in the United States, notably Thomas Jefferson, Lasch argues that they knew well-constructed democratic institutions were the necessary but insufficient condition for a vital democracy – they had to be peopled by individuals who were engaged in the democratic process and had a stake in the outcome.

In the 1990s, it is the steady diminution of engaged stakeholders with a republican commitment to civic values and the process by which communities solve their problems through debate and voting that is causing democracy to implode into sound-bites, posturing and single-issue pressure groups.

Lasch looks back to a Jeffersonian golden age in the nineteenth century when sturdy American farmers, urban artisans and the burgeoning merchant classes, underpinned by deep religious belief and united by a common stake in neighbourhood, made the institutions of democracy work. The leaders of society, as its most important stakeholders, set an example by energetically engaging themselves in the democratic process – and as such were the custodians of a system that underwrote the values of a wider civilization. Democratic rights were associated with civic obligation; tolerance with a willingness to set and stand by absolute standards; differing approaches and values did not harden into exclusive ideological rivalry.

The image looks back to a mythical golden age, but Lasch uses it to telling effect. The contemporary American elite has revolted from its obligations and so betrayed democracy, hence the title of his book. The quest to boost profits over ever-shorter time horizons, and the dismantling of national boundaries, have transformed the operation of American capitalism, forcing it to be more ruthless and footloose.

A division has opened up in the American labour market between blue-collar workers whose real wages are falling and a class of detached and well-paid professional specialists – ranging from investment bankers to advertising

* C. Lasch, *The Revolt of the Elites and the Betrayal of Democracy* (New York: Norton & Co., 1995).

executives – who service this increasingly cosmopolitan, unrooted capital-ism.

This would matter less if the elite had retained its stake in neighbourhood together with the acceptance of responsibilities for the commonweal and an engagement in the democratic process. But it has not. It has exploited the new potential offered by the market to set itself apart from the networks of common schools, clubs and common interest, building instead a world of private schools, pensions, health and even personal security.

It ceases to have a stake in what is commonly held, and sees no point in enlisting in the democratic process or in paying taxes towards the common pool. It has privatized itself and gone offshore – like the firms for which it works. Left behind is the disaffected mass of common men and women whose capacity to be stakeholders is undermined by the new forces in the labour market and the wider marketization of society.

A de-civilizing, de-democratizing brutishness is emerging, infecting everything from the way children are educated and parented to the culture of shopping. America's malls and supermarkets, in which even the physical layout is subordinated to the need to maximize sales per square foot, are no substitute for the neighbourhood high street, for example. Nor are children, distractedly parented, able to take advantage as much as they used to of eavesdropping on a multiplicity of local and family conversations as part of their educative growing up; such conversations don't take place as neighbourhood and family implode.

Lasch was dying of leukaemia as he completed his book, and his solution is little more than a sketchy appeal to a new spirit of community in which the primacy of neighbourhood is asserted, along with obligations accom-panying rights. This is the same airy communitarianism to which Tony Blair appealed in his *Spectator* lecture last week, when he talked of the need to be tough about truancy at school and noisy neighbours.

The sentiments can scarcely be challenged, but unless they are embedded in a vigorous political economy they are whistling in the wind. The collapse of neighbourhood and the crisis in the family – where Britain is advancing down the same road as America – are at the end of the chain of causation rather than at the beginning. They are caused by the operation of a particular kind of capitalism, justified by a particular ideology of free markets.

The Reagan and Thatcher revolutions, and the resurgence of classical economic theory that lay behind them, truly believed that the exercise of individual choice in free markets would produce the good economy and society. Neither wanted individual choice to collapse into opting out and corrosion of civic virtue; it was meant to be underpinned by forces independent of the market, notably religious belief.

But in a secular society those beliefs are under siege – and, as Lasch says, belief cannot be reinvented because it might serve a helpful social and moral purpose. The task is more complicated. It is to reinvent a value system in which obligations are stressed along with rights – and so underpin democracy and the wider society.

The way forward must be to transform the institutions of market capitalism so that, instead of embodying networks of unravellable spot-market relations, there are new legal obligations to acknowledge a reciprocity of obligation. Moreover, the work must begin at the top.

Thus, shareholders may have rights to sell; but they should also be accompanied by obligations of commitment. Managers may have rights to hire and fire, but there should also be the obligation to consult, inform and incorporate their workforces in decision-making. Rich parents may have the right to educate their children privately, but only if private schools discharge an obligation to educate equal numbers of the disadvantaged who need the resources supplied by private schools. The list could go on.

But this stakeholder economy and society needs to be buttressed by a revived democracy that offers the capacity for local elites to engage in debate and in which public service is worthwhile; nobody, from the upper middle class to rank-and-file volunteers, wants to become a cipher of ideas decided upon at the centre – the condition of local democracy in contemporary Britain.

Just to identify the task underlines its magnitude – and the degree to which Britain's opted-out middle class has deserted ordinary people in its quest for self-advancement. Yet if it cannot be brought back to share in the commonweal, if the primacy of neighbourhood cannot be replaced, then the future is as Lasch portrays it. Our civilization will be irremediably damaged – and what will take its place?

Guardian, 27 March 1995

Darkness at the Heart of Privatization

Auckland is the first city where it has happened, but it cannot be long before its experience is repeated in Britain. For the past three weeks the central district of a city of a million people has been totally without power. Apartment blocks have been evacuated. Business has ground to a halt. Bankruptcies and unemployment are growing. Normal life has been suspended. It could be more than a month before power is restored.

It's this kind of reality that rams home to ordinary people what otherwise exists only as a theory. Electricity is not a commodity like a designer dress where an interruption of supply poses no wider consequences; it is a precondition for successful modern life. If the owner of the power and distribution system fails to maintain supply and so loses revenue, this is not just an issue for the shareholders of the enterprise. It is an issue for everyone. In economic terms, electricity is a public good.

This means electricity companies – like water, gas and rail companies – cannot be run on the same commercial terms as firms in markets where there are many suppliers and the consequences of poor decision-making are restricted to the firms themselves. They have to carry more investment and capacity than is necessary on strict commercial grounds; must have higher safety margins; and operate with a high standard of propriety. Because they are monopolies, the best way to meet these criteria is for the companies to be owned by the consumers; in other words, they should be structured as non-profit-making trusts, or mutuals, or even have their shares owned by government.

But over the past fifteen years all forms of public ownership have been derided as bureaucratic and inefficient. The international consensus among finance ministries and international economic institutions such as the OECD and IMF is that the private sector has no incentive other than to be efficient and mistake-free because of its overriding need to make high profits. Only the public sector has incentives to make mistakes and be inefficient. Thus the privatization of public assets, especially utilities, will simultaneously raise efficiency and boost the public sector balance sheet. Privatization is win/win.

But Auckland has discovered this is baloney. Mercury Energy, supplier of the city's electricity, has been privatized around a similar privatization structure to that in Britain. It is a distribution company buying electricity from two power generators who, so far, remain in public ownership. Its board is controlled by the nominees of a law firm, Russell McVeagh McKenzie Bartleet, and its job is to distribute the electricity it buys in central Auckland.

However, Mercury's commercial objective has not been to distribute electricity. It has been to raise the financial returns from its assets, lift its cash flow and so finance its ambition to take over its rivals, notably Power New Zealand, to become the monopoly supplier in New Zealand's North Island. More fees for Russell McVeagh; higher directors' salaries; and more fun. After all, running a utility is dull.

Inflating profits is easy to do. You reduce the workforce; you scale back the surplus capacity to make the operation lean; and you defer investment that does not meet normal commercial criteria. In other large cities in New Zealand the engineers that up until now ran the electricity distribution system as a public interest have insisted that there are up to ten major power cables delivering power. Some of the cables are never used: they act as standbys to avoid total power loss if the main cables fail. But it is uneconomic: in effect, it is an expensive insurance policy. Private shareholders should not be expected to bear this cost for the wider good; their interest is to act as Mercury Energy did.

Mercury only had four cables distributing power in Auckland. What the firm should not have done was go on the takeover trail; it should have invested in the distribution system even if it did imply additional overheads. So when freak conditions put all four cables out of commission, Mercury had no back-up. The system crashed and Auckland is without power.

Auckland's lessons should not be lost on us, especially for 3 million electricity consumers in East Anglia and North London. The ownership and control of Energy Corporation, a distribution company which owns the old Eastern Electricity, is being fought over by two American utilities – Oregon-based PacificCorp and Dallas-based Texas Utilities. When the auction began, Energy was around 650 pence a share: now Texas is offering 840 pence a share. It is prepared to pay £4.5 billion for assets that produce profits of $400 million and which have little scope to grow.

It is absurd. The sums only work because Wall Street is so high, taking the share prices of Texas Utilities and PacificCorp to silly levels; but once the deal is done, the pressures will be to run Energy in exactly the same way as Mercury. Britain's tiny regulator, Offer, will be given the runaround – and, anyway, it does not have the power or mandate to investigate closely how the assets are managed and run; its job is to set prices. Its feebleness is one of the reasons US utilities are prepared to pay so much for British electricity companies.

The British doctrine is that the decision over whether to sell and at what price should solely be at the discretion of the Energy Group board serving the interests of the shareholders – and that the interests of any new shareholders in Oregon or Dallas can only coincide with electricity consumers' in Britain. We know that cannot be true. It may be too late to renationalize the electricity companies, but at least if there were a body of corporate law built around stakeholder principles, Energy and companies like it would have to take into account other interests than those of shareholders. Regulation could be beefed up – and utilities put on notice that they will be taken back into public ownership in the event of sustained power failure.

New Labour, we know, won't go that far. But it is considering toughening up regulation next year in its Utilities Bill. Events in Auckland should redouble its determination.

Observer, 8 March 1998

PART V

Taming Mammon:
The Growth and Regulation
of the Global Economy

Reviving Bretton Woods

It has come to a pretty pass when Nelson Mandela's ANC and Silvio Berlusconi's Forza Italia pursue similar policies. But this is 1994 and every government must bend before the imperatives of the global capital markets. A government that wants to borrow internationally, avoid a run on its currency or attract inward investment must accept the markets' imperatives as its own.

Sound money, balanced budgets, low taxation and free markets are the order of the day. Governments no longer have autonomy in constructing their domestic social and industrial policy – what we might call a social settlement. Every move is cast with an eye on the markets' reaction.

For the right, this is a welcome development. The global capital markets oblige governments to enlarge the scope of capitalist endeavour and to roll back the state – which the right believes are preconditions for growth and prosperity.

But for those who believe a good society must allow scope for social solidarity and public choices, the situation is more alarming. Social solidarity involves redistributive taxation and some attempt to regulate the labour market. And if democracy is to have any meaning, it is surely to permit elected parties to shape their economies and societies rather than abandon the process to the dictates of the bond market. In short, in a world of deregulated finance social democracy is in peril.

Even the right has to concede that the results of the new policy bias have been disappointing. The industrialized world may have the lowest inflation for a generation, but it also has the highest level of unemployment. Include discouraged and involuntarily inactive workers and the jobless total among OECD countries exceeds 50 million.

While some point to technological innovation or the growth in low-cost imports from the developing world, no account of the rise in unemployment can exclude the very high levels of real interest rates that have prevailed for nearly twenty years – regularly in excess of 5 per cent – or the incapacity of governments to assure private businesses that future demand will be buoyant. And these phenomena are closely linked to the new role of international finance.

Once economies start to operate below their trend growth rates, governments get locked in a vicious circle: the lowering of the tax base and the inflation of social security spending makes persistent budget deficits part of the structure of the economy. This makes expansionary fiscal policy more difficult – a difficulty compounded by the power of the global financial markets, which are reluctant to lend to indebted governments. The only way out is to cut government spending, and this involves limiting the scope of the welfare state and the social democratic settlement.

The classic casualty has been Sweden. The link between the decline of its social democracy and rise of the power of international finance is a textbook case.

In the early 1980s, the development of an offshore Euro-krone market became a source of credit for Sweden's banking sector to make big inroads into the regulated banks' markets – the secondary banks lent on keener terms. As their market share declined, the big banks lobbied for deregulation in order to fight back; and this set in train the credit boom of the mid and late 1980s. The result was inflation persistently exceeding government targets and thus eroding the value of the collectively agreed wages, which in turn undermined the legitimacy of Sweden's famed concerted wage bargaining arrangements.

The government faced a conundrum. It did not want to undermine investment by containing inflation with high interest rates; and it could not re-regulate the financial system. So it attempted a prices and wages freeze to interrupt the inflationary cycle and stop unions breaking away from centralized wage bargaining. In order to slow domestic credit growth, however, the government had to limit its own borrowing and spending plans. Even before losing the 1991 election, Sweden's Social Democrats were cutting back on their famed welfare state; the arrival of the right only confirmed the new reality. Nor is it clear to what extent the Social Democrats, after regaining power in September 1994, can do other than continue the process they themselves began in 1989.

In short, the international framework is the key to domestic policy – something that is becoming as obvious to us as it was to the designers of the postwar economic order at Bretton Woods, New Hampshire, in 1944. And they were successful: the early 1950s to the early 1970s were the most remarkable decades the industrialized world has known. Growth averaged close to 5 per cent, investment was high and in most countries there was nearly full employment. Compared with what came before and after, it was a golden age – not least for social democracy.

This postwar boom inaugurated the age of the common man and woman. The generalized prosperity and social mobility it fanned into being allowed millions to escape the drudgery of their parents' lives. Full employment meant an expanding welfare state, package holidays and a new sexual equality.

The preoccupation of those at Bretton Woods was to avoid the mass unemployment and political tensions of the pre-war years. The world must have a robust financial framework that would foster growth and trade. The values of the currencies used for trade would have a fixed relationship with each other. And when differential economic performance – ranging from inflation to exports – forced devaluation and revaluation, the changes would be policed fairly by a new supranational financial institution, the International Monetary Fund.

The IMF would, at times of crisis, provide financial assistance to help countries avoid measures damaging to either their own or international prosperity. Above all, destabilizing private capital flows would be controlled and regulated. The IMF's articles specified that countries should move towards currency convertibility and that they should and must retain the capacity to control capital flows.

Thus beggar-my-neighbour policies and protectionism would be avoided. The debates at Bretton Woods emphasized the interdependence of growth-generating free trade and orderly finance. In the 1920s, the collapse of the international payments system, the cessation of currency convertibility and the lack of regulation of US markets had caused the world financial system to implode, with calamitous effects on trade, output and employment. Bretton Woods aimed to ensure that would never happen again.

At the same time there was an enlightened effort to organize aid flows to the less developed world, to give it access to funds from other than its colonial masters. The World Bank would channel loans to poorer countries and help them develop their economies. So the postwar epoch began.

For some, especially on the right, the subsequent boom had nothing to do with Bretton Woods – which was in any case, they said, fatally flawed because of the gentle rise in inflation that it sponsored. Europe had to rebuild itself after a devastating war and, by copying US production techniques, would inevitably experience a leap in productivity to generate economic growth. The international financial order had little or nothing to do with it, said the right.

Liberal opinion concurred. The IMF did little in its first ten years; the World Bank provided little capital compared with the private sector, even in the years after the war; world trade growth was financed not by the IMF, but by dollar loans and the Marshall Plan; and full convertibility of leading currencies was not achieved until 1961. And in the 1960s, runs the argument, Bretton Woods was defined as much by inflexibility over exchange rate movement as by its supposed capacity to give countries a framework in which to make economic adjustment. The postwar international order has been unreasonably lionized; the golden age had other explanations.

Yet the most recent economic scholarship decisively rejects this interpretation. In a recent paper published by the Centre for Economic Policy Research, Barry Eichengreen states that, even after allowing for catch-up and spring-back effects, European growth between 1950 and 1973 was 50 per cent higher than subsequently. Above all, investment in Europe – with

Britain a sad exception – climbed from 20 per cent of GDP to more than 30 per cent.

Eichengreen argues that the European economies were able to lock themselves into a virtuous circle, and that the new international institutions permitted a new set of domestic policy options. In short, claims Eichengreen, there was a social democratic 'grand bargain' that pushed the growth process forward. The system of predetermined – or pegged – exchange rates was among the most important of these.

European workers moderated their wage claims secure in the knowledge that, with pegged exchange rates, inflation could not rob them of the fruits of their moderation, and that high investment would continue to deliver growth and jobs. Governments succeeded in maintaining high investment – even in the downswings – because they could boost demand, knowing it would not be dissipated in inflationary wage claims.

The countries that made this bargain work best were those with regulated financial systems that supported industrial investment; competitive export sectors; strong unions that could make moderate wage settlements hold; and business organizations to bargain with labour and then exploit the results in high investment. In other words, the international system rewarded, rather than penalized, those countries that could construct a social democratic settlement. In this environment a Sweden or a Germany could flourish.

The Bretton Woods exchange rate regime made sure the benefits of the domestic bargain could be seized – through currency convertibility, opening markets and orderly exchange rate adjustments. The domestic bargain and the international bargain were mutually reinforcing.

What wrecked both, in Eichengreen's view, was the growth of capital mobility, as controls were circumvented and then lowered as they became harder to police. At Bretton Woods, Keynes had correctly insisted that capital controls were essential to the effective functioning of the system. But as the 1960s wore on, business exploited the loopholes to invest abroad and undermined the domestic bargain. Capitalists now had an exit and did not have to bargain with governments or unions.

Equally, the growth of capital mobility made it harder to defend the fixed exchange rates set by the IMF. In the early 1970s, the combination of US trade weakness and destabilizing speculation laid waste to the system. Right-wing commentators hailed its collapse as signalling a new period of growth, just as they did after the European Exchange Rate Mechanism fell apart in 1993. Financial freedom would rescue the world from regulation, corporatism and government-led efforts at creating full employment. In fact the world growth rate has halved and currency instability exploded.

In the mid-1990s the world financial system is spinning out of control.

The stock of cross-border lending now exceeds one-quarter of the industrialized countries' GDP. International bank assets are double the value of world trade. The volume of business in the currency futures markets exceeds even the flows generated by daily trade in currency. In other words, the tail of the futures market is wagging the dog of the spot market. Groundless fears about what may happen in two or three years' time move current spot prices and interest rates. The world has been turned on its head.

The governments of the US, Germany or Japan do not have the financial clout to take on the new volume of speculative flows. And many developing countries do not even have sufficient reserves to cover the purchase of eight weeks' imports. Capital's right of exit has been converted into economic supremacy – with London's financial markets playing a pivotal role.

Yet the new freedom for capital to move at will has not produced the high investment of the postwar years. By allowing capital to look for the highest return, governments have raised its price and inadvertently caused investment to shrink. There has been a race to the top for the highest short-term return.

Britain and the US have the freest financial systems, which also achieve among the highest returns in the Organization for Economic Co-operation and Development (OECD). As a result, they have the lowest levels of investment, and consequently the lowest levels of savings.

Thus, meeting the markets' concern to achieve low inflation has been prosecuted in a low-investment environment. The combination of restrictive policies and low investment has produced high unemployment and a slowdown in the trend rate of growth. This has blocked expansion of savings even further and driven up the price of capital, while below-trend growth has produced budget deficits.

The leaders of the Group of Seven at the IMF and World Bank annual meeting in Madrid in October 1994 ordered an investigation into the origins of low savings and falling bond prices. To them, the problem is high budget deficits. But these are consequences not causes of the new phenomenon. The real enemy is global deregulation and volatile capital flows. Postwar stability has been replaced by a new instability – good for the brokers and traders, bad for employment and investment.

The world needs to reinvent the bargain it abandoned. A regime in which capital movements are contained and rendered less destabilizing is easily outlined. The real issue is whether it is politically feasible.

For example, instead of floating currencies there need to be adjustable bands in which currencies move predictably. The world's chief economies need to support these bands. The low-saving, high-consumption US will have to contemplate tax increases to change its propensity to import and thus run a structural trade deficit; and high-saving, low-consumption Japan will need to cut taxes to attack its structural trade surplus – and so together remove the incompatibility in their economies that make it impossible to maintain a stable dollar/yen exchange rate.

Beyond the immediate dollar/yen crisis, there will have to be policy coordination to sustain economic convergence for the key European players. This will mean hard decisions on public spending, taxes and interest rates. But they are better taken in the context of a wider order, with the IMF holding the ring, than at the behest of central bank governors and finance ministers appeasing the markets' latest whim.

Europe will have to reconstruct a parallel system of flexible exchange rate bands, and the speculative flows in the futures and options markets will need to be regulated everywhere. This will be deplored by those earning telephone number salaries in the financial markets and their supporters in the media. But governments are there to promote the welfare of all.

The less developed world needs more buying power, more aid transfers on generous terms and more intelligent support of its effort to alleviate chronic poverty. Its capacity to convert its own reserves into hard currency via the IMF system of Special Drawing Rights (SDRs) should be greatly extended. And the world's rich countries need to recognize their own interest in offering hope to the people of the poorest countries by multiplying, many times over, the resources they currently transfer.

Above all, the terms on which the IMF and World Bank lend to Third World countries – their so-called structural adjustment programmes – need to be radically overhauled. The belt-tightening and free market economics which everywhere promote inequality and a fall-away in investment need to be modified.

With such an international financial system, countries such as Sweden – and indeed Britain – will have a chance of moving on to a higher growth trajectory as real interest rates fall, savings rise and the capital markets' veto on expansionary policies is weakened. The growth of the tax base will help tackle chronic budget deficits, and relieve pressure on the welfare state. Stability in exchange rates, meanwhile, will protect co-ordinated wage bargaining from sudden swings in price levels that produce unanticipated changes in real wages. It will also allow developing countries to construct similar social democratic settlements if they choose – for example, allowing South Africa greatly to expand its social housing programme.

Yet to cite the wish list of necessary changes is to realize that, as things stand, they are virtually unattainable.

In Madrid the G7 opposed even a limited extension of SDRs for the developing world proposed by IMF managing director Michel Camdessus, on the basis that it was 'inflationary' – a position Germany's Bundesbank held with special ferocity. The compromise extension to the 'countries in transition' was blocked by an enraged developing world. If this cannot be agreed, what possibility is there of agreement over a new international exchange rate regime? Is there any appetite to contain capital flows or regulate the derivatives markets? As a matter of principle, would leading industrialized countries consider surrendering economic policy to the IMF?

And in practical terms, do countries have sufficient policy levers to surrender the one they do possess – interest rates – to the maintenance of a given exchange rate? With the success of expansionary fiscal policy threatened by structural budget deficits, and in the absence of capital controls, any exchange rate regime means interest rates have to be devoted to holding the exchange rate target. To give up this tool in the hope of greater autonomy later requires an enormous act of faith. After all, who expects the US and Japan to make the changes that would produce yen/dollar stability?

Yet countries need a grand bargain abroad to permit social democratic bargains at home. The inability of the developed world to insulate itself from the grim march of poverty, disease and migration that now haunt the developing world is a further incentive to build a more sympathetic economic order. The IMF and World Bank are beginning to realize that they have done the cause no good by turning their backs on their Keynesian roots and embracing the free market right – which ultimately spells their own demise.

One day the spirit of Bretton Woods will return because it has to. Meanwhile, private capital and markets rule – and social democracy must learn to live in a cold climate.

New Economy (Winter 1994)

Crisis in Mexico should Puncture the Conservatives' Complacency

The world is different now. The scale of trade and financial flows has raised the interpenetration and interdependence of national economies to an unprecedented degree. The old, shallow business of economic relations between states – tariffs, exchange rates, market access – has given ground to how their entire economic and social systems relate to each other.

The structure of a country's tax or banking system can be a source of tension more than its tariffs; but arbitration and co-ordination of these potential conflicts go right to the heart of what a country is.

It is not enough, as the British rightly insist, to argue that the resulting crises can be managed through letting markets have their way and intergovernmental collaboration. This new territory requires new approaches. At least, that was the working assumption at this year's World Economic Forum at Davos where around 1,000 businessmen, financiers, ministers and academics gathered to assess the world economy. They would find the internal debate in the British Conservative Party truly naïve.

Nation states do have decreasing sovereignty, whatever the protestations of Michael Portillo or Teresa Gorman, at the same time as the range of issues requiring international governance is exploding.

Nor can the world economy be simply organized as a series of competitive spot markets – in labour, foreign exchange, products and capital – whose stability and beneficial working can be taken for granted. Davos is both a comfort that capitalism has won and a puncture to Conservative complacencies.

The titles of some of the sessions give the flavour. 'The coming of the global society – nations or networks', in which media magnates and academics will debate if transnational communications are reconfiguring the jurisdiction of the state. But it continues 'Bribonomics: corruption and the world economy', 'The new challenge of old infectious diseases' and 'New initiatives to combat global crime'. Here the practitioners of world capitalism get serious about world trends.

For example if cholera is reappearing and being spread more rapidly by the new flows of trade and people, then how is this dealt with except by new institutions of global governance which can compel countries and companies to comply with higher health standards? The same is true of organized crime, standards of ships' seaworthiness and pornography transmitted by satellite television, etc.

A clutch of proposals have been aired here emerging from bodies as disparate as the Commission on Global Governance in Geneva (*A Call to Action*) and the Brookings Institution in Washington (*A Vision for the World Economy*), trying to come to terms with the new exigencies. The core assumption is that economic integration has thrown up an array of common crises whose resolution requires a new framework for public action that supersedes the nation state.

The Commission on Global Governance proposes a strengthened and democratized United Nations, including a new Economic Security Council – while the Brookings Institution strikes a more subtle note, advocating the establishment of a network of international clubs to set global rules and exchange information, of which the UN would be one element. Its model is the Bank for International Settlements in Basle which sets minimum standards of capital adequacy for world banks – or the International Labour Office that does the same for labour standards. The idea could be extended from the foreign exchange markets to generic scientific research.

The British response is an immediate distrust of any initiative that smacks of international bureaucracy attempting to obstruct the smooth operations of markets. The private is axiomatically better than the public; and inter-governmental collaboration much better than any supranational interven-tion – whether it is building up the capacity of the IMF and World Bank or giving the United Nations an economic arm.

But there is one spectacular recent example which shatters all such preju-dices and which has cast a long shadow over this year's Davos . . . Mexico.

The extent to which events there overturn the entire house of cards upon which objections to building some better system of global governance are rooted can hardly be overstated. Every aspect of the Mexican crisis, with its shock waves radiating out across Latin America and the undeveloped world, is eloquent testimony to the instability of 'spot-market' capitalism and the limits of trying to manage its tensions by intergovernmental collaboration.

For what was wrong with the way Mexico approached the financing of its economic growth was that the terms on which Wall Street provided Mexico its vital capital inflows were so immediately reversible. Instead of the committed long-term investment of private banks and multinationals, who would benefit as the country prospered, Mexico was compelled to organize its capital inflows through a series of short-term spot-market trans-actions in the capital markets.

The investment attraction was that Mexican stocks, shares and dollar-denominated bonds (Tesobonos) could be bought and sold at will; but that also proved Mexico's downfall.

When sentiment changed as it became obvious that the vast build-up of short-term dollar-denominated liabilities could not be serviced by a coun-try in chronic trade deficit, each link in the spot-market chain unravelled as it was preset to do.

Mexico could not continue to sell its short-term dollar bonds to US Mutual Funds (equivalents of British unit trusts), who were and are terrified that their short-term investors would move their assets into bank deposits as news of the huge losses on Mexican assets, following the devaluation and stock market slump, grew.

The shock was all the greater because the Wall Street investment banks themselves – as David Hale, the irrepressible chief economist of the giant US investment house Kemper Financial Services, observes – had no inter-est in letting US Mutual Funds know that Mexico might be a high-risk investment. That might have interrupted the deal flow and so threatened their salaries.

The private capital inflows upon which the development of a country depends cannot be organized solely as a series of spot-market transactions. Somewhere there have to be relations of commitment.

To attempt to restore financial confidence, Mexico has indulged in swingeing spending cuts and tax increases, threatening to destabilize its delicately balanced social fabric.

Yet that has not been enough; it will need $40 billion (£26.6 billion) of credit lines arranged by the US government to assure the world investment community that it has sufficient firepower to meet its short-term obligations as it restores its domestic and international finances.

Time was when the International Monetary Fund would have had the resources to do the job; but western governments have allowed its scale to shrink so that its maximum $7.76 billion stand-by loan is chicken-feed beside the scale of the problem. Enter the intergovernmental collaboration so desired by the Conservative right as Mexico turns to governments for help.

This too is inherently unstable. The US loan is deadlocked in Congress, as the Republicans try to capitalize upon President Clinton's difficulties; and the Germans, who lead the European consortium, have said they will do nothing until the US gets its house in order. So commercial banks squabble over who gets better terms and the situation drifts, causing untold economic harm and threatens more.

Already some $200 billion has been wiped off the value of Latin American stock markets, and with sky-high Mexican interest rates, a wave of Mexican corporate collapses seems inevitable. It is in the interest of the world that Mexico in particular and Latin America in general do not suffer another decade of disinflation and social disintegration. The world financial system is increasingly vulnerable to weaknesses in any one part – and Mexico's problems, if unattended, could impact on Britain and Europe.

But to get a different out-turn the private sector has to operate along different principles.

The spot-market capitalism of which Mexico has been victim is the most extreme form of the Anglo-Saxon way of doing things; what is required is the more relational capitalism of northern Europe and East Asia. If Mexico had relied more on long-term bank finance and direct investment, its chances of finessing the crisis would have been greater.

And when the stress points are international, there have to be supranational institutions with the resources and competence to respond – in the Mexican case a strengthened and more Keynesian IMF could have averted the embarrassments of the living standards of a continent being dependent upon the day-to-day congressional tactics of Newt Gingrich.

This is certainly the emerging consensus of Davos; and it is one more reason why the French and Germans here – along with the president of the European Commission, Jacques Santer – strike such a determined note about accelerating the process of European integration together with a single currency. Intergovernmental collaboration and spot-market capitalism makes no more sense for Europe than it does for the world – and Europe has an obligation to move forward.

Against this background the political discourse in Britain comes from another planet – but it is difficult to see how and why it might change.

Guardian, 30 January 1995

Job Worries Contain Message of Import

What is happening to jobs and work across the West is beginning to worry the political and economic establishment everywhere. Whether it is President Clinton ruefully blaming the scale of the Democrats' electoral defeat on the new world of work insecurity or the CBI and TUC urging action to alleviate long-term unemployment, the backwash of endless rounds of downsizing and rationalization is causing mounting concern.

Yet still national elites tend to cast solutions in national terms, apparently unaware of the global nature of the forces at work. Plainly there were specific US factors in the Democrats' defeat – but Clinton is right to identify the impact of the tidal wave of low-cost imports on the US labour market as a source of political disaffection. We live in a world where the social gains of the last forty years – the forty-hour week, rising real wages, paid holiday entitlement and employers' contributions to pensions – are under assault. The impact is most acute in Britain and the US, where exposure to free trade with minimal welfare systems is most marked, but the phenomenon is universal.

Right-wing free marketeers and social democrat liberals alike want to deny that this wave of low-cost exports from the underdeveloped South to the developed North has any significant relationship to the collapse in demand for unskilled labour. The right blames the welfare state and the burdens it imposes upon employers and state budgets; the left cites insufficient commitment to training and labour market intervention.

Both can tell part of the story, but to imagine that the collapse in demand for unskilled workers in industries as disparate as textiles and shipbuilding, from Japan to Canada, is independent of trade conditions is wrong. It may be a global imperative for the North to keep trade flows continuing, without which the South is condemned to penury – but the North needs to diagnose correctly the source of its ills.

In the 'golden age' after the war, western societies were able to accommodate the adjustments resulting from free trade comparatively painlessly – because the international financial system allowed governments the room for manoeuvre to run expansionary macroeconomic policies, develop active labour market policies and improve social safety nets. But now, when the trade flows have become much more significant, the new international financial regime has denied governments such initiative.

Global financial deregulation has raised the cost of capital, intensified the speed with which shocks like the rise in US bond yields are transmitted worldwide and made the markets more volatile. To keep borders open and sustain social cohesion, western governments need a properly governed international financial environment.

Those who defend the current position should reflect on the likely impact on western labour markets of ten years of Chinese and Indian exports growing in double figures on top of the existing exports from the newly industrialized countries (NICs) if the present emphasis on deficit-cutting, high real interest rates and roll-back of the welfare state remains. It will be a murderous cocktail – and heading off protection in the US and Europe will be very difficult. These conditions are the recruiting sergeants for political extremism from both left and right.

For those outside the national debates the commonality of the experience is more obvious – as are its roots. The international institutions charged with regulating trade, financial and labour standards increasingly realize the interconnectedness of developments – and how the love affair with unfettered markets can destabilize social systems and economies. A sign of the way opinion is moving is that it is no longer just the International Labour Office (ILO) that recognizes the rights of workers to basic labour standards as a fundamental precondition of not just social cohesion but the wider wealth-creating process, and that this is being derailed by excessive trade and financial deregulation.

In Geneva on Friday, the ILO hosted a seminar with the World Bank and the IMF as part of its seventy-fifth anniversary celebrations – and both Robert Picciotto, director-general of the World Bank's policy evaluation division, and Jack Boorman, director of policy development at the IMF, signed up to the basic proposition. Indeed, Mr Boorman said that unless the unfair income distribution resulting from global market pressures was properly addressed there was a growing risk that market capitalism would become discredited, while Mr Picciotto insisted that an uninhibited laissez-faire labour market could not work. The labour market, like the financial market, had to be given boundaries to its operation.

Neither dissented from the importance the ILO attached to agreeing a social clause that would be incorporated in the constitution of the new policeman of world trade, the World Trade Organization. This would require all signatories to establish procedures that would permit workers to be represented by trade unions and to engage in collective bargaining. The idea, says the ILO's director-general, Michel Hansenne, is a kind of grand bargain between the industrialized West and the less developed world. We keep our markets open; they put in place procedures which ensure that competitive advantage is not won by rank exploitation of labour. It is a minimalist measure, but recognizes the force of the pressures in train. But even if the ILO can persuade the less developed countries to agree such a clause, which the Third World may see as a form of cultural imperialism that compels stable societies like Singapore and South Korea to import mechanisms for social and worker dissent, it is not obvious that agreement will be reached to insert it into the WTO. Or even if it were, it might not be robust enough to do more than simply stem the worst forms of unfair competition. The Asian NICs are determined to protect the combination of social authoritarianism, state-directed investment, and export-led growth that has brought them so far – and worker representation is not part of the picture. Others in Latin America share that view.

For liberal regimes in the industrialized West this poses a formidable challenge. They want to keep their markets open to capture the gains from trade; but they have to manage the gathering dislocation, insecurity and social privation at home, while deregulated global finance increases the cost of capital for the private sector and exerts an effective veto on public initiative. The IMF, designing a special loan facility for industrialized countries at the receiving end of unwarranted speculative attack, trying to build its special drawing rights as a proper world reserve currency and canvassing support for a more rules-based international financial system less prone to instability and volatility, desperately wants to contain and shape the new forces – a belated return to its Keynesian roots.

But, as Mr Boorman remarked, if the US, Germany and Japan are not prepared to cede sovereignty to make a new order work, then the hopes of a more progressive Bank and IMF reshaping the world financial system are minimal.

The right does not, of course, share such views, but the concerns expressed in Geneva show just how shallow that position is. It may be that free trade has tripled world per-capita incomes over the last fifty years; but income disparities have doubled and are set to widen further, with insecurity adding to the brew. In the past, the poor could consider that the system required their exploitation and thus gave them some leverage in return; now it simply ignores them. Can you run the domestic and international economy in this way for long? I doubt it – but those prepared to heed such fears grow less confident and less powerful by the day.

Guardian, 14 November 1994

Myth that Sets the World to Rights

The modern world is different, we are told. Communications, ever-freer trade, mushrooming capital flows and transnational companies are creating a global market with a global workforce.

In a race for global competitiveness, the nation state has no option but to accept the lowest common global denominator – whether of TV standards or employment.

This is the globalizer's world view. It is the language of the economic pundit and western finance minister alike, and will be the shared assumption at the world economic summit in Halifax, Nova Scotia, next weekend. The dignitaries will tut-tut over the instability of the foreign exchange markets and worry about the trends in their societies – but they won't promise to do anything. We knew that anyway, but last week's leaked draft final communiqué confirmed it.

The conviction that states are helpless before the new forces can spark evangelical delight for the free market right, which sees a global free market producing all they ever hoped for – well expressed in John Redwood's book *The Global Marketplace* – or near-despair for the social democratic left. Senior ministers in Sweden's social democratic government privately speculate whether social democracy is still possible for even a medium-sized industrial power – a worry echoed in the upper reaches of Germany's SPD. Those who wish to protect national cultures and institutions, both on the right (Sir James Goldsmith in France) and the left (Richard Gephardt in the US), are espousing protection and a retreat from the global market.

But the whole argument is based on an incorrect premise. The capacity to dial direct to the world from Beijing, to relocate production to a Malaysian free-trade zone, or of a British merchant bank to bankrupt itself because of its unmanaged dealings in Singapore and Osaka, are important phenomena – but stop a long way short of globalization. There is a fundamental distinction between accelerating internationalization, which is what is happening, and globalization, which is not. And there are very different political conclusions.

The notion that there is now one global, borderless, stateless market – as Paul Krugman said in his LSE lecture last week – is 'globaloney'. Much of the talk about gigantic global capital flows, huge global direct investment and tidal movements of global trade turns out to be hyperbole. The numbers may be large and growing rapidly, but they are not 'stateless' in the sense that the funds have slipped national preoccupations. Indeed, much of the activity is national capital using offshore tax havens and the so-called global financial system to escape national controls or to secure tax advantages.

For example, between 1991 and 1993, foreign direct investment (FDI) in the less-developed countries jumped from $36.9 billion to $56.3 billion. But all of that rise was accounted for by increased inward investment into China, most of which was 'round-tripping' by Chinese enterprises which by exporting capital and bringing it back into China could secure the favourable tax treatment offered to 'foreign' investors. Without the Chinese figures, FDI flows into less-developed countries were static. In any case, 90 per cent of the FDI went to nine developing countries and the Chinese coastal provinces.

It is a similar story wherever you turn. Huge 'global capital flows' turn out to be largely exchanges between the leading industrialized countries. Total portfolio investment in emerging countries totalled $60 billion in 1994 – 0.3 per cent of world output – and will fall this year after the Mexico crisis.

Migration is not on the scale of the pre-1914 period; and what is interesting about the growth of exports from the less-developed countries is how few succeed rather than how many – and how small a proportion of world trade – the numbers represent. Can China and India really transmute themselves into capitalist superpowers?

Nor, despite the capacity of capital to cross national frontiers, is there any sign of an equalization in savings ratios between industrialized countries or in rates of return on business investment. Neo-classical theory predicts that savings converge to an international average as part of the construction of a global capital market, but the dispersion of national savings rates around the average is if anything increasing. In 1994, Japan's gross national savings were 34 per cent of national output, compared with 19 per cent in France and 13 per cent in Britain; a significantly wider range of outcomes than in the mid-1970s.

The 'transnational company', freed from the constraint of national shareholders and national jurisdiction, and with a genuine transnational operating capacity, also turns out to be a chimera. Ford may produce a global car, but 80 per cent of its fixed assets are in the US; even the 'global' Pepsi Cola and McDonald's have more than half of their fixed assets in the US. One survey shows that on average two-thirds of the sales and assets of German, Japanese, American and British transnational companies are at home.

The companies also conform to their national cultures, preoccupations of their national shareholders and demands of their national jurisdictions. For example, the hurdle rates for new investment set by Japanese companies are very nearly half of those set by British companies; and again the evidence is that the dispersion has widened rather than narrowed. There are companies operating in many countries, but none has slipped the national leash to become a stateless body operating in a borderless world with common average hurdle rates and metropolitan organizational cultures.

Multinationals are important – as they have been throughout this century. Two-thirds of the trade in merchandise goods between industrialized countries is between their subsidiaries – but that again gives the lie to the globalization thesis. The global market is not an anonymous market: it is operated by companies with legal and ownership roots in distinctive national capitalist systems.

It is true that the collapse of capital and exchange controls together with cuts in tariffs have given multinational companies and investment houses more power in relation to national governments. And typically they exploit it against their own governments. Thus, the weight of the recent speculation against the Swedish krona was from Swedish financial institutions operating off-shore, just as the bulk of the speculation against the French franc inside the ERM in August 1993 was by French banks and pension funds.

Yet it fell to governments to bail out those same financial institutions when they were stricken by the disasters that accompanied deregulation and globalization. Despite all the brave talk of the efficiency of unregulated financial markets, the international financial system is, as much as any domestic one, organized around a fundamental asymmetry. It wants to be able to make as much money as it can, free of any regulatory constraint, when times are good; but when its actions put individual banks, or the entire system at risk, it looks to governments to act as the safety net.

Whether it is the French government bailing out Crédit Lyonnais or the IMF's $17.8 billion of stand-by credits for Mexico – both records – the story is the same. The apostles of global capital markets scuttle for government help the minute the system shows signs of cracking, exhibiting the same passion as they employ to reject any form of government control.

The globalization thesis is no more than an argument deployed by the right to cow the left – but is in danger of rebounding on the right. Because, while it may serve the political purpose of persuading workers in the industrialized West that they have to accept ever-worsening pay and conditions, and social democrats that welfare systems are costly burdens that must be privatized, it also denudes the few international institutions that exist of the political and financial support necessary to upgrade their capacity to shape and manage current trends.

This global market needs superintending and policing. Governments can and should co-ordinate their policies to manage it – and set rules by which the trade and financial game is played. The institutions of international co-operation – the IMF, the World Bank, the World Trade Organization – are more, not less important. Their authority hangs by a thread almost as thin as western governments' conviction that the power of capital can and should be challenged. If the global market really was global, perhaps they would be right; but because it is not, there is a capacity for action – and a necessity that it is discharged. The myth of globalization may rebound on us all.

Guardian, 12 June 1995

Restrain these Corporate Godzillas

We live in an era of corporate gigantism. In January 1998 two British drugs companies, Glaxo and SmithKline Beecham, agreed to merge to create the world's third largest company – the biggest deal yet in a corporate Britain in the middle of its most extensive and ambitious merger boom of modern times.

Its authors say it is a logical response to the challenges of globalization. That may be true, although beware globalization arguments that have such obvious benefits for their proponents. What is certainly true is that the new company represents an astonishing concentration of corporate power. Everything to do in Britain with drugs – how scientists are trained, where they work, where R&D is directed, the location of labs and factories, the future of the high-street chemist and how and which drugs are sold to the NHS – will revolve around this new company. The poor DTI and DHS will be helpless before its ambitions. Public authority will be little more than a cipher.

So do we want such mergers? Do we believe they serve a wider public interest? Is the framework of company law and competition policy in which they take place any longer adequate for the new world of corporate gigantism – both domestically and internationally? Are current affairs programmes and news media alive with debate? No. Instead there is silence, even as the economic structures that determine our lives are transformed.

This is not to argue that Sir Richard Sykes, chief executive of Glaxo, who instigated the deal, is a bad man. On the contrary. He is a refreshingly diffident grammar-school-educated scientist who runs a great research-oriented company with *élan*. But English company law requires that he has no duty to any constituency in Britain other than his shareholders for whom he must maximize profits, earnings and dividends year by year. It is not his remit to worry for a second about the impact of his new company on Britain's health service, labour market, scientific community, manufacturing capacity or even public health.

If this were but one isolated case, it would matter less. But the drugs merger is only one of many. In accountancy, advertising, music, investment banking, publishing – indeed wherever you look – the trend and the arguments for merger are the same.

None of this is desperately surprising. Competitive markets are frightening and difficult to control. Growth is hard to achieve, demanding innovation and a capacity to spot the next technological transformation and exploit it. The much easier route to rising profits and dividends, and a securer environment, is to buy a competitor.

In Britain and America, dominated by hungry and short-termist stock markets, the merger trend is at its fiercest. But the emergence of super-challengers in the Anglo-Saxon world is forcing the rest of the industrialized world into a parallel response. In Switzerland, for example, the two largest banks – Union Bank of Switzerland and Swiss Bank Corporation – are currently merging. In Germany, Bertelsmann and Kirch are set to merge to become Europe's most powerful publishing/media company.

In ten years the major industries of the world will be dominated by one or two global players; in the newspaper industry, for example, one likely force is News International. But if the *Times, Telegraph, Independent* and *Guardian* were all to merge into one super-daily broadsheet paper – justified, say, because it could sell at 20 pence and thus represent better consumer value – would readers' choice be enhanced or reduced? The answer is obvious, as it should be in pharmaceuticals, banking or advertising when the same bogus arguments are proffered.

Yet the policy response to all this is pathetic. In the recent four-hour 'wonkathon' at the White House, you can be certain that such issues were not raised or explored – in part because the conclusions require national leaders to take on the rich and powerful rather than 'welfare reform' of the poor and weak. For example, the British business establishment's reaction to any widening of company responsibilities was amply revealed in the final draft of the Hampel report. Charged to review the legal framework in which companies are managed, the report said it would not stand in the way of 'wealth generation' and the overriding importance of shareholder interest.

It proposed trivial changes to the voluntary code asserting principles for corporate governance. Prosperity should come before accountability, it fatuously claimed. The managers of the new gigantic super-monopolies admit no responsibility to any constituency but those who want to buy cheap and sell dear. In the run-up to the last presidential election, Bill Clinton vetoed plans for tax incentives for 'responsible' corporations. He was frightened that the Democrats would upset corporate America. Tony

Blair, having briefly championed stakeholding, abandoned it for similar reasons. But if national frameworks are not built to make the new concentrations of corporate power work more accountably and for a wider constituency, then we must look to supranational authorities.

But here the track record is feeble. The European Union does its best, but so far its rulings have been characterized by their inability to overrule individual member states' objections – usually on the grounds that the new proposed 'super-corporation' will safeguard jobs and competitiveness. But size guarantees no such thing; it is the handmaiden of sclerosis, lazy cutbacks in investment and over-pricing.

We need stakeholder companies, progressive rules for corporate governance and tough competition rules at home and abroad as much as we need so-called 'welfare reform'. The chances of getting anywhere? On current form, nil – although I hope I'm proved wrong.

Observer, 8 February 1998

PART VI
European Dilemmas:
From ERM to EMU

The Chancellor, the Banker, and Deaf Ears in Bath

The German finance minister's restraining hand on Helmut Schlesinger's arm as he stood up to leave the meeting in disgust was not noticed by everyone in the room – but then it seemed few had taken in what he had said only a few moments earlier.

The president of the Bundesbank, a hawkish guardian of both stable prices and his bank's independence, had told Europe's finance ministers and central bankers gathered in Bath's Assembly Rooms that if they could agree to a realignment of currencies inside the Exchange Rate Mechanism, then the way would be open to cuts in German interest rates.

It was a remarkable offer in the context of the Bundesbank's history of independence and its place in Germany's constitution; if it were ever to be disclosed the political storm in Germany would be intense. Dr Schlesinger was risking the charge that he was qualifying his bank's independence by conceding to the demands of foreigners; and all to preserve the future of the ERM. Yet, as one finance minster was to say afterwards, it was as if no one had heard.

The meeting of European finance ministers in Bath that first Saturday of September had gathered under the shadows of an intensifying financial crisis. A day earlier the lira had come under speculative attack, prompting the Italians to raise interest rates to 15 per cent and the Bundesbank to supply Rome with billions of marks to support the lira in the ERM. How much longer could the lira hold out?

Although in public the Italian government repeatedly ruled out devaluation, privately it recognized that the lira's parity would have to change – and it had reason to believe other countries would join it. Indeed, its central bank had been quietly sounded out by the Bank of England, which also spoke to the Bank of Spain during August about Italian ideas over realignment.

In the run-up to the Bath summit on 5 September, the Italians repeated in secret discussions with the Germans what they had already told the British: although the weakest link in the system, they refused to devalue alone but would consider moving as part of a more widespread realignment of currencies.

The Germans were in a bind. Under the ERM's rules the Bundesbank was obliged automatically to provide marks to support any currency in the system; but the marks they were now printing to lend to the Italians to sell to currency speculators would end up in the Frankfurt money markets, undoing eighteen months of effort to hold down the growth of German money supply and risking, as the Bundesbank saw it, an acceleration in inflation.

There were other rules demanding some reciprocal action from the borrower country. If interest rate increases and austerity measures failed to hold off speculative attacks on its currency, the next step was devaluation. Italy, with 15 per cent interest rates and a package of budget deficit cuts already announced, was still suffering from acute currency speculation and was plainly at the stage where it could no longer expect unconditional German support.

The Germans could see that the Italians had a point; if Italy devalued alone, that would only whet the foreign exchanges' appetite for more. Other currencies would come under assault; the Spanish peseta and British pound were obvious candidates, and even the French franc was a possibility. All would look to the Bundesbank for support, and an operation already costing billions of marks could cost tens of billions without any long-run chance of success.

The cleanest response would be a simultaneous adjustment of as many currencies inside the ERM as possible.

The question that preoccupied the German finance ministry in the run-up to Bath was how to persuade others to join the Italians in a downward movement against the mark. At the Thursday Bundesbank council meeting it was decided that German interest rates would no longer rise; and privately Bundesbank officials let the finance ministry know that if there was a realignment then the upward movement of the mark would so lower inflationary pressures that the council would feel justified in reducing interest rates.

But constitutional propriety could not allow a straight deal; the linkage would be that lower inflation justified lower interest rates rather than their being prompted by an explicit bargain between the ERM countries and the Bundesbank. The German delegation arriving in Bath on Friday evening knew it could and should trade interest rate reductions for as wide a realignment as possible.

On the Saturday morning Horst Köhler, the German state secretary for finance, met Norman Lamont. Mr Köhler now tells colleagues he spent half an hour pleading with Mr Lamont to place realignment and German interest rates on the agenda. As Britain held the European Community presidency, the Chancellor was hosting the meeting and controlling the agenda. He refused to accept realignment as a formal item, but was also in a bind.

Although the Bank of England had been trying to find some common ground over realignment in confidential bilateral talks for some weeks, Mr Lamont knew that politically he and John Major could not be seen to be departing from their ERM commitment to hold sterling at DM2.95. The party manifesto and every ministerial pronouncement for months had stressed that ERM membership was at the heart of efforts to defeat inflation.

If Mr Lamont allowed realignment on to the agenda and the discussions leaked, what would happen to his credibility? After France's referendum on Maastricht two weeks later, when Paris had hinted it might reconsider its opposition to devaluing the franc and so allow the mark to appreciate against the rest of the ERM, the position might have to be considered, but then only in utter secrecy. After all, Britain had let it be known in July that it would not be opposed to such a general realignment. But in the full glare of publicity Mr Lamont did not dare risk discussions that could only end in Britain joining Europe's second tier by devaluing without France; the better tactic was to go for a unilateral cut in German interest rates.

In any case, Britain was still wedded to following the French example. Since 1985 they had held the franc against the mark in the 'franc fort' policy; a strong franc put downward pressure on prices which improved competitiveness which justified the strong franc. Low inflation was locked into a virtuous circle. The British were not alone in being impressed. Besides the policy of the strong pound there were the 'lira fort', 'peseta fort', 'krone fort', 'punt fort' etc. Realignment, code for devaluation, meant abandonment of these policies.

Therefore it was not difficult for Mr Lamont, chairing the meeting, to make realignment a dirty word – as Dr Schlesinger was to complain later; especially as no one wanted to do anything to upset the French referendum vote on 20 September. Instead Mr Lamont intended to use his chairmanship to put irresistible pressure on the Germans to cut their interest rates.

The Chancellor began by acknowledging that the agenda on Gatt and eastern Europe was window dressing and what they had to discuss was the currency question. He asked for everyone's consent to the agenda change and invited the Italians, whose currency was under most pressure, to speak first.

Piero Barucci, the Italian finance minister, was in an invidious position. Italy had done all it could to restore confidence in the lira, he said, but it now needed 'positive help'. The Italians had hints of German thinking, and wanted to use the meeting to flush realignment out into the open; the positive help they had in mind was realignment linked to a cut in German interest rates – and the more substantive the realignment the greater that drop might be.

Mr Lamont then turned to Michel Sapin, the French finance minister. It was a calculated manoeuvre to stem talk of realignment; as one delegate present says, Mr Lamont knew 'bloody well' what the French thought. An invitation to the Dutch or Germans to speak at that stage might have opened up the arguments in favour of realignment and if, say, the Irish, Spanish or Belgians backed them up the anti-realigners would be on the defensive.

Sapin delivered, ruling out realignment as jeopardizing the outcome of the French referendum. It would smack of indecision and suggest 'we weren't collaborating economies'. Nor would the devaluation of the lira be limited; the first ERM realignment for five years would shatter the system's credibility and the markets would start looking for the next currency to devalue. The fall-out would be general – indeed it might extend to the franc. The heart of the problem was not currency relationships, but high German interest rates.

With Mr Lamont in the chair, John Cope, the Paymaster General, was deputed to speak. He said Britain was also concerned that pressure on the franc would follow any devaluation of the lira – not admitting that the British accepted that the pound might have difficulties. The Spanish finance minister, Carlos Solchaga, said devaluing the lira would open the dam and joined the demand for lower German interest rates.

Only the Dutch picked up Barucci's challenge. Yes, German rates were too high, but all measures should be looked at – an implicit reference to the 'R word'.

Finally, it was the Germans' turn. Theo Waigel, the finance minister, blamed the low level of US interest rates for the strains in the system – forcing the mark higher and making it hard for the weaker ERM currencies to follow suit. If US interest rates continued to fall, then a small fall in German interest rates would not help – and if the Bundesbank had been seen to bow to international pressure then the Germans would be less likely to vote for Maastricht. For this, he said, tight monetary discipline was needed.

Then Dr Schlesinger made his intervention. He stressed the significance of the decision not to raise interest rates the previous Thursday, but warned that German inflationary pressures excluded any cut in rates. Then he broached the subject of realignment as delicately as he could. Speaking as a 'technical expert', he said, he would advise against ruling it out – in particular because of its implications for interest rates. Although the Bundesbank could not cut them now, 'an interest rate cut as part of a general realignment of the entire system would, of course, be quite another matter.' He held back from making his offer explicit, but the offer was there.

Dr Schlesinger's views were hardly a surprise. Soon after the Berlin Wall had fallen in 1989 the German government sounded out its ERM partners about their willingness to realign, allowing the mark to appreciate and thus heading off the potential inflationary dangers of reunification. Although the proposal had received a dusty response, the Bundesbank and Ministry of Finance never passed up an opportunity to remind the rest of the ERM that in the German view it was a fixed, but adjustable, system of exchange rates.

The Germans equally had their doubts about the spread of 'franc fort' policies. Unless hard currency policies were backed by solid programmes of anti-inflationary adjustment then they implied unnecessary economic dislocation and unemployment, almost certainly ending in collapse. The foreign exchange markets would not be fooled and, worst of all, because of the Basle–Nyborg agreement obliging the Bundesbank to supply effectively unlimited marks for up to ninety days for currencies in distress, the Germans would be pulled into the vortex.

Throughout the negotiations for monetary union, the Germans expressed their doubts about the idea that the ERM should become a conveyor belt to a European single currency with fixed parities; but by December 1991, when the Maastricht treaty was signed, they resigned themselves to the notion that realignments were off the agenda. When the Bundesbank felt the need to raise its key Lombard rate to 9 per cent that December, it shrugged off the criticism; the rest of Europe had made its bed, it could lie in it.

It was the Danish 'no' vote on 2 June that shattered the monetary calm. If there were doubts about the ratification of the Maastricht treaty, then maybe there would be realignments – and with the French announcing their intention to hold a referendum the day afterwards those doubts increased.

The Italians were first in the firing line; the following day, 4 June, they raised long-term interest rates as the lira came under pressure. The crisis was beginning. The following week the Bank of England began internal assessments about the desirability of an ERM realignment. On 6 July Italian short-term interest rates went up to 13 per cent; but the hammer blow was to come on 16 July when the Bundesbank raised its discount rate to 8.75 per cent.

Two days earlier at the European central bank governors' meeting in Basle, the Germans had warned that interest rates would go up; and even though the rise was confined to the least internationally sensitive rate the impact was profound. The Italians lifted their rates to 13.75 per cent.

In recessionary Britain there could not be a rise in interest rates, indeed they needed to fall. To ensure lower German interest rates British officials began to wonder if the better option might be an ERM realignment, raising the mark and so lowering German inflation.

After the 16 July Bundesbank meeting there was growing agreement among Europe's central bankers that there would have to be a realignment after the French vote on 20 September; France signalled confidentially it might join in.

Despite ministerial protestations that devaluation was the soft option, the Bank of England began to 'kick around' the idea of realignment with feelers being put out to the Spanish and Italians during August. Sterling's devaluation, it was felt, should not be less than 5 per cent – but ERM rules disallowed any devaluation larger than 10 per cent. The economic logic was obvious but politically there were constraints. Britain could not let France join Germany, and almost certainly Belgium and Holland, in moving upwards, leaving the pound to move down with the less strong currencies.

The UK was willing to consider a general realignment with the mark appreciating against all other ERM currencies; a feeling picked up in Paris where, in the second half of July, officials reported that Britain was known to favour this. French and German officials talked confidentially about the need to organize a change in parities, including a 5 per cent British devaluation, but the impetus never picked up. Indeed, in the first half of August, the urgency retreated. The Italians cut their discount rate by 0.5 per cent, having just secured agreement on ending the automatic indexation of Italian wages. Perhaps Italy could hold out until 20 September.

But by the beginning of the last week of August the stresses were back with a vengeance. French opinion polls were signalling a surge in the 'no' vote – on 25 August one showed a majority against Maastricht. Realignment talk returned, with private conversations between Group of Seven deputies preparing for the IMF meeting in Washington, and the markets picked up the tremors.

The Chancellor was determined to quell them immediately. On Friday, 28 August he rang Mr Sapin, Mr Waigel and Mr Barucci and insisted that the EC's finance ministers issue a joint statement committing themselves to no change in ERM parities. It was a bold move but put the British so far out on a public limb that any private realignment negotiations became more difficult.

As pressure on the Italians mounted Mr Lamont went one step further, announcing on 3 September a 10 billion ecu (£7 billion) loan; the proceeds would be used to support sterling. It was an important gesture, as much to the Germans and French as the markets. If there was to be a realignment, it implied the British would move upwards too.

After lunchtime at the Bath summit the exchanges grew testier. Mr Lamont pressed the Germans to lower interest rates by even a 'token amount' – three or four times, according to one participant – but the Germans stonewalled, with Mr Waigel insisting that currency relationships could not be locked in stone until 1997.

In the late afternoon, the Belgians picked up Dr Schlesinger's morning comments about realignment. But it was now too late. If the Dutch, Italians, Germans and Belgians had acted together earlier then a deal might have been secured – but Mr Lamont's chairmanship had ensured that they could not co-ordinate their position. The Germans, one delegate said, had been too low-key.

On two occasions when realignment surfaced Mr Lamont was asked, 'What about you?' and 'Are there any other candidates [for realignment]?' On neither occasion did he respond one way or the other. He had brushed aside Mr Köhler that morning; now he simply ignored what were pointed requests for Britain to open realignment negotiations.

Outside the formal session ministers and officials conferred in *ad hoc* bilateral discussions, with one delegation learning for the first time of the 3.5/3.5 per cent realignment option – the mark rising 3.5 per cent, some currencies staying the same and others devaluing by 3.5 per cent.

But all that could be agreed at the end of the Bath summit was a commitment for no realignment which few believed was credible, and an understanding that Germany would not raise its interest rates. A summit declaration communicating the lowest common denominator position was painfully drafted.

When the meeting broke up there was a general sense of foreboding. The lira and pound were as overvalued as ever. The last opportunity to save the ERM had been passed by.

Guardian, 30 November 1992

Black Wednesday Massacre

The eleven other EC central bank governors were appalled. There is a convention that no one speaks to the press after the regular second Tuesday of the month meetings at the Bank for International Settlements in Basle, but on 7 September Dr Helmut Schlesinger insisted that he was going to put the record straight.

What had upset him was the supposed guarantee he had offered at the Bath summit that the Bundesbank would not raise interest rates. He could make no such cast-iron guarantee; nor had he any confidence that the existing parities inside the ERM would survive. He wanted to attack the way the Bath summit had been presented.

There was widespread consternation. The prospect of his telling the press these things would provoke the crisis that had been looming for weeks. Dr Schlesinger said that of course he was not going to talk about currencies but he had to reassure the German public that the Bundesbank still reserved its rights over interest rate policy. He was not to be deterred.

Warming to his theme as the meeting progressed he said that the level of Bundesbank support for the lira, approaching 100 billion marks and with no end in sight, was unsustainable. He reminded his peers that the ERM had responded to similar crises in 1986 and 1987 with a realignment. He did not signal that he would be making a formal request for a realignment conference over the coming weekend but, as one participant said, 'We were put on notice.'

Even as they were talking the foreign exchange markets were in the process of taking the first of the many scalps they were to claim over the next two months – the Finnish markka.

The Finns had pegged the markka to the ecu as their own version of a markka 'fort' policy, informally shadowing the ERM but without any of the ERM's support mechanisms. Interest rates had been forced up to 18 per cent the previous Thursday, but by that Tuesday evening the force of speculation forced Finland to abandon the peg.

On Wednesday the markka fell by nearly 15 per cent, giving the speculators an instant huge profit; the hunt was now on for bigger game, with banks' foreign exchange departments around the globe who had not made a killing holding inquisitions, and those who had scenting blood.

There could be no more obvious target than the lira. The markets had got wind of realignment talk, and selling the lira seemed a one-way bet. The austerity package was bogged down in parliament, forcing the government to defer vital decisions for a week; Italy's foreign exchange reserves were falling rapidly and the Bundesbank had made no secret of its view that Italy should devalue. On Wednesday the waves of selling reached new peaks.

The following day the Italian government, amid further massive intervention, announced that it would seek emergency powers in the event of an economic crisis. The 'announcement effect' was tiny, and by Thursday evening it was clear in Frankfurt, Bonn and Rome that Italy's position was no longer tenable. The lira would have to be devalued.

At this stage the *Guardian* understands the Italians let it be known that they wanted the EC Monetary Committee, which governs the ERM and is composed of senior finance ministry and central bank representatives from all members, to hold a full meeting over the coming weekend.

From Bath the Italians knew that the Dutch and Belgians would support a realignment; and the German position could hardly be clearer.

Even though the British and Spanish had signalled their opposition surely they would see that, if the lira devalued alone, they would be in the same position as the Italians when the markka was knocked off its perch – the next in the firing line.

Although accounts have focused on the weekend of 12/13 September it was the events of Thursday morning to Friday evening that made a solo Italian devaluation certain. The Italian request to hold a full monetary committee meeting was obstructed in London, Paris and Madrid, although it is not clear whether the request was ever clearly communicated. Certainly the

Treasury do not consider that any such request came before Saturday night.

Even then it would have not been too late for the British to signal their readiness for a full meeting, forcing Spain to abandon its opposition. The way would have been open to discuss, if not a general realignment, then what Horst Köhler, the German state secretary for finance, calls a 'broad' realignment. The guilder, mark, and Belgian and French francs would have revalued and some other currencies, including sterling, would have moved lower with a German interest rate cut to lubricate the process. It was not to be.

The British line was that with the French referendum only seven trading days away sterling could survive unscathed. What happened afterwards would very much depend on the vote – giving lots of political cover if, for example, a 'no' vote forced a general realignment. Indeed, the British had already decided that if such a realignment was on offer, with the mark unilaterally revaluing against the rest of the ERM, they would go along with it.

For months certain British officials had been increasingly convinced that sterling devaluation was inevitable.

A difference of opinion was emerging between a still confident Treasury and more sceptical Bank of England, who could see the scale of the support required to support the lira and knew that for sterling, much more widely traded, the scale of the speculative attack would be colossal, but the official line remained that the problem was the strains thrown up by the divergence between high German and low US interest rates rather than sterling's parity with the mark. Devaluation was off the agenda.

The prime minister's support could be taken for granted – that summer he had taken out a fixed-rate mortgage at 9.8 per cent – and Andrew Crockett, executive director at the Bank of England, had informed central bank deputies in Basle only on Monday that the government was under immense political constraint. If it raised interest rates support for the Maastricht treaty would evaporate. Equally, as Mr Major's famous 'no devaluation' speech to the Scottish CBI underlined, it was so far out on a limb that anything less than a general realignment was politically impossible.

Moreover, although the lira was under terrible pressure, sterling seemed to be holding comparatively well, even if it was at the bottom of its permitted ERM band. What point was there in joining a realignment now? The manifesto, the repeated commitments not to devalue, the joint EC finance ministers' statement that Mr Lamont had initiated, the ecu loan and Mr Lamont's chairmanship of the Bath summit could not be repudiated.

The Germans knew they had a first-class crisis on their hands; they accepted that if Italy devalued alone, not only would it be bad for the Italians but also for those weaker currencies which had passed up the opportunity, and the Germans would be faced with a mark intervention running to tens of billions.

A general realignment against the mark was impossible for the French to accept before the Maastricht referendum, but what about a 'broad' realignment, in which the pound joined the lira, peseta, escudo, and even the Irish punt and Danish krone, in moving down against a mark block, including the franc and perhaps the Dutch guilder?

To sweeten the deal Germany was prepared to lower its interest rates, but it is not clear from telephone calls made between Rome, Frankfurt, Bonn, London, Paris and Madrid how far advanced was the Germans' thinking or how explicit their offer. Certainly Carlo Ciampi, governor of the Bank of Italy, believes that with a 'broad' realignment the Bundesbank could have lowered German short-term interest rates by a full percentage point instead of the quarter percentage point that emerged. The idea may have been floated but it never became a hard bargaining position.

Horst Köhler is on record as saying that the British were offered a 'broad' realignment but did not accept. Nigel Wicks, Köhler's opposite number at the Treasury, is known to have received a telephone call from him on Friday but says it concerned arrangements for the visit of Treasury officials to Germany the following week. If so, both men's coolness during the biggest financial crisis the ERM had yet encountered can only be admired.

By Friday afternoon it was likely that further realignment negotiations were going to take place by telephone over the weekend, rather than the full EC Monetary Committee meeting which might have produced a 'broad' realignment. The exchange of views initiated by the Germans had not produced any basis on which to proceed. As Chancellor Kohl, Finance Minister Theo Waigel and Horst Köhler met Dr Schlesinger and his number two, Hans Tietmeyer, at the Bundesbank on Friday evening it was clear that the cumulative Bundesbank intervention totalling around DM290 billion (£107 billion) had to be staunched.

Mr Kohl agreed; and Mr Köhler and Mr Tietmeyer were deputed to go to Rome on Saturday to agree an Italian devaluation. Mr Köhler would first fly to Paris and ask Jean-Claude Trichet, head of the French finance ministry and chair of the EC Monetary Committee, to contact other members and try to keep open the options of 'broad' realignment and a Sunday Committee meeting. But realistically the Germans had already conceded that the most likely outcome would be a unilateral Italian devaluation.

On Saturday evening Nigel Wicks, the Treasury's representative on the Committee, was contacted by Mr Trichet and told the outcome of the Rome discussions. The lira was to be devalued by 7 per cent. The Germans would lower their Lombard rate by 0.25 per cent and their discount and money market intervention rates by 0.5 per cent. It was a 'done deal', as one British source said.

Formal British assent required a meeting, and Mr Wicks attempted to round up the key players for 7.45 a.m. on Sunday at the Treasury. He could only contact Sir Terence Burns, Permanent Secretary to the Treasury, by mobile phone and, frightened of security, talked elliptically of 'problems with our sick patient' (Italy).

At the Treasury the following morning the Bank of England team, Professor Alan Budd, the government's chief economic adviser, and other Treasury officials were assembling as an upbeat Sir Terence and the Chancellor entered the room. One participant describes them as 'cock-a-hoop', another as 'relieved'. There was no disguising their welcome for the German interest rate cut as the signal to the markets that might see sterling safely through the next week to the French referendum.

The Bank of England representatives were more pessimistic, as was Mr Budd. They felt the markets' focus on the pound might be unsupportable. As the implications were discussed Sir Terence called the meeting to order.

His questions were – do we object and do we want to join in? Everyone, whatever their private misgivings, knew the answers and the decisions were almost instantaneous. Britain could hardly object, and at this late stage there was no point in reversing the long-standing policy of resisting a broad realignment without the French. Even had bigger German interest rate reductions been available with British participation there was no forum to discuss them; it was far too late to call a full meeting of the EC Monetary Committee. The Irish had only been informed at 11 p.m. on Saturday and the Bank of Holland was ignorant as late as midday on Sunday.

There was the technical question of how the devaluation should be presented and confirmation needed from the Germans that Mr Trichet's description of the deal was accurate but within forty-five minutes Mr Wicks was in a position to give British assent.

In retrospect almost everybody believes that not holding a full EC Monetary Committee meeting was a mistake. The Italians are still smarting from the insult, with Guiliano Amato, the Italian prime minister, saying it was 'scandalous' that the lira's devaluation was treated as an everyday matter. Some Bank of England officials felt at the time and still do that it would have been better to get the whole issue into the open.

The reception of the deal on Monday morning was better than the pessimists had feared, although there was Bank of England unease at the way Downing Street sources expressed such jubilance at the prospect of immediately lower British interest rates. Like the withdrawal of the high interest National Savings instrument First Option because it might have led to higher mortgage rates, it was another reminder to the markets of how anxious the government was to lower interest rates and how resistant it was to increases.

As Tuesday wore on the danger signals multiplied. The selling of sterling was becoming intense and the pound was at its floor. The markets were increasingly convinced that whatever the result of the French vote sterling was a one-way bet. If there was a 'no' vote the ERM would break down and sterling would devalue; and if there was a 'yes' vote, a general or at least very broad realignment including sterling looked equally certain. The markets were right; and the British had walked knowingly into the trap.

Inside the Treasury the strain was intense. With the peseta feeling the fall-out Carlos Solchaga, the Spanish finance minister, telephoned Norman Lamont to ask him how things were. 'Awful', came the reply; 'I'm just living from day to day.' Many others echoed this.

At 6.45 p.m. that Tuesday there was a stock-taking meeting at the Treasury to report on the last few hours' trading and decide the strategy for Wednesday. The Governor and Deputy Governor of the Bank of England were there, along with two or three other senior officials; the Treasury team included, as always, Sir Terence Burns and the Chancellor.

Would raising interest rates be a warning of distress, a signal to the markets that the end was nigh, or a pre-emptive strike? It was clear that as trading began the Bank of England should intervene by buying sterling as aggressively and openly as possible but what should follow?

Although Eddie George, the Deputy Governor, laid out the classic intervention strategy culminating in higher interest rates, the Bank team was clear what it wanted: agreement in principle that interest rates could be lifted on the Wednesday if necessary, with some prepared to argue for a pre-emptive rise when the markets opened.

It was while the discussion was in full flow that the Governor read out loud the message from his press office. Helmut Schlesinger had given an interview casting doubt about whether existing parities would hold – a clear hint that he thought sterling would devalue.

The meeting was stunned. The Governor, Robin Leigh-Pemberton, was asked to make immediate contact with Dr Schlesinger to ask for clarification and rebuttal of the news if true. At least one member present is heard to have said that the news was devastating; the game was up. In the centre of the table, where the principal decision-makers sat, there was extreme concern but no open admission that defeat was staring them in the face – rather a recognition that the witching hour was fast approaching.

The following morning at 9 a.m. Mr Leigh-Pemberton, Mr George, Sir Terence Burns and the Chancellor met at the Treasury. Overt intervention was not going well – indeed in one exchange that morning a senior official is known to have counselled that the entire exercise would be fruitless. The selling pressure was growing with the pound still at its ERM floor. At 11 a.m. interest rates were lifted to 12 per cent; and by 11.30 a.m. the same four had decided they would have to tell the prime minister, ensconced in Admiralty House, that in the face of overwhelming selling the pound's parity could not be held.

Europe's central bankers, who held two telephone conferences that day, discerned a 'sense of panic' in the British camp by mid-morning; the scale of selling was outside the British experience. At lunchtime first the prime minister himself and then his conclave of inner ministers, including Douglas Hurd, Michael Heseltine and Kenneth Clarke, learnt the news. A decision to hike rates to 15 per cent was taken and announced at 2.15 p.m. with hopes not completely dead, but when that failed the dénouement was inevitable.

It was not even clear that the pound could get through the day without its membership of the ERM being suspended. Other ERM countries urged Britain to hold on, to go for a unilateral devaluation rather than suspension or simply to announce a temporary suspension.

Pierre Beregovoy, the French prime minister, rang John Major twice encouraging him to stay in the ERM rather than leave it. But by 5 p.m. the decision was taken to rescind the 15 per cent minimum lending rate (MLR), and by 7.45 p.m. the Chancellor announced sterling's suspension from the ERM.

At the hastily convened European Monetary Committee meeting in Brussels that night Nigel Wicks from the Treasury and Andrew Crockett from the Bank of England explained the British decision. Mr Wicks began by confessing that the last hour before the market closed had been the worst in his life, while Crockett explained that Britain had spent £11 billion in reserves, nearly half its total.

They wanted a complete suspension of the ERM until after the French vote, arguing that a simple sterling devaluation was impossible because any medium-term defensible exchange rate was so dependent on the referendum result.

Indeed the Dutch had told the Bank of England during the afternoon that any devaluation would have to be over 10 per cent to be credible – outside ERM rules. And what if the market judged any devaluation to be insufficient? That would mean a rout. By Wednesday afternoon the trap had snapped shut; there was no way out. British membership of the ERM had come to an inglorious end.

Guardian, 1 December 1992

Nothing but the Actualité?

So it's now clear that despite the ringing speeches from the Prime Minister and Chancellor ruling out devaluation over the summer a more realistic appraisal of sterling's prospects inside the ERM was being taken at the highest levels of the Treasury and Bank of England.

The much-mocked government turnabout from doughty defenders of sterling to warm endorsers of devaluation was much less than we knew; the idea that sterling would have to be devalued, at the very least against the mark, had been accepted months before Black Wednesday.

In a sense that is how it should be; the only moment when a government can concede the case for devaluation is when it does it – anything other than complete public commitment to the exchange rate can only encourage speculation that will force the issue.

The trouble was that Mr Major and his Chancellor believed their own propaganda, making it impossible to engineer any compromise before the French referendum on Maastricht that fell short of a comprehensive general realignment of every ERM currency downwards against the mark. It was a weakness that was to prove the government's undoing and exclude the only effective route it had of staying inside the ERM.

The difficulty was that Europe had decided to peg its various exchange rates to a German mark wrestling with the inflationary consequences of reunification provoking high interest rates; but no one country wanted to incur the markets' wrath by breaking ranks and being the first to argue openly for a German revaluation to unblock the logjam.

That might lower German inflation and interest rates, but at the same time it would threaten 'credibility'. Indeed in Britain not even the Labour Party was prepared to challenge the consensus; and in France there was a similar cross-party coalition in favour of maintaining a strong franc.

But the collective resolve was only as strong as its weakest link; and that was Italy. Over the summer the Bundesbank became increasingly desperate at the prospect of spending possibly hundreds of billions of marks to support an unsustainably high currency, and wanted a solution. But France was not going to abandon seven years of 'rigueur'; and Britain, holding the chair of the EC presidency, was not going to abandon its sterling 'fort' policy either. Neither country was going to initiate change. Nor was Spain.

Thus Mr Major's account of the run-up to Black Wednesday is not contradicted by the new information revealed in the *Guardian*'s investigation. He has consistently claimed that an offer of a general realignment of the

ERM was not on the table – either formally or informally. That was the reality.

The French, despite hinting that things might change after the referendum on 20 September, were not going to budge beforehand, so all that was possible was not a *general* realignment but a *broad* one – a slight verbal distinction but one of immense political importance.

For a *broad* realignment in which the pound, lira, peseta, escudo, and perhaps the punt and krone devalued against the mark, guilder, and French and Belgian francs would have put Britain firmly into Europe's second division; and that Mr Major felt he could not countenance, even if the Germans offered a sweetener of an accompanying cut of up to 1 per cent in interest rates.

It is this *broad* realignment that Germany was trying to bring off at both the weekend of the Bath Summit and of the Italian devaluation; and which it maintains was offered to Britain. Mr Lamont says it was not.

Again a concrete package was not assembled, and in those terms Mr Lamont's account is correct – if disingenuous. For the chief reason there was no *broad* realignment on offer was because Britain opposed it and made sure it did not get onto the agenda at Bath; and without British interest the trigger for Spanish and Portuguese participation did not exist.

Even so discrepancies exist between the German account and the British, for Horst Köhler, the German state secretary for finance, claims that something more concrete was put to the British. If so, when?

It might have been at Bath, but at that stage even agreement on an Italian devaluation was not secured – so it must have been later. The evidence gathered by the *Guardian* points to the following Friday when Köhler was frantically sounding out his principal ERM partners to find a way of stemming the now £100 billion haemorrhage of marks – whether they would agree to a realignment conference to discuss a *broad* realignment over the weekend, on what terms, and if not whether they would accept a unilateral devaluation of the lira which they had opposed at Bath.

After all a lira devaluation would put Britain, Spain and even France in the firing line. Köhler would want to know their reactions because that evening Chancellor Kohl was to confer at the Bundesbank with Dr Helmut Schlesinger, its president, and the German finance minister Theo Waigel. What were Germany's options?

Sir Nigel Wicks, Köhler's opposite number at the Treasury, is known to have received a telephone call from Köhler that Friday; but the two men, at least according to the Treasury, did not broach the subject that must have been totally preoccupying Köhler only hours before the Bundesbank meeting. The following evening Wicks was available to receive the key telephone calls from both Rome and Paris even though others were out at parties and functions; and he was able to contact the Permanent Secretary, Sir Terence

Burns, immediately. Were the British really as ignorant of what was going on as they claim?

In any case it took only five or six hours on the evening of Black Wednesday to convene a full EC monetary committee meeting; even by Saturday night it was not too late to organize a meeting to consider a *broad* realignment beginning, say, at mid-morning on Sunday. This the British, together with the French and Spanish, refused to accept.

Apart from the fullness of Norman Lamont's account, does any of this matter? The Italians got bounced out of the ERM even though they devalued, argue the government, so had Britain followed suit it would have made no difference.

But a co-ordinated broad realignment, accompanied by a significant German interest rate cut and with the Bundesbank prepared to give unconditional support, would have been a very different proposition in the run-up to the French referendum weekend from allowing the foreign exchange markets to pick off currencies one by one. The ERM would probably have survived; and for a government which made it the centre of its economic policy the attempt must surely have been worth making.

Sterling would now be trading between DM2.50 and 2.60, and interest rates would be higher – probably between 8.5 and 9 per cent reflecting still high German interest rates; but at the same time the government would have saved £11 billion of foreign exchange reserves and confidence would not have been buffeted by Black Wednesday.

Moreover the earlier and more extensive a realignment could have been made the lower German interest rates would now be; a general realignment last autumn, for example, might have so lowered German inflation that their interest rates might be 7 per cent or so by now. In other words had the ERM been managed more flexibly, British policy could have been more expansionary far earlier – and the worst of the recession might have been avoided.

Yet Britain remained in the thrall of a deflationary experiment, rescued finally by the markets. There has been much talk of fault lines in the ERM but in effect there was only one: the refusal of national governments to accept that exchange rates are prices and can change. But if Mr Major and Mr Lamont were culprits, they reflected a European consensus; the ERM's best hope is that it has been dashed for good.

Guardian, 2 December 1992

Winds over the West

Written with Martin Kettle

In a world short of certainties, one fixed point in the British compass is Europe. It is always there, pressing on towards ever closer union, and laying dangerous snares for British politicians. The British can opt in or they can opt out; but 'Europe' is guaranteed to be moving forwards to meet its destiny as forming the heart of a new block.

Yet over this year it has become clearer that the assumption no longer holds. The pace, direction and content of the European project have rarely been as uncertain and problematic as they are now. In Germany the principal opposition party, the SPD, opposes a single currency. Italy cannot and will not pay the price of monetary union. In France the Gaullist president Jacques Chirac alternates uncertainly between the pro-Europeanism of his predecessors and the assertion, particularly in nuclear testing, of French national power. It is not that goodwill is fading; it is just that it is no longer obvious what that Europe should be. It is certainly not the Europe of the Maastricht treaties.

It is more clear now than ever that the European Union was a postwar solution in a Cold War context. It was established to prevent another Franco-German war and its agricultural policy was designed to prevent mass starvation in Europe. The EU evolved within a divided Europe constantly threatened with nuclear war, the rise of communism, the American military presence, and its own relative, global, post-imperial decline. Inevitably it developed as a 'third way' project, a putative European bloc between the two superpowers, and for nations like France and latterly Britian as a plausible post-imperial redefinition of a global role. The EU conceived at Maastricht was true to that tradition.

Yet the context has now radically changed. We are fifty years on from the last European war. The prospect of an inter-state European war seems incredible, although civil war in former Yugoslavia is a salutary reminder that it is not purely theoretical. Europe now not only feeds itself but agriculturally over-produces on a vast scale. And we are six years on from the end of the Cold War.

There are no longer two superpowers between which to forge a third way; the idea of an essentially middle-way western European bloc is anachronistic. Yet we are left with the agenda of those earlier times – common institutions, convergence of regulations, citizenship etc. – all of which made clear (if controversial) sense in a Cold War context, but whose boundaries and purposes are now highly problematic and not properly defined.

There is thus a pressing need to define the European project afresh, so that it is not encumbered with an agenda which cripples rather than equips it in a changed world. The momentum which drives both the institutional change and the rhetoric ('building Europe' etc.) is absolutely no longer adequate to the real decisions and choices of the post-Cold War world. It needs to be scrapped, rethought and put in place afresh.

If we do not do that, then there is a profound danger that the very institutions and projects which were originally intended to bring Europe together will turn into their opposite and begin to force it apart. This can be seen in all kinds of localized contexts – the persistence of the Eurosceptic ascendancy in the UK, the Chirac government's deferral of its Schengen obligations, German mockery of monetary union, the public-sector revolts in France and Italy as their governments attempt to cut public spending at a pace that will meet the 1999 deadline for monetary union. The Treaties of Maastricht may come to be seen in some parts of Europe – perhaps even in Germany – as the Treaty of Versailles came to be seen in inter-war Europe: the source of the problem, not the answer.

The deflationary effects of the Maastrichtian ambition to create a single currency must not become so overriding that they create the very social division and friction they were intended to heal. If Maastricht is seen as the cause of the dismantling of the welfare system and the social wage upon which millions of the poorest in Europe have come to depend, then it will spark inevitable populist backlashes.

The immediate question facing the countries of the EU is their relationship with the central and eastern European nations. The western nations will the end – incorporation of the eastern neighbours – without willing the means. We say we want to widen, but we persist at the same time with the illusion that this wider union, let alone the deeper union of which some still speak can possibly exist on the terms of the existing union.

For example, the eastern countries cannot become full members of the EU without breaking the Common Agricultural Policy or provoking such a radical increase in the EU budget that it would spark a chain of domestic political crises in the existing states, as governments demanded higher taxes to pay for the adherence of the eastern Europeans. The Germans managed, just, to follow that route successfully following German reunification; that they succeeded was due, fundamentally, to national solidarity. There is no such solidarity to fall back on in a pan-European context.

It is this lack of European solidarity that will fatally undermine the attempt to construct quasi-federal institutions and the expectation that they can exercise supranational competence for which they have no political legitimacy – and which widening will stretch to breaking point.

Nor is it any solution to construct a Europe of a variable economic and political geometry. The Italians, as senior politicians, bankers, officials and academics confirmed at this year's Anglo-Italian Pontignano conference, would recoil from any construction which left them – one of the original six – as second-class Europeans.

The way forward is to remove the sources of destabilization and recognize current realities – while offering the various European publics positive reasons for loyalty to the European ideal. The creation of a single currency by 1999 with its convergence criteria needs to be put aside; in its place there might be a parallel currency and a loose exchange rate mechanism – but anything more will be destabilizing.

The current European constitution – a council of member states with veto powers serviced by the Commission – is the best compromise available for the governance of Europe; and the big powers need firm guarantees that their vital interests will stay protected. Majority voting can only be allowed on second-order matters; and the European Parliament cannot expect co-decision-making. Only associate membership can be offered to eastern and central Europe; more threatens to wreck the Europe we have. Ever closer union cannot happen until there is more European solidarity – for which education, massive mobility and an increasingly common culture are necessary preconditions. They must be worked for from the bottom up – not imposed from the top down.

This is a political rather than economic agenda, and requires tough decisions and the spelling out of some unpalatable truths. There cannot be both widening and deepening; economics cannot alone propel European integration. There is much at stake. Britain cannot and must not opt out; but it is imperative that it is clear which Europe it wants.

Guardian, 2 November 1995

The Cost of Going it Alone in Europe

It has become the new centre of gravity of British politics. Europe should be a partnership of nation states. The gains of forty years of European integration should not be thrown away, certainly, and where there are grounds for friendly collaboration it should be undertaken. But the clock should now stop on anything more visionary.

Malcolm Rifkind, presenting the government's white paper on its stance for the Intergovernmental Conference to the House of Commons yesterday, defined a position that was plumb centre in the rows that rack the Conservative Party – while tacking back from some of his more Eurosceptic remarks to adopt a more pro-European tone. The bedrock of the European Union might be the independent democratic state, as John Major says in the document's foreword – but that has not prevented the government from backing, if guardedly, the idea of a 'single figure to represent the foreign policy of the Union to the outside world'. Quite a concession from an administration beleaguered by Euroscepticism and now Sir James Goldsmith's Referendum Party.

But the basic thrust remains an undying commitment to intergovernmentalism, the sanctity of the nation state's powers over defence and foreign policy, and the case against extending majority voting – a position that Robin Cook was careful not to oppose. He was as much for the nation state as his counterpart, while managing to open up some red water between Labour and the government over employment and social legislation. But in truth there was not much more to go on; Labour has no intention of being labelled as Brussels's poodle, so it is compelled to find merit in the government's position. That in turn draws its sting in the areas where it does want to criticize.

Yet Britain's political parties should be cautious about congratulating themselves on establishing a position which while selling the pass on the case for European integration is still sufficiently pro-European to inflame the ranks of the Eurosceptics – thus successfully pleasing nobody. For Europe, however reluctantly and unwanted, finds itself playing for very high stakes at the IGC. The notion, quietly promoted in the white paper, that 'there may be areas in which it is perfectly healthy for some member states to integrate more closely or quickly than others', will be picked up by the Germans who reluctantly have come round to the same view. A Europe constructed as a series of initiatives which, once in place become *acquis communautaire* – community gains – is to be jettisoned. In its place a new Europe is emerging in which a pace-setting group of nations will define the structure of Europe, which others can then take or leave.

Yet the reality for most European states is that not being part of this construction is not a conceivable option. This is partly a matter of sheer practicality given the range of issues that require some standing secretariat to propose common solutions, the functional reason for Brussels's existence; and partly about the shrinking capacity in today's world of the celebrated nation state to achieve what it wants on its own.

Yet at just this moment Europe is moving from being built by consensus to a new model which will allow it to be built by the instincts of its most pro-European members – and that means Germany. This represents a transformation in European politics, and nobody can be certain that it can be executed with the old ethos of pro-Europeanism being kept alive. It will be divisive before it is integrative.

The breach was already made at Maastricht, not only because Britain negotiated its opt-outs from the social chapter and the single currency, but in addition because of the nature of the convergence criteria for monetary union. It was never likely that every member of the EU would be able to qualify in 1999, and thus the beginning of multi-speed Europe was launched. The IGC, with Britain's connivance, will elevate it as the new principle around which Europe should be constructed.

Thus to argue for Europe as a partnership of nation states completely dodges the issue which will be at the heart of the IGC. Liberated from the necessity of moving Europe forward as one, the Germans and the French, with the Dutch, Austrians, Belgians, Irish, Italians, Finns, Spanish and even Swedes actively helping, will set about brokering the deal that is at the heart of the single currency. Germany will surrender the D-Mark only if there is change in the process of political integration – and that is the implicit agenda of the IGC.

For it is not only British Eurosceptics who have noted that there is a crisis of legitimacy of European institutions. Michael Mertes, one of Chancellor Kohl's closest advisers is on record as saying that it is difficult for the new Europe to be democratic, because there is no European democratic public – no European *demos*. But as Michael Maclay, a former adviser to Douglas Hurd, writing in this month's edition of *Prospect* says, the German conclusion is rather different from the British; it is not to turn back from political integration – rather it is to find ways of accelerating it.

Britain does hold some cards. It can block development of the European parliament and it can insist that any initiatives that draw on the European budget have to be agreed unanimously – but unless it gives some ground given the new environment it risks being confronted by a *de facto* European ultimatum. It will be offered opt-outs and derogations from the changes to the new institutions; but it will not be allowed to veto what a majority of the other states choose to do.

Striking a new tone and offering a few concessions will not avert a crisis that in some respects is as dangerous as permitting Sir James Goldsmith's obsessions over Europe to effect a new direction in British national policy – yet another extraordinary development in the deformed structure that is Britain's political system. The parliamentary sovereignty that the white paper invites us to defend to the last is one so fragile that it can be snared by the attentions of a politically ambitious billionaire.

Lack of knowingness about what is happening abroad is thus matched by self-deception about what is happening at home. A British white paper that is as uninhibitedly partisan – for example talking dismissively of many continental politicians who press for 'more Europe . . . and corporatist economic solutions to the perceived deficiencies of the free market' – degrades the very notion of a white paper. The British state plumbs new lows. Self-delusion and false premises were never good guides to policy. Now they are the new gods, but they will lead to isolation in a world in which the US is no longer a reliable ally – with costs that the British are neither ready nor prepared to pay.

Guardian, 13 March 1996

Imperial Echo Defies Logic

The British Commonwealth is becoming fashionable again. It boasts five out of the ten fastest-growing economies in the world, claim its new proponents. Commonwealth countries in the Asia–Pacific Rim provide a unique bridgehead into the world's most rapidly growing region. For Eurosceptics, the Commonwealth is an asset Britain has for too long neglected.

It is not clear how this new importance is going to take shape – since the threat of expulsion did not stop Nigeria hanging Ken Saro-Wiwa any more than the prospect of censure at last week's Commonwealth meeting inhibited John Major supporting French nuclear testing. But that does not prevent it from being a useful artillery piece in the increasingly bitter exchanges over Britain's interests and future.

The gradual transformation in the Commonwealth's image, from a tiresome responsibility in which Britain exchanged aid for immigrants and slow-growing markets, to a potentially positive resource, has matched the rise in Conservative Euroscepticism. Tony Baldry at the Foreign Office, David Howell as chairman of the Commons Foreign Affairs Committee and Lord Young as President of the Institute of Directors have all recently spoken about the Commonwealth in glowing terms. Why tie ourselves to Europe when old imperial glories are waiting to be revisited?

But while it is true the Commonwealth offers opportunities, it falls a long way short of being a genuine alternative to Britain's growing economic and political commitment to Europe. Eurosceptic zeal has got in the way of hard thinking.

None the less there is a real change afoot, and the doubts about the

Commonwealth's worth have begun to be dispelled. It trapped British exporters into low-growth, low-tech markets, ran the old argument, and locked the British economy into deflation as the Treasury and Bank of England fought to maintain the convertibility of sterling area assets, held by the Commonwealth, into hard currencies.

Escaping from this nexus was an argument used by Edward Heath and then Harold Wilson to support British entry into the then Common Market. Britain needed to redirect its exports to fast-growing European markets and confront its industrial competitors head to head; competition and access to continental-sized markets would give industry just the boost it needed. The Commonwealth would be allowed to wither on the vine.

Last week the Royal Institute of International Affairs released a paper – *Economic Opportunities for Britain and the Commonwealth* – that is the best effort yet at making coherent the newly developing pro-Commonwealth case. In a global economy Britain has to think globally, argued author Katherine West. The Commonwealth could be more than just a soft network of countries united by a common past; the rusting skein of ties needed to be revived and made into a more robust association of states and business networks.

The relationship between Britain and Australia is an examplar of why the Commonwealth still matters. Australian investment in Britain is eight times higher than it should be, given the size of the British economy, while by the same calculus British investment in Australia is seven times higher. For Australian companies, Britain provides a jumping-off point for the European single market, while a growing number of UK companies are using Australia as headquarters of their Asia–Pacific operations.

The scale of this interpenetration demonstrates, Katherine West says, how useful it is to both to have a shared business culture at each end of the world which allows them access to great regional markets. With a common legal tradition, similar financial systems and parallel organization of government, businessmen can find their way round each other's economy much more easily than others, from outside. This is an advantage that should be enlarged and better exploited.

So far so good, but Ms West wants to go further. Europe is such a low growth zone that Britain should reorientate its diplomatic and trade efforts to burgeoning Commonwealth markets. Here there is a familiar litany. By 2010 the Asia–Pacific economy, including Japan, will surpass the combined economic weight of North America and Europe. Malaysia and Australia were strong markets for British exports in 1994, while in 1993, exports to Europe rose by only 5 per cent. Behind the trade flows there is a build-up of British direct investment, too. For example, the value of UK net outward direct investment in Hong Kong, Malaysia and Singapore doubled between the end of the eighties and 1991–3. The message is clear: here, and not in Europe, lies Britain's future.

But Ms West is partisan, as are Conservative Eurosceptics. It is true that 1993 was a poor year for exports to the EU. After twenty years in which the Union steadily grew as the destination of British visible exports, 1993 saw a sharp reverse, with the proportion falling from 60 per cent of the total to under 55 per cent. Europe was in recession. But in 1994, which Ms West neglects to mention, Britain's visible exports to Europe jumped by 14 per cent as the European economies recovered – with the European proportion picking up again to 57 per cent.

The inclusion of invisible earnings lowers the proportion of overall export earnings to below 50 per cent. But that is partly because Britain's overseas Commonwealth investments, having accumulated over two or three hundred years, are so mature that the flow of dividends and profits from any pound of direct investment in the Commonwealth is significantly higher than from any pound of EU investment, so reorienting the figures.

But that has not deterred UK business, uniquely focused on making high short-term returns, from continuing to build up its investment in the EU. An article in last week's Bank of England quarterly bulletin reports that British foreign direct investment in western Europe has consistently outstripped investment in the rest of the world, of which the Commonwealth represents the lion's share – and over the last five years the cumulative investment in the EU has exceeded that in North America.

Business plainly believes the returns it wants lie in Europe, where the rise in direct investment is on course to match the proportion of British exports.

The investment figures for Hong Kong, Singapore and Malaysia are enhanced by the boom in the early 1990s, and the growth now looks much more modest. The five Commonwealth countries that rank in the world's fastest-growing ten economies are Mauritius, Botswana, Belize, Hong Kong and Singapore. These do not offer a serious alternative to Europe, even as examples of deeper trends, and their heterogeneity underlines the differences within the Commonwealth rather than mystical shared values. Australia is the exception, not the rule.

In any case, German exports to Asia have grown at nearly twice the rate of Britain's over the last decade, without any ideology that Germany's vocation in Europe is now redundant. Industrial and corporate vigour are the recipes for success as much as long-standing emotional ties.

And how should Britain act, even if it accepts the Commonwealth case? Ms West proposes more funding for Commonwealth initiatives and the establishment of a Commonwealth Global Communications Network to enable better inter-country networking. Fine. These are deserved in their own right and worth supporting, but their very modesty demonstrates the difficulty of making the Commonwealth a viable trading and political unit.

After all, what does Nigeria fear most – Commonwealth or EU trade sanctions? Britain can and should keep its Commonwealth networks alive and vigorous; but its interests and destiny remain firmly European. There is no escape to the Pacific. Geography is compelling.

Guardian, 13 November 1995

X Marks the Spot for Start of Euro Race

Power politics are never pretty. Events last week showed just how ugly they can get when the Chancellor flew home from Brussels on Monday night in high dudgeon. He had been excluded from 'Council X' – the grouping set up to run the economic policy of the single currency.

It fell to the French finance minister, Dominique Strauss-Kahn, to explain his anger: 'The euro is a monetary marriage. The countries in the marriage do not want anyone else in the same bedroom. Those who share the same money want more intimate relations.' In Madrid the next day, after a Franco-Spanish summit, the minister added emphatically: 'We are no longer seeking a compromise.'

It was a decisive moment in Europe's affairs in which the choices facing the British over not merely the euro, but the character of our economic and social structures, were thrown into sharp relief.

In short, the euro will start on schedule; there is a high probability of subsequent success; and the founders, having taken all the risks in creating the new currency, are going to play hardball over how the wider benefits are distributed.

For non-member Britain there is no prospect of helping to shape the European project; outside the euro zone, two fundamental pillars of British economic and employment policy – the reliance on inward investment and the City – are seriously threatened. But as Britain looks at relegation in the new international order while also facing challenges to its economic structures, silence reigns.

As determination grows in mainland Europe to make no more concessions even to the friendly Mr Blair – or at least until he shows more leadership over the issue – the government has been able to rely on the Eurosceptic indifference of the press and the Conservative Opposition to make sure that the importance of Monday's rebuff is unexplored and unremarked. Tony Blair still hopes that he will manage to talk Chancellor Helmut Kohl round at this week's summit in Luxembourg. The aim remains to have our cake – taking no risks in the formation of the euro or any potential failure – and eat it, sharing in economic policy formulation and only joining when the project is an unmistakable success and it is to our unmistakable advantage to be a member.

There is a chance, however diminished, that Blair may succeed. He is pro-euro, pro-European and believes that Britain's long-term interests lie in being part of the inner directorate that runs Europe. He has made this clear to Kohl, who is sympathetic. But the German leader has other, more menacing concerns. The French left, now in government, and the German left, potential victors in next September's elections, could qualify or challenge what Kohl regards as his European achievement.

At one time, the Franco-German left had such serious wobbles over the euro that it looked as though it might be delayed. But this autumn both have recommitted to the euro – largely because they have been recasting the project as more growth-orientated than the Maastricht treaties allowed.

Kohl and French Prime Minister Lionel Jospin quietly agree: Council X's task will be to co-ordinate growth-orientated fiscal policies across Europe to take advantage of the low interest rates that will accompany the euro. They will not let this be scuppered by the veto of a non-member – Britain – who is taking none of the risk. Hence Strauss-Kahn's uncompromising language and Kohl's difficulty in offering Blair concessions.

Gerhard Schröder is the most likely candidate to compete for the Chancellorship against Kohl, but to get the nomination he will have to accommodate the views of SPD chairman Oskar Lafontaine – who represents the heartbeat of the party. In Hanover last Tuesday, he opened the party conference with a passionate pro-European speech, insisting that the expansionary options sparked by the launch of the euro be seized in order to lower European unemployment. Be sure that the Jospin government saw a copy of the speech before it was made.

In this debate New Labour is largely a bystander, preaching the conservative orthodoxies of flexible labour markets, shrinking the welfare state and balancing the budget. The Germans, along with the French socialists, do not buy this stuff. Rather they want, ultimately, nothing less than to recast the European and world financial order.

This is power politics with a vengeance; the kind of thinking that was second nature to the British in the days of Empire. As Professor Jonathan Story writes, the EU is about faith and will. The British now define the political task as adapting to market forces whatever the social cost; the Europeans see the task as shaping market forces to sustain dearly held social and cultural values.

One of the least understood aspects of the single currency is the way dealing in euro assets is going to disadvantage the City. Barclays's and NatWest's withdrawal from the capital markets means that London dealing is now wholly based around foreign banks. But when they deal in euro assets, they will need to be members of the new euro intra-bank cash settlement system to get the best terms for their clients – in other words they will move their dealing operations to Frankfurt, Paris and Amsterdam. This, given the scale of the euro as the emerging world reserve currency along with the dollar, is immensely significant. London, now an offshore financial centre run by foreigners, will become secondary to Europe.

It is a similar story with inward investment. The multinationals seeking global spread in their production and distribution systems will aim to be locked into the euro area. Last week, Toyota announced that their next wave of car investment will be in France; more will follow.

Britain thus loses every way; but there is little debate about what we should do. The government would have liked to have joined the euro on 1 January 1999, but feels the unpreparedness and scepticism it inherited make the task impossible. Instead, it is hoping to keep its options alive while preparing public opinion for entry – although only Gordon Brown has made any attempt to take on the sceptic consensus.

Instead the British debate is dominated by the risk of entry – not by the risks of the rough and tough world of staying outside. Story quotes George Canning, the British foreign secretary when Britain decided it would leave the European diplomatic network woven by Metternich after the Napoleonic wars: 'Every nation for itself, and God for us all.' Canning was confident that God was on Britain's side, an easy assumption when running a world empire – but one which still informs British attitudes. But God, we may find, follows power and those brave enough to exercise it.

Observer, 7 December 1997

Hot Money Goes Euro

It has been gathering momentum for months, and now it looks like a done deal. On 1 January 1999, at least six and perhaps as many as ten members of the European Union will start using the euro as their currency. It will be another three years before euro notes and coins are used universally. But it is now nearly as certain as any event in politics that European Monetary Union will go ahead. A momentous period in European history is about to begin.

It is a trip into the unknown – with the fears and hopes on both sides well known. Pessimists see it as an act that will divide Europe, plunging it into a deflationary economic nightmare, robbing nation states of their sovereignty and devaluing the legitimacy of national political institutions. Optimists portray it as an act befitting the millennium; a statement of solidarity that, by spreading low interest rates across the continent, will trigger a pan-European boom while prompting the further peaceful integration of disparate states. Love it or hate it, the single currency is emerging as the most salient European economic and political fact in our times.

Even a year ago, the odds against it starting were more finely balanced. The newly elected President Chirac, with his commitment to lowering unemployment, was hinting broadly that he wanted to break with the orthodoxy of the dying Mitterrand and France's elite *énarques* and side with those in his own party who favoured a national, growth-orientated economic policy. In Germany, the Social Democrats were flirting with becoming the pro-Deutschmark and anti-euro party. There was little stomach in Bonn or Paris for the budgetary discipline needed to meet the Maastricht guidelines, and strikes by French public-sector unions against a wage freeze and welfare cuts led to self-congratulatory British *Schadenfreude*. Monetary union was finally imploding.

This weekend, it looks very different. Even the Bundesbank cannot complain about the current convergence of interest rates and inflation rates around the average performance of the best three countries in Europe that the treaty demands before monetary union can go ahead. Moreover, currencies within the newly reconstituted and much laxer ERM have moved within the narrow margin of fluctuation that Maastricht provides for. As for the treaty's criteria for governments to lower budget deficits to 3 per cent of GDP or less in 1997 for EMU to go ahead, there has been considerable progress: over the past ten days, the Germans, Dutch and French have all produced budgets that will do just that. If there is any slippage, creative accounting tricks can ensure that the figures will be met. In any case, the famed article 104c of the treaty allows for flexibility in the way meeting the deficit target is interpreted.

But beyond economics, the political argument has swung back in EMU's favour. The German SDP has found that being against the euro pays no electoral dividends, and bouts of speculation against the franc whenever the French government betrays scepticism about the single currency have helped persuade Chirac that going it alone is not an option. If France passes up this chance to bind Germany into a Europe that they would jointly lead, it will cede European leadership to Germany. Chancellor Kohl, for his part, believes that he is discharging his generation's obligations to Europe by ensuring that Germany takes a lead; building a European Germany, as he puts it, rather than a German Europe.

If all this was not enough, this weekend's informal meeting of EU finance ministers in Dublin set the seal. In essence, countries have agreed to pass up ultimate control of their budget deficits, and thus fiscal policy, to Brussels and Frankfurt; if they run deficits above 3 per cent of GDP they will take remedial action or face a fine. The fine is less than the Germans wanted originally, but Kohl now has a deal that he can sell to his public; Europe's governments are not going to free-ride off Germany in the new single currency area. In any case, the Germans take treaties seriously; its provisions are binding on the signatories. The criteria for a single currency are going to be met; there are instruments in place to ensure Germanic disciplines remain and the political will is evidently there. French and German banks and multinationals have committed hundreds of millions of pounds in investing for the change; going back now is not an option. The euro is about to become a reality.

There is, notwithstanding Ken Clarke's insistence that Britain would be wrong to give up the option of joining in 1998, almost no chance of Britain being in the first wave. On two important criteria for eligibility – an independent central bank and a narrow margin of fluctuation inside the ERM – we fall at the first hurdle, and our budget deficit next year promises to be above 3 per cent of GDP. But politically the story is familiar beyond weariness. To enter would split the Conservative Party, and Labour, despite a greater disposition to be pro-European, sees no reason to take risks the Tories will not. Whoever wins in 1997, Britain will exercise John Major's opt-out.

If monetary union fails, this could be a great stroke of policy; but if a single currency succeeds, it will be a monumental blunder. The reasons for possible failure are well rehearsed. Countries need some autonomy over fiscal policy to manage the economic cycle. Exchange rates are a vital tool of economic adjustment. Success depends not merely on convergence of economic indicators, but of underlying institutions and variables like unemployment. Workers need to move as fluidly around a single-currency area as they do in their own country. Above all, do countries in general, and Britain in particular, want this degree of integration as a matter of principle?

Britain's economic establishment is united in viewing the exercise as fraught with hazard and bound to fail – perhaps the best reason for regarding it as having a better than even chance of success. After all, the convergence criteria, though tough, will be met. There are powerful mechanisms for ensuring they will continue to be met. The euro will be strong against the endemically weak dollar, and that opens up monetary policy and growth options that are little examined.

Consider. EU countries, in preparing for EMU, have adopted deflationary policies that have held the rate of economic growth below its true trend for more than five years; a large gap has emerged between actual output and that which would have occurred. When this continental-wide economic area enjoys nominal interest rates of 2–3 per cent, as it becomes apparent that the euro is both strong and here to stay, Europe will enjoy a boom as the output gap is clawed back.

Britain, of course, will enjoy some benefit as exports to Europe rise – but it will find that it has to peg its interest rates significantly above those in Europe. What's worse, our interest rates will move up and down in rhythm with those in Europe just as they have in the past with those in the US; the minor economic power's interest rate cycle always mirrors that of the major one. But we will be helpless onlookers in those interest rate decisions.

Worse still, Britain's position as a financial centre with large sterling liabilities will become a renewed economic burden – rather as the sterling area used to be. There will be three world currencies – the euro, yen and dollar. Smaller currencies, to avoid bouts of intense speculation, will have to adopt intensely conservative economic policies. Britain, with its massive sterling markets, will be a frontline victim and its macroeconomic policies will be compelled to be more conservative. The City, losing business to Frankfurt and Paris and terrified that a government of any hue will have to introduce capital controls to protect against speculation, will clamour for entry into EMU – as will the inward investors and British multinationals fearful of losing access to rapidly growing markets. Moreover, the political establishment, losing control of the political agenda and of economic decision-making to France and Germany, will take up the argument. Britain will join, but in the early years of the next century.

The euro, of course, might fail – but the ensuing turmoil will do Britain no good either. And here lies an important point of principle. Do we want this bold act of European integration to collapse? Would the resulting Europe of competing nation states dominated by Germany be in our national interest? Faced with this choice, is it not better for the euro to succeed?

There is no doubt that Europe would have been better off had it not suffered the past depressed five years; and EMU as structured does have grievous weaknesses. A fixed but adjustable exchange rate system within a world system of managed rates would be a better option. It would have been less risky had the next phase of European co-operation been around defence and foreign policy – or even education. Integration of eastern Europe is more important than grand monetary schemes.

But those are now old and redundant arguments. There is no purpose in saying, as Labour does, that Britain would join EMU, but not this one. Calling for a different EMU – one where growth and employment have a higher priority – is a perfectly reasonable game of political charades, but it is not the choice the country faces. The EMU that is on offer is the one whose outlines after yesterday's meeting are now clear. They are not going to change.

The mocked Tory grandees are right. There will be a single currency. It will probably work. And Britain would gain much by being in the first wave, both in shaping the system to our needs and gaining the credibility to build Europe in directions that suit us. After all, the Europe we have may not be the best – but it is better than any alternative. We know that Britain will not be in the first wave. But that doesn't make the sense of loss, and the futility of the Eurosceptic arguments, any less keen.

Observer, 22 September 1996

PART VII

The Political Economy of Penury: Taxation and Public Spending in the UK

Taxing Question should be a Matter of More, not Less

Britain remains in a fiscal mess. The government's current spending on everything from education to pensions has been pared to the bone, with stress points obvious everywhere. But its capital spending, already inadequate, is set to fall.

All this hair-shirted austerity should at least have brought some virtue to the government's accounts – but not so. The 'golden rule' requires that governments borrow only for investment and ensure that on average over the ups and downs of the economic cycle their spending on everything from teachers' wages to maintaining roads is matched by tax receipts. But last week we learnt that the government is set to breach this rule over the 1990s by tens of billions of pounds – the first time this has happened since the war.

This summer's Economic Forecasts – the snapshot of the economy and public finances which the government is obliged to publish twice a year – provide a sobering backdrop to the Conservative leadership campaign and to the Labour Party's confirmation that, once in power, it aims to meet the 'golden rule'.

They underline that, far from there being scope for reducing tax, the debate should be about tax increases, and that Labour in government would confront some agonizing choices if it is to be as fiscally virtuous as it proclaims – an awkward truth it needs urgently to address.

What the figures portrayed was a remarkable £4.9 billion undershoot in the Treasury's expectations for next year's tax take compared with its Budget forecasts just seven months ago – even though its projections for growth in the economy are almost exactly the same. As a result, the so-called current balance – the gap between the public sector's current spending and current receipts and the operational measure of the golden rule – will still be in deficit in 1996/97, to the tune of £9.4 billion.

Moreover, it is likely, unless all the rules of economic cycles are broken, that by 1996/97 – five years after the economic trough – the economy will once again be turning down. It may be a faltering in growth or an actual recession, but willy-nilly there will be some impact on the government's current balance. Taxation will fall and spending rise.

In any case, if the golden rule is to be met, there have to be financial years in which the current balance is in surplus to offset the deficit years during the recession. But there will not have been even one year in the current economic cycle in which this will have been true. To have achieved that, taxation would have had to have been at least £10 billion higher – or current public spending £10 billion lower.

Nor is that the only fiscal teaser, because public investment, chronically low, needs to rise. The entire basis of fiscal policy needs to change.

This is not as difficult as it seems. Britain is, by European standards, seriously undertaxed. The OECD projects that in 1996 Britain's general government current receipts will stand at 37.9 per cent of GDP, compared with a European average of 45.2 per cent. Britain taxes less than any other country in Europe apart from Greece. If the British moved into line, the government could raise an additional £55 billion.

By the same token, Britain has plenty of latitude to borrow for public investment. The OECD projects that by the year 2000 British public debt as a proportion of GDP will have fallen to 47.4 per cent – easily the lowest in Europe, where the ratio will average 70 per cent.

Britain could borrow £10 billion a year for public investment until 2000 and its public debt would still be at the bottom of the world league table. The timing and extent of tax increases and borrowing for public invest-ment would have to be well judged, but that is the direction in which policy must move.

Some readers may find this implausible. Isn't Britain groaning from tax-ation? Haven't the rules that make government borrowing for investment so difficult got to stay in place for reasons of fiscal prudence, as Andrew Smith of Labour's economic team told the Chartered Institute of Housing last week? The answer, in both cases, is a resounding no. It is true that the British tax system is extraordinarily inequitable, so that those on average earnings and below pay disproportionately more while companies, inward investors and wealthy individuals pay disproportionately little.

But that unfair distribution of tax only disguises that, overall, the tax yield is too low.

A responsible government and a responsible political debate would take such unassailable facts as a starting point; but we live in Britain, right-wing land of myth and self-delusion. The mendacious debate over taxation in general, and the standard rate of income tax in particular, could hardly correspond less to reality.

It is not only that the £17 billion of phased tax increases launched by Chancellors Lamont and Clarke were the absolute minimum the govern-ment could get away with – they were the direct consequence of the 'tax-cutting' 1980s that is now lionized by the Conservative right. The budgets of 1987 and 1988, together with the sale of nationalized industries for a fraction of their proper value, left Britain's public accounts structurally enfeebled. But it fell to the Conservative Party when it won the 1992 general election to confront the consequences. Justice was done, with political consequences that are still working themselves out.

The establishment's hope, on both sides of the political divide, is that growth can now solve the problem. If economic growth is sufficient to boost tax revenues while public spending is held back, ultimately the golden rule will be observed.

But there are a number of problems with this approach. The first is that the impact of growth on the government's fiscal position is, while good, no longer quite as good as it was. The emerging unequal and insecure society, with its plethora of part-time work and impoverished self-employment, has meant that the growth of the income tax yield in relation to any given growth in output (its elasticity) has weakened.

At the same time, the fall in the demand for male workers is structural, so that growth alone does not pull them off income support. Corporations are also ever more efficient at shielding their profits from the Inland Revenue.

In short, neither current public spending nor current receipts are as sensitive to growth as they were. In addition, as the Treasury acknowledges, 'virtuous' growth delivered by an improvement in the trade balance, low inflation and low consumption also weakens the growth of the tax take. These are the influences that have weakened the projections for next year's tax yield – and which will continue.

These trends, if growth has the same character and tax increases are excluded, mean that the other option is spending cuts. But, as John Redwood has discovered, there are no easy choices. Pupil-teacher ratios are now the worst for fifteen years. A million children are taught in classes of thirty-one or over. Are ministers, nearly all of whom have their children educated privately to escape such ratios, prepared to take the axe even more to education budgets? To health budgets? To the social security budget, where benefits have fallen by more than a quarter in real terms since 1979? As for cutting Civil Service running costs as a route to salvation, forget it; the total budget this year is only £15.4 billion. There are no easy savings.

Somehow or other the public sector must have extra resources. The private finance initiative is no great help; providers of private finance are not Santa Claus and expect the public sector to chip in its share.

In short, by supposing that matters can stay as they are, the Conservative left and Labour alike are dodging the issue, and thereby allowing the argument to be shaped by the increasingly hysterical right.

The structure and pace of economic growth have to be transformed, along with a wholesale redesign of how the British contribute to the commonweal. If the growth rate could be lifted, spearheaded by public investment, and social divisions made less acute, then the deteriorating relationship between the tax yield and growth could be improved.

That would help matters, but more has to be done. Lifting the top rate of tax to 55 or 60 per cent, toughening up on inheritance and capital gains tax, raising corporation tax and hitting the scope for evasion and avoidance would improve affairs still further. In total, government receipts would need to rise by 1.5 per cent of GDP to hit the golden rule. That would still leave tax below 40 per cent – well below the European average.

The blunt and unstated truth remains. Britain is undertaxed for the collective services it wishes and needs to consume. Somebody, somewhere, has to find the courage to say so – and keep on saying it.

Guardian, 3 July 1995

A Tax that Needs to Go Up, not Down

For those who doubt we live in right-wing times, there is no better corrective than the debate over inheritance tax. What was once seen as an important source of revenue, and a means of levelling up disparities in wealth, is now portrayed as the enemy of enterprise. The Conservative right confidently looks forward to further reductions in this month's Budget as the prime minister half promised in his conference speech – and some even dare to believe it could be abolished.

The track record is impressive. Before Mr Clarke's arrival as Chancellor, nine out of fourteen Conservative Budgets had included important concessions to a tax which in any case is largely voluntary. By gifting assets to their heirs or placing them in trust, donors can ensure that no tax is paid. But it was Mr Lawson's extraordinary 1988 Budget, one of the great economic mistakes in recent history, that made the biggest change.

It was the year of hubris. The 1987 election had been a famous victory, and caution could be thrown aside. In the following Budget all higher rates of tax were abolished and replaced by a single higher rate of 40 per cent. That was what provoked the political storm – but the fact that the top rate of tax on inherited wealth had become 40 per cent as well, a much more important concession, went virtually unnoticed. Yet as the Rowntree Commission on Income and Wealth was to observe, Britain's inequality of wealth is much more marked than its inequality of income; the top 5 per cent own 37 per cent of Britain's wealth – but have only 16 per cent of the country's income. Lawson had given the wealthy their biggest boost of the century.

And the larger the estate, the larger the gain under Lawson's changes – just as it would be if inheritance tax were abolished today. The vast majority of estates in Britain that are notified for probate each year come nowhere near the current £154,000 threshold for paying inheritance tax; indeed, in 1991/2, the last year for which the Inland Revenue provides figures, only a paltry 16,489 estates paid inheritance tax.

The question is whether the claim of those few thousands for concessions from the public purse outranks that of hospitals, schools or libraries – or of the low-paid to have income-tax cuts. The astonishing political reality is that the advocates of change – in the right-wing think-tanks, the media and in the parliamentary Conservative Party – have made as much progress as they have in developing their case.

There are two prongs to their argument. There is the practical point that, because of the various concessions of the past sixteen years, inheritance tax is paid only by the unlucky and the financially unsophisticated so that its yield – £1.5 billion – is now trifling in relation to its collection cost. In any case, it is the 'residential homes' component of the Revenue's figures that pay 41 per cent of the tax; not the great estates.

But the high-ground argument is one of principle. As John Major put it, inheritance tax damages investment and stultifies wealth. In this world view, what animates the entrepreneur and the wealth-creator is the prospect of passing on wealth to his or her bloodline. Moreover, it is argued, it takes wealth to create wealth, so that, if it is in ever denser concentrations, the rich can run greater risks.

Nor has society, in the form of the government, any moral or philosophic claim on personal wealth or any social obligation to promote less inequality. Property, in this Conservative universe, is held freely by individuals to dispose of as they choose. Only thus can capitalism work.

The arguments are wrong. Not even medieval societies accepted the immoral argument that property confers only *rights* upon its owners and no accompanying *obligations*. Property was held not as an absolute privilege, but conditional upon the Crown's will; in a simple feudal contract, lands could be passed on to heirs only if the new owners recognized their feudal duties and paid significant taxes to the sovereign.

The social contract may not be so explicit in the 1990s, but it exists none the less. The 5 per cent who own 37 per cent of Britain's wealth do not do so independently of the society in which they live so well. They depend upon the wider society's acknowledgement of their property rights if they are to enjoy them; indeed, without social order their rights are meaningless – and they have a greater stake in the order holding together than the rest. A down-payment, by way of inheritance tax at the time of assuming ownership of wealth, is that contribution. Nor is this a 'disincentive' to entrepreneurship and investment. Indeed these, like property, are rooted in the success of wider institutions and social structures.

What makes an entrepreneur tick? The prospect of profits in the here and now, or the chance of leaving his descendants millions? In any case the vast bulk of output, investment and innovation in any economy is undertaken by large or medium-sized firms that have long ceased to be owned by the original proprietor. The key to their success is the commitment of the banks and saving institutions which finance them, the supply of skilled workers and the professionalism of their managers. Which is hardly surprising, given that, despite the Conservative Party's claims, almost no inheritance tax is paid on entrepreneurs' estates: the vast bulk is paid by wealthy individuals on the cash, shares, land and residential property they will inherit.

Nor should crocodile tears be spilled over the middle class supposedly suffering from the depredations of an unfair tax. Those same Inland Revenue figures show that in 1991/2 just 2,090 estates worth more than £500,000 paid more than half that year's inheritance tax – including 'residential homes', a definition which encompasses stately homes as much as suburban villas. It is the rich who pay most tax.

And if the yield is lower than the £4–7 billion range (at today's prices) it used to reach in the 1940s and 1950s, that's because the concessions have gone too far – and the tax rate is too *low*. Instead it needs to be raised. That would break up large estates, so that in the country, for example, young farmers would get a chance to buy land – and in the towns young entrepreneurs would have a chance to buy small companies that might be brought back into the inheritance-tax net. The gross inequalities of wealth that have grown up over the past twenty years could be reduced, and up to £3–4 billion raised to reverse the damaging cuts in investment in the Budget to finance tax reductions.

Mr Major is 100 per cent incorrect. Higher, not lower, inheritance tax is the means both to boost growth and develop a society which, famously, would be more at ease with itself. Asking the mass of the British to suffer in order to feather the nests of a tiny minority for no good reason is outrageous. Mr Clarke should stick to his One Nation instincts and not lower the tax.

Guardian, 8 November 1996

We All Lose out in the Tories' Lottery Game

Now here's an excellent ruse to give the Exchequer up to £1 billion a year spare cash. It's a scheme that delivers a new, largely unnoticed tax while offering the government the political cover to withdraw from swathes of public-spending commitments. It offers a steady drumbeat of good news to disguise what is going on. It's a public-relations dream.

It is the National Lottery – a means of redistributing from the poor to the rich while giving the Treasury a handsome bonus on the way. Nor, despite the incredible success of a game which 30 million British play weekly, is there any evidence that the 4 per cent or so of national income that the British give to charity has been significantly affected.

Yet to criticize the lottery is to court the accusation of being a killjoy. The audiences for the Saturday evening National Lottery Line may be falling, and the demand for 'Instants' (the lottery scratchcards) beginning to subside, but the lottery has won its place in national affections. If our fellow countrymen and -women wish to play a game of hazard where the chances of winning the jackpot are only marginally higher than being hit by a meteorite, then it's only a harmless flutter. And the money does go to good causes, doesn't it? Despite the manufactured outrage over Covent Garden or Sadler's Wells receiving millions, more than a billion has been found for other causes. There is a general sense, broadly correct, that most of them are thoroughly deserving.

It's a mood the government has every intention of fostering. Each round of successful applicants for lottery funding – as long as they are sports centres in Hackney rather than money for the Churchill papers – is evidence of the general good intentions of conservatism, and some relief in the pall of gloom induced by constant stories of public-spending cutbacks and austerity. Without the lottery there would not be a cat in hell's chance of the millennium even being modestly celebrated; as it is, construction work on the first monuments can begin next year. Which is why the Chief Secretary to the Treasury, William Waldegrave, was so quick to deny that the leaked exchange of letters between his office and the Heritage Secretary Virginia Bottomley last week really meant that he was advocating even a roundabout way for substituting lottery income for government spending. She replied that the letter would break the prime minister's pledge that all lottery funds would be deployed in addition to existing public-spending plans – and thus his proposal could not be countenanced. He hastily endorsed her view.

But on Monday the Treasury confirmed that lottery spending *does* count as general government spending – in which case Waldegrave's letter made more sense. Why not lower Bottomley's public-spending allocation financed by the taxpayer – and substitute it with money from the lottery? You dodge the little matter of the PM's pledge by routing the money through an endowment fund, and use the interest to pay the department's bills. It will start small – but soon whole departmental programmes could be funded from the new trust.

Yesterday, there was further Treasury clarification. International convention demands that lottery spending, under the sponsorship of the government, should be counted as general government spending. But that should not be confused with the *control* total for government spending, the departmental totals over which ministers haggle. Waldegrave was arguing over the Heritage Department's *control* total – which does not include lottery-financed spending by accounting definition. The PM's pledge still held.

Well, that's plain – except it's not. The government directly and indirectly, via its grants to local authorities, gives £4.3 billion a year to British charities – most of it conditional on the private sector matching the contribution. On top, there are similarly structured grants to arts, sports and heritage organizations. And this is where the scope for significant public-expenditure savings lies, while retaining the PM's pledge.

Tuesday's news that the Welsh Tourist Office withdrew its offer of funding to the Brecon Jazz Festival because the other half of its funding was provided by the lottery is precisely because lottery spending counts as general government or *Exchequer* spending; the rules are that the state pump-primes such charities, leaving the charity to find the other half of the cash from the private sector. The lottery can provide half, or the Welsh Tourist Board can provide half; but, as public-spending agencies, they can't both provide half – as the Treasury guidance note yesterday confirmed.

Nor are such savings the only benefit to the state. There is also the lottery tax, now set at 12 per cent but tipped to rise to 15 per cent in the Budget. All in all by 1998/9 the Exchequer could be up to £1 billion better off than it would have been had the lottery never existed.

But this is coming from the steady 4 per cent of national income that the country gives to charity; and the money can't be spent twice. Charities will be dipping into a depleted pool to match the public-lottery money that is substituting for tax-financed money, and bit by bit their range of activity must shrink. Giving is already down by some 15 per cent, and falling.

And, as charities appeal to the altruistic instincts of the British to dig deeper into their pockets to compensate, they will find the tradition of charitable giving irreparably harmed by the culture generated by the lottery and its operator, Camelot.

No thought was given to the signal sent when the franchise was awarded to a profit-making bidder who proceeded immediately to pay the chief executive £200,000, plus a £120,000 performance-related bonus for his pains. If the government and its lottery operator place so little value on charity and altruism, why should the public think any differently?

If British public-accounting rules were less opaque; if there was more participation in how lottery proceeds are allocated; if the lottery was structured to set an altruistic example, the story would be different. But that's the point. They're not, precisely because the British system does not operate that way – and the government is pledged to keep things as they are.

The undemocratized state, with its archaic system of public finance and devotion to profit-making agencies, sulllies everything it touches. The lottery is no different.

Guardian, 18 October 1996

Cashing in on the North Sea Bubble

So at least one Conservative cabinet minister has been brave enough to come to the defence of the welfare state – and for that act of singular political courage the Chancellor deserves some praise. But such are the terms of the debate in the Conservative Party that Mr Clarke's speech yesterday still implies that education, health and social-security spending will come under heavy pressure in the years ahead. It is some comfort that the pressure is less than it might have been; but no one should be confident that Mr Clarke's attachment to the concept of the welfare state will be backed by sufficient action to halt its current rate of attrition.

The Conservative Party's priority over welfare spending is not need, social cohesion or even affordability – for the funds, as you will see, are there to finance a more generous welfare system if we choose. Rather, just as Stalin's planners decided that steel production should double whatever the circumstances, the central planners in the Conservative Party have arbitrarily decided that government expenditure should fall below 40 per cent of GDP. This is to be the yardstick of the good society – not, for example, class sizes, the speed of response of fire brigades to emergencies, hospital waiting-lists or well-stocked public libraries.

Indeed few politicians and even fewer commentators seem to be aware just how extraordinarily tight the government's spending plans are for the next three years. Mr Clarke may not have announced that he wants to get public spending down to 35 per cent of GDP – he knows it's crazy – but anybody with a stake in public services, consumer or worker alike, should be chilled by his commitment to keep public spending 'more or less constant' over the next three years.

Thus unlike the wider economy, growing at its average annual rate of around 2 per cent (miserable enough), the public sector is to be frozen. Ambitions to recruit more teachers or rehabilitate more prisoners – the kinds of expenditure one might expect as Britain grows richer – are killed stone-dead. Instead, the story will be of a public sector struggling to offer minimal pay rises to its staff, financed by job losses and a deteriorating service. Already the loss of 3,000 prison officers, the strains in the fire service and the ending of the reading-recovery programme bear testimony to what lies ahead. This comes on top of benefit rates which are continually falling back in relation to average earnings and to which entitlement is ever tougher. The continual leeching of youth-training programmes and the cutback in TEC budgets are well known. Free dentistry and eye services have long since gone, and formal and informal rationing in the NHS grows. Tertiary education is in near-crisis as expenditure per student falls calamitously – hence the vice-chancellors' flirtation with charging undergraduates £300 entry fees. This is the 'strong welfare state' to which the Chancellor claims he is attached, and which he believes is the handmaiden of flexibility because it reduces fear and opposition to change.

Yet to argue for better invites the inevitable charge that it has to be paid for – and that in turn allegedly means higher income tax. Every radio and TV interviewer in the land, faithfully rehearsing Central Office's lines in the name of 'balance', knows how to turn up the heat on anybody who dares to challenge the idea that depredation, dilapidation and decay have to be the order of the day. It is a false premise. Income tax provides only a quarter of all tax revenue. Indeed, it could even be cut and still there are potential funds in abundance to finance the kind of welfare state the British want.

For example, unremarked and largely unreported, there is a boom in North Sea oil and gas production which already comfortably exceeds any year in the 1980s and will do so for the rest of the decade. Yet the tax yield is derisory – even to the point where the taxpayer is subsidizing more new wild-cat oil-well drilling in British waters than in any other oil province in the world. The usual explanation for declining oil revenues is falling oil and gas prices, but an important paper sent to me recently by Sheffield University's Ian Rutledge and Philip Wright shows how that is only partly true; the real driver of the extraordinary collapse in oil revenues is what they describe as 'the weakest petroleum taxation regime in the world'.

Over the past twelve years the government has emasculated the tax system bequeathed it by the 1974–9 Labour government. Oil royalties have been abolished. Advance petroleum revenue tax (PRT) has been phased out. In 1993 PRT for old fields was halved and abolished for new fields. Exploration, appraisal and, amazingly, *development* costs can be offset between fields. With the lowering of corporation tax to 33 per cent, some companies with smaller fields are being subsidized by the taxpayer, with Rutledge and Wright citing Ranger Oil as just one of many that seem to have recovered a substantial part of their tax payments.

Forget falling oil prices; taxation for any pound of North Sea oil profit is a quarter of what it was ten years ago – and gross trading profits are actually higher! Just restoring the tax regime to where it stood in 1987 would deliver another £3 billion of revenues; and if we choose to be tougher, restoring oil royalties and a stricter system of reliefs, the take could increase significantly again.

The net effect is that Britain comes second in the world league table for lax taxation of oil revenues prepared by the Geneva-based oil consultants Petroconsultants. The government takes just 33 per cent of oil-company cash flows, lower only than Ireland. But as Petroconsultants say, normally countries run light tax regimes when the prospects for discovery are poor and the infrastructure for landing, refining and shipping oil is weak. Extraordinarily and alone Britain represents the opposite: a light tax regime along with good discovery prospects and infrastructure – hence the sobriquet of being the world's weakest petroleum tax regime.

Oil and gas executives deny the undeniable, but North Sea extraction rates give the lie to their protestations that the tax regime is just. If there were fifteen years of oil reserves at current production levels in 1983, now there are fewer than five – with a similar pattern for gas. The industry is exploiting North Sea reserves of oil and gas mercilessly because the tax is so light – and before the regime changes.

And if the government had an ounce of propriety the regime would be toughened. What is the case for accelerating the depletion of British reserves of hydrocarbons, minimizing the tax take and running an ever more threadbare welfare state as a result? These islands have become a milch cow as our social infrastructure rots – and all against a chorus that there is no alternative. It is as offensive as it is unjust.

Guardian, 7 February 1996

Millennium Fiasco that is a Monument to Failure

We managed it in 1851 and in 1951 – why not in 2000? The idea of a landmark exhibition to celebrate the next millennium, along with ten other accompanying monuments around the country, should capture all our imaginations. Yet just as Crystal Palace and the Festival of Britain reflected the country in those years, so the progress of the Millennium Exhibition in Greenwich reflects contemporary Britain.

It's a bog-up, whose failings can be reliably traced to our masters in the Conservative Party and conservative establishment, along with the ideology they embrace. Insiders rate the chance of building the Millennium Dome on time as little more than fifty/fifty, with an ultimatum being delivered this weekend to the organizing company, Millennial Central, drastically to lower its ballooning costs, fast approaching £1 billion, by early January.

The private sector has proved remarkably reluctant to subsidize a government propaganda coup. And a letter last week from the Shadow Heritage Secretary, Jack Cunningham, reproducing exactly the harsh approach to public engagement and initiative of the Conservatives by insisting that a Labour government would not bail out the project, has lowered its chances of success still further. The biter has been bit and a project that had the capacity to bind the country together in an optimistic millennial moment, regenerating eastern London and leaving a monument for future generations, has become a politicized exemplar of the country's failings.

It should never have been like this. From the start the approach should have been truly bipartisan, with as many stakeholders as possible incorporated in the early planning so that its success was owned by a cross-section of us all. And, above all, it needed to be recognized that projects whose aim is to further the public good with little identifiable cash return need to be funded, or at least substantially pump-primed, with public money. It might have seemed a good wheeze to establish a quango, the Millennium Commission, pack it with Conservative supporters and a token Labour voice, and then try to achieve something for nothing by arming it with lottery money and expecting the private sector to finance losses to an almost equal degree.

But it was a profound misconception. It is not only that projects of this type need to be genuinely public rather than live in the demi-monde of quangoism if they are to be legitimate, but they also need to be activated directly and largely funded by the state. It is as the economic momentum gathers pace that the multiplier effects set in, with the private sector joining in to take advantage of genuinely profitable opportunities. If you rely on the private sector to assume too much of the risk as the motor of such projects, then the returns it demands prohibit its participation and the whole affair stalls.

We know from the example of the road projects that have attracted private finance that the state needs to guarantee returns three times more than the original stake money if private capital is to become involved in road construction. Yet the Millennium Dome is organized to have a one-year life with an uncertain number of paying visitors, and its subsequent ownership is murky. Companies are not charities, and especially not in Britain whose financial system enshrines maximizing shareholder value as the sole objective of business. The reluctance of all but ciphers of Central Office, like British Airways, to get involved was all too predictable.

For the Tory idea was that the Millennium Exhibition was to be a private-sector triumph. The notion was to revisit the glories of 1851 when Crystal Palace was built and funded wholly by the private sector. Yet the breathless ideologues wanting to ape the Victorians missed the point. Crystal Palace was the high-water mark of Britain's celebration of technology and science; it was a demonstration by the new industrialists and engineers of their modernity and awesome engineering power. An Isambard Kingdom Brunel or a Robert Stephenson was in business not to maximize shareholder value or secure guaranteed riches via underpriced share options; they wanted to act on the world and improve it, and business was the means to that end. The paradox is that, if you want a successful capitalism, the least good way to secure it is to enthrone profit and markets as the sole mobilizing force. Today's right understands neither our present nor our past.

Moreover Crystal Palace's organizers balanced their need for profit with genuine altruism, attracting the working class with the famous concessionary 'shilling days'. Yet as Millennial Central struggles to attract private finance, ticket prices are projected at £20 or more. This is a celebration that will be affordable only by the top 40 per cent in Britain's fragmented society. And the corporations approached to fund it do not react like their Victorian forebears. In any case, why save the government money for an exercise it should be funding itself?

As a result, Michael Heseltine and Virginia Bottomley, the two ministers seconded to the Millennium Commission, are spending an increasing amount of time desperately arm-twisting companies to come up with the goods. One chief executive told me he had been tracked down in the Far East; another that he will only speak to either minister if a colleague is listening in to assure his board that his remarks have not been falsely portrayed in an effort to create a bandwagon effect that is non-existent. It's an extraordinary spectacle: ministers behaving like second-rate hoods in an extortion racket – and companies having to protect themselves by trying to build a common line of resistance. The air is rife with rumours of illicit sweeteners and side-deals to produce the necessary funding.

It need not be like this. If Britain had a political system which admitted a degree of bipartisanship, or if the Conservative Party had more honour and sense of national obligation, then the whole process would be substantially depoliticized. If Britain had a financial system that placed more emphasis on businesses as organizations that add value rather than as short-term profit maximizers, we might have companies with more freedom to express engineering, scientific and technological values. And if we could lose the absurd prejudice against spending public money to achieve public goals, we could equip ourselves with the wherewithal to build lasting public monuments and plan regeneration around them.

Possessing none of these things – and with little prospect of change even with a new government – we will end up with a shadow of what could have been. And degrade every participant in the process as we fail.

Observer, 15 December 1996

PART VIII

An Age of Insecurity?
Polarization, Poverty and the
Fraying of our Social Fabric

High-Risk Strategy

The British are increasingly at risk. The chances of their jobs disappearing, of their incomes falling, of their homes being repossessed or being impossible to sell, of their families breaking up, of their networks of friendships disintegrating, have not been higher since the war.

There is a new source of inequality abroad. On top of the long-standing concerns about the growing gap between rich and poor, there is an increasing awareness of a new range of risks that are bringing fresh patterns of social distress and exclusion. Unemployment and low pay are no longer the sole measures of inequity and lack of social well-being; with the rise of new forms of casualized, temporary and contract forms of employment, even those on average incomes and above can become the victims of pressures beyond their control. They too can be left partially or completely excluded from their social networks.

The developments in the labour market have led to a new categorization of British society. There is a bottom 30 per cent of unemployed and economically inactive who are marginalized; another 30 per cent who, while in work, are in forms of employment that are structurally insecure; and there are only 40 per cent who can count themselves as holding tenured jobs which allow them to regard their income prospects with any certainty. But even the secure top 40 per cent know they are at risk; their numbers have been shrinking steadily for twenty years. The 30/30/40 society is a proxy for the growth of the new inequality and of the new risks about the predictability and certainty of income that have spread across all occupations and social classes.

Each category faces its own dilemmas and crises. For the bottom 30 per cent the risk is that poverty will turn into an inability even to subsist, and that marginalization will change into complete social and economic exclusion. Eight per cent of people are unemployed; 4 per cent have been out of work for more than a year – which means complete social exclusion. The work the unemployed do find is part-time, casualized or insecure, so that their lives consist of unemployment interspersed with periods of insecure semi-employment.

The worrying figure is the 21 per cent of the working population who are now economically inactive – of working age but not making themselves available for work. Twenty years ago this segment was mostly made up of women voluntarily withdrawing from the labour market to bring up children; now it is largely peopled by men of working age and single parents.

The 30/30/40 society

Percentage of all adults 16–59/64

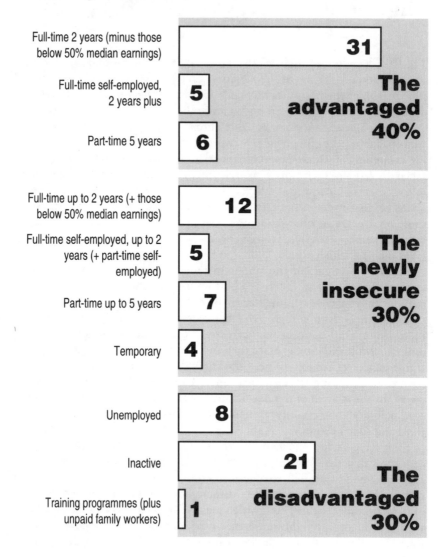

Full-time 2 years (minus those below 50% median earnings) — **31**

Full-time self-employed, 2 years plus — **5**

Part-time 5 years — **6**

The advantaged 40%

Full-time up to 2 years (+ those below 50% median earnings) — **12**

Full-time self-employed, up to 2 years (+ part-time self-employed) — **5**

Part-time up to 5 years — **7**

Temporary — **4**

The newly insecure 30%

Unemployed — **8**

Inactive — **21**

Training programmes (plus unpaid family workers) — **1**

The disadvantaged 30%

One in four men in Britain of working age is now unemployed or economically inactive. This statistic has risen inexorably through recession, while the recovery has checked its growth only in the past three months; it is likely to go up again as the pace of recovery slows down. These are the men who have retired early (nearly half the men between fifty-five and sixty-five are now economically inactive); these are the million unskilled men who claim the renamed 'incapacity benefit'. Then there are unemployed women, and, worse, women who would like to work but find themselves trapped in unemployment, because under the social security rules every pound they earn is subtracted from their husbands' income support, leaving the household no better off. In 1979, some 6 per cent of households had neither adult partner working; now, computes Paul Gregg of the LSE, this is 16 per cent. Life for these people is tough beyond the imagination of most of us.

But it is no bed of roses for the 30 per cent who are newly insecure. More and more risk has accrued on workforces as successive Employment Acts have reduced employee protection and as companies have come under intense and growing pressure from pension fund and insurance company shareholders to deliver the highest financial returns over the shortest period in the industrialized world. Companies can more profitably manage the ebb and flow of demand over the business cycle if they reduce their core staff to a minimum and hire additional workers on contracts which will allow them to be shed quickly if times get tough. The company bears less risk. The risk is borne by their fluctuating labour force. The famous example is of Burger King, where young workers clocked on when customers appeared; this reduced their wages to a derisory level but ensured they were only paid for the *minutes* they were needed.

There has been a marked growth in forms of work that are not 'tenured'. With full-time workers only qualifying for tenure after two years, the recent pick-up in full-time work means little. They can be laid off within two years as easily as they were hired. The rapid growth in the numbers of part-timers without any formal job security, contract workers, workers sacked and then rehired as self-employed, temporary, part-time and agency workers is the true indicator that employment conditions have changed; self-employment alone has doubled over the past ten years. Even those employers who want to hold out against the new trends are forced to conform. If they allow their wage costs to rise above the industry average, they face loss of market share and financial distress.

Here there is a gender effect. Most of the growth in part-time and insecure work has fallen to women, typically less unionized and more compliant. Many married women respond in surveys that they like such work because it allows them to juggle family responsibilities with earning. But as 70 per cent of all *new* part-time jobs are for sixteen hours or less, and so do not attract employment protection or any benefits such as holiday or sickness entitlement, such workers are highly at risk. Such work is becoming essential for family incomes – and women are slowly becoming less content. When the capacity to avoid repossession depends on earnings from an employer who can sack you at will, family stability hangs on a thread.

The last 40 per cent are the advantaged – from the workers still covered by union wage agreements to full-time, tenured employees working in the great organizations in the public and private sectors. The full-time self-employed, like John Birt in his old contract with the BBC, come into this category too. But their numbers are shrinking by 1 per cent a year on average. Market-testing, contracting-out, downsizing and delayering are steadily transferring workers into much less secure work patterns. By the year 2000, full-time tenured employment, around which stable family life has been constructed along with the capacity to service twenty-five-year mortgages, will be a minority form of work. And as the risk of insecure or no employment grows, so the social institutions and systems built up over the past fifty years to protect against risk are decaying. The welfare state is more threadbare, and eligibility for income support – itself worth less and less in relation to average incomes – ever tougher. Trade unions' capacity to protect against sudden and sharp deteriorations in working conditions has been reduced. The British labour market, reports the OECD, ranks bottom in the league table of industrialized countries.

The individual means to protect against risk are no stronger. With nearly 70 per cent of homes owned by their occupier, one bulwark against financial calamity has been rising house prices. For forty-five years, the average British household steadily grew more wealthy on the back of the great house price boom; but the fall in house prices in real terms over the nineties caused the most savage reverse in personal wealth since the war. The operation of the housing market, with more than a million home owners having mortgages that exceed the value of their house (negative equity) and every mortgagee paying high real interest rates to own an asset that is falling in value, is now a source of insecurity in its own right.

Private insurance companies have become more selective about insuring those whose circumstances indicate that they might claim, making basic protection more expensive, sometimes impossible, to obtain. Millions hold personal pension plans that will pay them a minimal pension in retirement, worth substantially less than the former state earnings-related pension. What financial calamity in the event of unemployment or loss of income really means is captured in one telling statistic from the Institute of Fiscal Studies: half of British households have *£450 or less* in savings. Risk has grown, but the protections have shrunk.

All this has been justified by a narrow conception of 'efficiency'. It is said to be efficient for firms to have lean core workforces; for the provision of welfare to be privatized; for unions to be less powerful. But perversely the promotion of uncertainty, risk and insecurity has made the operation of the economy as a *system* less efficient. It has weakened the growth and stability of demand; it has reduced firms' incentives to invest in their workforces and their infrastructure; it has inflated current public expenditure and reduced the tax base.

One of the features of the recovery has been weak investment growth – with firms repeatedly saying in surveys that they are worried by the need to make high financial returns in the context of uncertain future demand. Consumers have become price-conscious, leery about buying big-ticket items and undertaking long-term commitments. How can they behave otherwise? David Miles, chief economist of Merrill Lynch, calculates that the average variability of income for average workers has grown by half since 1968; we are 50 per cent more likely to have a violent downward swing in our income. The individual firm may find it efficient to reduce its core workforce and displace risk on to part-timers and contract workers; but in aggregate the impact is to make incomes more volatile and individuals more cautious. Demand becomes weaker and more variable. To explain the crisis in the housing market, and the implications for the house-building and construction industries, look no further than the 30/30/40 society.

Nor does it make sense for government finances. Tax revenues this year will undershoot the Treasury's projections by up to £4 billion; low-paid part-timers and short-term contract workers do not generate the same income tax yield as their full-time equivalents, and their spending, biased to subsistence goods that attract no VAT, means that indirect taxation grows less rapidly as well.

Simultaneously social security spending, despite ever tighter eligibility tests, increases as the numbers qualifying for housing benefit assistance and income support rise remorselessly. The freezing of the growing 30/30/40 society would have saved the Chancellor the £3 billion in spending cuts he is searching for this autumn.

The changes make no sense in terms of Britain's wider social structures. The struggle to maintain living standards has meant ever-longer working hours. According to a survey last week by recruitment agency Austin Knight, two-thirds of British workers now work more than a forty-hour week, while a quarter work more than fifty hours. The rise in stress is marked, and such long hours necessarily reduce the leisure-time that parents can spend with their children or with each other.

Nor is it only parenting that suffers; the capacity to sustain friendships outside work, to become a member of local clubs and societies, to play a part in the local neighbourhood, reduces as hours worked rise. The forty-hour week, along with paid holidays, pensions and sickness benefit, is one of the great social achievements of the twentieth century. It, too, is at risk.

The forces generating the 30/30/40 society could be arrested. A more determined assault on long-term unemployment; extending employment rights to those not in full-time work; relieving companies of the pressure to make sky-high financial returns; constructing more solid systems of social support; placing less emphasis on home ownership as the only form of housing tenure – all would help. To act in this way is supposed to be inefficient. But *not* to act in this way is more inefficient still. In the long run a 30/30/40 society is neither desirable nor sustainable. One day the pendulum will swing back because it must.

Guardian, 30 October 1995

What Comes after the Gold Rush?

We live in a world in which increasingly the winners take all. It has never been unusual for pop stars or sportsmen to attract fantastic earnings but the phenomenon now spans the spectrum – from bankers to software writers, lawyers to surgeons. Those deemed to bring success command ever more startling returns.

If this is becoming true in Britain, it is even more true in the US. Just twenty years ago, chief executives of top American corporations earned thirty-five times more than the average worker – now they earn 130 times more. It is estimated that the top 1 per cent of the US population has captured 40 per cent of all economic growth since 1973. The growth of income inequality in western labour markets is being driven not only by developments at the bottom, but by those at the top.

It is a new twist in the entire debate about inequality – and the argument over job insecurity. The usual framework is to cite the change in demand for skilled and unskilled labour, so the unskilled are worth less in a techno- logically driven environment while the educated and skilled are worth more. Competition from low-cost developing countries exacerbates the trends, while tax cuts for the well-off, coupled with stagnation in welfare payments in real terms for low-income groups, have made the situation still worse. Add cor- porate downsizing, and the normal terms of the argument are set.

All are plainly significant, but a new best-selling book in the US – *The*

Winner Take All Society,* published here last week – claims that they rate behind the magnitude of forces which are creating super-rewards for the top performers. Nor, argue the authors, Professors Robert Frank and Philip Cook, is this growth in inequality economically healthy. The lure of achieving these top prizes is causing floods of workers to clamour for jobs in the professions where they exist – such as law and investment banking – and ensuring a dramatic fall-off in other sectors – the Civil Service, teaching and engineering – with knock-on consequences for growth. The authors estimate that a doubling of student numbers in engineering would increase US gross domestic product by 0.5 per cent, while a doubling of law students would cause it to decline by 0.3 per cent – but that is precisely the direction in which the winner-take-all society is going.

As the numbers of disappointed winners grow, you might expect them to learn by their mistakes – but as Frank and Cook argue, people continually overestimate their chances of success. Miners rushing to a Klondike are not rational about their chances of finding gold; neither are the numbers flooding into investment banking or the law.

But winners' salaries are not falling as you might expect, given the laws of supply and demand. Indeed the super-earnings grow exponentially. Why? Frank and Cook blame the creation of a highly flexible labour market – for the super-successful. With faster dissemination of information, each industry knows which individuals bring success and to what degree, and with the weakening of moral and employment rules that used to bind top earners to their firms, such people are less loyal to their companies. Top lawyers, security traders or surgeons are in the same position as chat-show hosts – their success is ever more visible as is their capacity to take it with them. It is the new market in 'winners' that is generating super-salaries.

By itself this would matter little. The trouble is, say the authors, it is causing a ferocious misallocation of talent. In Britain, graduate applicants for the Civil Service are dropping, while the numbers anxious to secure City jobs or become the next Chris Evans rise. Inequality driven in this way, if the US parallel holds, will not help the British growth rate.

The authors scoff at the notion that winners need lower taxes to motivate them even more; instead, they turn the argument on its head, saying that while confiscatory taxes for the rich are counterproductive, progressive taxation could boost growth by reversing the misallocation of resources. They don't favour higher income tax, though, but rather a progressive tax on consumption – so the winners have to pay more for luxuries, making the value of winning rather less.

All this places the British argument in a different context. Defenders of the status quo insist simultaneously that Britain has a highly flexible labour

* R. Frank and P. Cook, *The Winner Take All Society* (New York: Free Press, 1995).

force, which is a launch pad for growth, and that job insecurity is a fiction. They claim everything has changed but nothing has changed. But there *is* a developing winner-take-all tendency at the top of the labour market, and at the same time, as Paul Gregg shows in *Business*, there has been a sharp fall in the number of years that men can expect to hold their jobs.

So while the winners capture ever-higher salaries, middle earners become more insecure, and those at the bottom actually see hourly rates fall. We are invited to laud all this in the name of promoting growth and efficiency; but if Frank and Cook are right we should be highly sceptical. We have ever-higher-paid winners and more desperate losers. It will bring nothing but lower growth and much social pain.

Observer, 16 June 1996

Why the Poor Remain Silent

How unequal must society become before it touches raw nerves and compels some response? If statistics alone could inflame concern, the point would already have been reached – but the facts about the scale of inequality in Britain still fail to ignite a popular outcry.

Part of the explanation is the reticence of rich and poor alike. The rich, apart from the new kids on the block – the directors of the privatized utilities – have learnt discretion about the scale of their income and wealth. Old money knows that the best way to protect the outrageous inequalities permeating British life is to keep mum.

But there is an equal and telling silence at the bottom. The Rowntree Foundation Inquiry into Income and Wealth last week reported that the numbers living on less than half of average incomes had tripled since 1978. Up to 30 per cent of the population, the inquiry found, had not shared in the gains in economic growth since 1979 – and it portrayed a degree of inequality which it believed was fully appreciated by neither policy-makers nor the wider public.

Among the sufferers, too, ancient British attitudes come into play. When Seebohm Rowntree revealed in his landmark study in 1902 that 28 per cent of people in York were living in poverty, *The Times* thundered that a large proportion of the poor were 'miserable mainly from their own fault' – a reaction not seriously shaken as another Rowntree inquiry ninety years later reports similar findings.

So overwhelming is this view in popular culture that the poor share it;

even if they resent their lot, they believe that they have no right to expect any different – and those that do, find marginalization so lowers their self-worth that they become accomplices in their own devaluation.

Validating these prejudices is laissez-faire economics. Even if the poor deserved better, it would require such increases in taxation and additional action by the state to change things that the remedy would be worse than the cure. Taxation and government action, as we have been told relentlessly for the past fifteen years, are economically inefficient and corrosive of moral values.

To its credit, last week's Rowntree report argued eloquently that neither the silence nor this justification for inequality can continue. If the rich are compelled to live in a drawbridge society, then their lives are gravely diminished. Moreover, if millions are idle they can be neither consumers nor workers; instead, they inflate social security spending and become an even greater burden on the groups above them.

The new right argument, that alleviating inequality entails more inefficiencies than letting it grow, must be challenged. For it is not merely the trend growth rate that is lowered by running economy and society with a vast overhead of unskilled and marginalized people; the variability about the cycle increases as well.

Inequality in society translates into instability in the economy – raising chronic difficulties for economic management and business investment. Not only the pattern of demand, but also ultimately of supply, is structured by the offence of mounting inequality. In any upswing, for example, the first beneficiaries will be the rich, but the more their spending is fuelled by tax reductions and the expectation that their incomes will rise faster than the average, the more their spending will increase for any given change in income and output.

This in turn will fuel a real appreciation in the asset prices on which they spend their income, ranging from houses to yachts, making them feel wealthier, improving their feel-good factor and persuading them to spend even more.

As the upswing gathers pace it will suck into employment those living on poverty-level income support linked to prices and not wage growth – especially if labour laws have been relaxed to encourage a hire-and-fire approach to employment, increasing the amount of job-churning. As the 30 per cent who are marginalized move into the next highest categories of income, definitionally there is a sharp improvement in their spending power.

Thus, as the upswing radiates around an unequal society, the economy has to deal with lumpy increases in demand: first-round effects from the rich and second-round effects from the poor.

The same works in reverse in the downturn. As incomes fall away, the asset prices underpinning spending from the wealthy fall, intensifying the feel-bad factor; as the less well-off find themselves moving from work to deteriorating levels of income support, the fall-away in their spending is proportionately greater.

As inequality grows with each cycle, firms will be surprised by the lumpy demand increases in each upturn, leaving them short of capacity and so generating inflationary bottlenecks. Equally, they will be surprised by the extent of the downturn, because they do not realize the extent to which lower social security payments reduce overall demand levels, causing them to intensify their investment cuts and lay-offs – which in turn will have multiplier effects on demand and employment levels.

This framework helps explain the switchback ride of the 1980s and early 1990s. British monetary policy, with entry into the ERM, made things far worse – but the basic unstable motion of the cycle was there anyway. For all the talk of stop-go in the 1950s and 1960s, it is no accident that the most violent postwar economic cycles have coincided with the growth of inequality.

But as the cycle grows more volatile, it makes firms warier about long-term investment. The structure of demand begins to impact on the structure of supply, turning firms even more into opportunist traders rather than social organizations committed to production and innovation. Why train your labour force if you know you will have to lay them off during the downturn? Why build up capacity when you know you will have to carry it during the downswing? The best strategy is to under-invest and simply exploit the cyclical peak by raising prices and margins, boosting profits and not having to worry about surplus capacity in the downturn.

This is the economic structure, together with the unequal income distribution, that the Treasury and Bank of England are trying to manage just by relying on moving short-term interest rates. If demand presses against capacity constraints, everyone fears that will generate multiplier effects which will cause the economy to overshoot, as in the 1980s boom; but while hikes in short-term interest rates may depress the growth of demand, they also must lead to deferral of investment decisions – so that the economy gets even more trapped in a low-investment/low-skills equilibrium.

That does not mean interest rates can be frozen over the economic cycle; but it does mean that some of the dangerous, self-feeding instability of the economy can be better handled by supplementing monetary policy with measures to make the structure of demand less volatile – to create a more equal society.

Yet whatever the economic rationality of more equality, in Britain the value system is hostile to such notions. To reduce inequality implies redistributive taxation and, as the Rowntree inquiry argues, targeted public investment. It is true that the marginalized need to be made stakeholders in the wider society; but to make them so requires those that foot the bill to believe that they as stakeholders, too, want to extend a helping hand to those beneath them and trust in state structures as the vehicle of that help.

The British undoubtedly have strong altruistic sentiments, but they do not believe themselves to be stakeholders – and they do not trust their political system to deliver. The tradition of citizenship, the key to unravelling this conundrum, is weak – even non-existent. If confronting inequality were only a technical question requiring economic efficiency as its justification, the task would be easy – and Gordon Brown and Tony Blair would find more resonance for the political arguments they make about Britain's divided society.

But it is not. Reducing inequality might smooth Britain's economic cycles and raise its growth rate – but even if the rich and the Conservative Party believed that to be true they would not place that wider purpose before their own. Inequality is here because they want it, and because the moral and social forces that oppose them are so weak.

Guardian, 13 February 1995

Why a Minimum Wage Offers Maximum Returns for All

Fairness has a powerful grip on the popular imagination. In vain do right-wing politicians, free-market economists and the business elite plead that the rich need and deserve incentives while the only way for the poor to price themselves into work is for there to be no potential minimum to their wages. It is seen as one law for the rich and another for the poor – and so it is.

This week the business elite's double standards will be vividly on display. Today the Greenbury committee reports, arguing for some minimal changes and safeguards to limit the more outrageous abuses but essentially leaving the existing structures in place. Tomorrow the CBI will reaffirm its opposition to the minimum wage.

Market forces, business will claim, must do their felicitous work at each end of the income scale. If the country feels that the results leave those at the bottom too poor, then it should supplement their income with benefits for which the taxpayer foots the bill. At the top, the processes by which pay is determined should be transparent and properly taxed – but beyond that the market must rule.

In this conception the market is a somehow impersonal arbiter of economic fortunes. The great forces of power and equity that lie at the bottom of market relations, and the social and political institutions through which they are mediated, are abstracted away. It is all supposedly a matter of supply and demand. The rise in executive salaries is explained as a price signal showing that there are too few people coming forward with the ability to run British companies. So their price gets bid up.

But as Paul Ormerod argues in *The Death of Economics*, the notion that the pay of directors, investment bankers and the like has anything to do with supply and demand operating in a competitive labour market is palpably absurd. Tens of thousands apply to get on the management training courses of the top 100 companies or City investment banks, but still their salaries spiral upwards rather than are bid down; meanwhile, there are chronic shortages of applicants for jobs on the railways – and still Railtrack resists paying more than 3 per cent. The one thing that you can honestly say about the labour market is that it does not operate according to the laws by which British business claims that it does.

Leading theorists in economics are now challenging the simple nostrums that inform the British debate, which amount to little more than a return to the axioms of early nineteenth-century political economy, in which the price of labour is meant to be like the price of tomatoes: lower it and more is demanded – raise it and less is sought.

Late in 1994, David Blanchflower and Andrew Oswald published the most rigorous cross-country survey of the labour market ever undertaken – *The Wage Curve.** Over four years the two used 9,000 computer hours to survey the relationship between wages and employment of 3.5 million people in twelve countries, delivering results that show that every word the CBI, the government and the *Economist* magazine – the British *Pravda* to the Conservative elite – utter on the labour market is balderdash.

Employment is not highest where real wages are lowest, and lowest where real wages are highest. Nowhere has lowering real wages led to higher employment. Put another way, unemployment serves to lower real wages by a predictable degree – a doubling of unemployment lowers real wages by about 10 per cent everywhere – but that lowering of wages does not lead to a rise in employment.

There is no disputing the numbers; the task is to find an explanation that fits the data. The answer lies in the way wages are fixed and maintained. The dynamic component of the labour market is not the price of labour; it is the demand, and wages are fixed not in relation to what terms the unemployed might accept but an internal calculus by individual firms of the worth of their workforces. This 'efficiency wage' comprises the best

* D. Blanchflower and A. Oswald, *The Wage Curve* (Cambridge, Mass.: MIT Press, 1994).

combination of incentives, the cost of rehiring, the value of knowing the capacity of the existing workforce and its marginal productivity – all traded off against the value of what is produced. It is a complex mix in which the level of unemployment is at best only one element, at worst peripheral.

Unemployment therefore does not lower real wages to price the unemployed into work; it acts to discipline the wages and behaviour of those who are employed. It is only if the demand for labour rises that the unemployed will find work – which is why Blanchflower and Oswald find that high employment and high wages go hand in hand, and that low wages and high unemployment are similarly correlated.

Top executives' pay is one proof of this theory; they are the beneficiaries of high demand for their services and the need to secure their loyalty to one firm rather than a competitor – a kind of efficiency wage for senior directors. Their pay has nothing to do with the competitive interaction of supply and demand, as in a textbook free labour market.

Another proof is new evidence from the US that a minimum wage for the low paid is also an instrument for promoting efficiency in the labour market, and that as long as it is set at reasonable levels it promotes rather than reduces employment.

In *Myth and Measurement,* Professors David Card and Alan Kreuger from Princeton University show that just as in the wider labour market unemployment acts as a discipline on wage levels for those in employment rather than an active force for lowering the jobless totals, so this same process is at work at the bottom of the labour market. The difference is that here wages are so low that they create social difficulties for those earning them.

Free market theory predicts that a minimum wage must lower employment because it raises the price of labour. In a variety of empirical tests, notably in the US fast-food industry, Card and Kreuger show the opposite is true. In a free market, firms set their wages so low that they have high turnover rates and longer periods in which they cannot find workers. Although this may appear to boost margins in the short run, the actual wage is below the efficiency wage. A minimum wage reduces turnover rates, raises skills and even increases output by having extra manpower to service customer needs. A minimum wage raises employment as long as it brings the efficiency wage and money wage into line; but if the minimum wage is set above the efficiency wage, job losses will result.

It also serves to promote social cohesion and alleviate poverty. In Britain it used to be argued that low wages were not a cause of poverty – single parenthood or bad pensions were the main reasons for low incomes. But that was before the labour market was deregulated, with the wages of the bottom 10 per cent falling in real terms since 1979. Two-fifths of the workers who would benefit from a minimum wage of £3 an hour live in the poorest 10 per cent of households.

The CBI and government are united in opposing a minimum wage in principle, preferring to boost the incomes of the poor through family credit. But this is no more than a contemporary version of the Speenhamland system which at the beginning of the nineteenth century locked the working class into appalling dependence and poverty for a generation. The idea was that the very poor were to be saved from starvation by being offered a subsistence income devised by local magistrates and funded by the ratepayer. But, just like today, the free labour market bid down wages, and the ratepayers found themselves subsidizing rapacious employers. Poverty exploded, the rates became insupportable and the economy began to wind down as levels of demand fell away. It was inherently absurd.

Yet that is the path Britain is now set upon. Spending on family credit has already exceeded £2.4 billion and must increase as the processes bidding down the wages of the bottom 10 per cent extend up the income hierarchy. Essentially the taxpayer is funding cheap labour.

It is the oldest story in capitalism and over the next two days of special pleading for the rich and assault on the idea of a minimum wage for the poor, never, ever forget it.

Guardian, 17 July 1995

Investing in Social Capital can Help to Counter the Spate of Evil

The first shock is the event, awesome in its evil, horror and irrationality. The second shock is that British society has become so deformed we can produce the individuals who commit such crimes. Dunblane, we sense, will be followed by more.

The reflexive instinct is to legislate for anything that might help. Tighter gun and knife control; more security guards outside schools; more intervention by the police. All may help at the margins – yet even their most ardent advocates know that the next Thomas Hamilton could evade such controls if he were determined enough.

Real protection demands a profound change in the character of British society and culture. Individuals – especially the growing number of marginalized men living alone – need to be integrated better into the networks of mutuality and reciprocity on which a well-functioning society rests. Then at least there may be some chance of making the deviant recognize the consequences of breaking basic human rules on such a scale – and of embedding him in social relations that can act as a constraint. The spate of awful crimes highlights what we know in our guts: that Britain's stock of social capital is diminishing and unless it is replenished there is no long-run relief in sight.

Here, unexpectedly, some new thinking in economics offers insights. A new wave of theorists, concerned that market mechanisms alone cannot signal the economic rewards resulting from collaboration and co-operation, is exploring the role of social capital in advancing economic development – and how it is fostered. The capacity of an economic grouping to forge trust and recognize a mutuality of interests is emerging as no less important in fostering growth as is investing in physical and intellectual capital.

A group whose members trust each other can achieve more economically than a non-trusting group; the classic example is how farmers can economize on farm tools if they can trust in the capacity to borrow from other farmers. Equally, they can have leaner labour forces if, for example, one can be trusted to bale hay for another when idle, in the expectation that the favour will be returned. These trust relations can be formalized into co-operatives and even local agricultural banking – so that, the stronger the social networks, the more prosperous the farming economy.

Economic historians are picking up on the theme, emphasizing trust as an important animator of industrialization. Trust is the cement that creates industrial clusters, innovative supply chains and long-term supportive finance; but trust cannot be created without a strong civic society and clusters of social networks.

Professor Robert Puttnam, a political economist at Princeton, and Professor Douglass North, a Nobel prizewinning economist at Washington University in St Louis, have been prominent in arguing that social capital along with an economy's institutional structure are fundamental to its performance.

But economists working in a similar vein range from Harvard's Professor Michael Porter, who famously advocates that social clusters and networks of firms create self-generating growth circles, to Reading University's Professor Mark Casson. The latter argues that even entrepreneurship is based on trust, because the production of high-quality, innovative goods demands an integrity of relationship between the workforce, suppliers and financiers. Integrity of production requires the integrity of trust relationships.

Social capital has, however, been on the decline in the US and Professor Puttnam is concerned about its impact on the economic and social development of American capitalism.

The vast US legal industry is founded on the breakdown of trust as individuals turn to lawyers to police contracts; the financial services industry is overblown because individuals need financial instruments that protect against risk as trust relations diminish; the explosive growth of crime and the prison population is intimately related to the orgy of corporate downsizing, causing falling real wages and marginalizing unskilled men.

The new, untrusting American corporations generate productivity not through creativity and organic growth but by destroying what seems to be costly social layering.

This may have short-run benefits, but in the long run it imperils the good society which sustains any successful economy. Nor is the US alone. In Britain there is the same erosion of trust relations which leads to industrial and financial short-termism, and is corroding trust relations in the wider society – reflected in these moments of horrific social breakdown. Hamilton, left alone to his own macabre devices in his Stirling house, became a moral outcast unable to empathize with the plight of his victims or their families. The decline of social capital infects economy and society alike.

Yet whence social capital? Professor Puttnam's study of Italy, *Making Democracy Work* (Princeton University Press), shows how when the Italians regionalized their political system in 1970 it was those regions with the great civic traditions and rich in social capital, with dense networks of clubs, associations and civic action groups (including trade unions), notably Emilia-Romagna and Umbria, that exploited the opportunities best. In the poor south, the typical unit is the individualistic, inward-looking nuclear family which stays aloof and apart from civic life – and those regions were less successful.

They found it much harder to launch themselves on the same virtuous circle of autonomous government reinforcing the civic tradition and so enhancing social capital.

Nor was this just a political and social gain; in the north the benefits spilled over into the dynamic small-firms sector – itself profiting from the same trust relations and high social capital that allowed small firms both to co-operate in the development of new technologies and production processes as well as to compete. Successful regional governments put in place structures to support that collaboration – and those in turn became part of the local social network.

Some of this civic tradition and social capital has roots that go back to the Middle Ages – with the depressing implication that if a society has not got the historical underpinning for social capital it is preordained to be a loser. History matters. On the other hand, Professor Puttnam notes that after twenty years there are the first signs that even in the Italian south a civic participative tradition is beginning, with knock-on effects on the economy and society. New institutions can make a difference; but it takes time.

In Britain, however, social capital and trust have been under assault from two directions. In the first place, the insistence that only individual bargains in markets can organize economy and society efficiently has helped generate a winner-take-all culture.

Individuals are exhorted to capture as much gain as possible and structures have been created – from the NHS to the labour market – in which that exhortation is matched by a new pattern of legal and economic incentives. Mutuality of obligation is secondary to self-interest; strong public services are secondary to tax cuts.

The other impact on social capital has been the marked decline, which Professor Puttnam observes in the US, of civic and social life, and the weakness of Britain's political and social institutions in offering any counterbalance. The Americans are joining and participating less, he reports, a trend that is matched in Britain.

But, rather than blame the so-called dependency culture, he focuses on new forms of recreation, which require less social interaction, as one of the causes. For example, he is not so concerned with the growth of violent films on TV so much as the rise of television-watching itself as displacing social and civic activity. And that activity in turn is less attractive because the new rootlessness of aggressive market economies makes it hard to have any long-run stake in the outcome of activity that is based in one permanently changing neighbourhood.

These arguments point to a more subtle response to Dunblane than looking for top-down legislative mechanisms of social control and coercion to solve the problem – while in the economy further promoting atomistic market relations. The task is rather to rebuild trust and social capital.

Guardian, 18 March 1996

Priceless Gifts within Everybody's Reach

Christmas is a standing offence to the idea of economic rationality. The entire population launches upon an orgy of gift-giving, card-sending and party-throwing, abandoning any rational calculus of self-interest.

After all, who can know with any certainty whether and when that card, Christmas gift or party will be reciprocated?

Here is a whole array of unpriced economic acts in which people are doing no more than trying to earn good will, create social obligations and cement their relationships to generate, in its broadest sense, mutual regard. They are pitching into the world of social horse-trading and gift-giving without any robust means, except a combination of trust and instinct, of assessing whether their sallies will pay-off.

Contemporary free market economists – advocates of the primacy of market relations and flexible prices as the sole and most efficient means of organizing economic and social activity – are at a loss. The dynamics of giving on this scale fall outside their theoretical categories. While plainly a gift is the first step in a hoped-for exchange, with no prices and with psychic rather than monetary gains sought, there is neither a predictable equilibrium nor an internally consistent model to explain what is going on, Christmas is nonsense in economic terms.

Neoclassical economics hangs on the demonstration that efficiency is only produced through the impersonal relations of a market. Market actors need to know nothing more than the price and availability of a good, and armed with that information they buy, sell or do nothing. The gains from trade are the only ones available. The economic actors do not need to know who is offering the good for sale, worry about whether they are liked or disliked, care about their reputation, or as social beings desire the company of others. Like automatons, they just buy and sell, based on a calculus of economic advantage.

This is the theory that, in the labour market for example, has demanded the removal of all restrictions to the hire and fire of workers – so they can be treated like commodities as in any other market. Thus will wages fall, employment rise and the general good be delivered. An employer who pays his workers well, refuses to sack them during a recession or does not cut their wages to the level that the unemployed might accept is behaving irrationally. He or she is forgoing profits to do no more than gift good working relations to the workforce – an economic Santa Claus.

Adam Smith, writing in his *Theory of Moral Sentiments*, understood such action well. The purpose of bettering one's condition was much more than simply maximizing profits to live – that did not require much money, after all. It was to 'be taken notice of with sympathy . . . and approbation'. Human beings are in a restless search for status and the good opinion of others; and betterment cannot be understood as merely an economic act.

This, of course, is what is taking place at Christmas. But are there any rules or clear dynamics to this gift-giving – what Avner Offer of Nuffield College, Oxford, describes in an intriguing and subtle paper as the satisfaction of 'regard'? This economy of regard, allowing human beings to express their humanity and desire for sociability, is as important to the good society as market exchange – but it lacks any systematic explanation. This Dr Offer sets out to remedy.

The key point about regard is that this is a commodity of which the traders are true monopolists; only they can supply it. But herein lies a great paradox. As soon as someone places a cash value on their good opinion of you, the regard is devalued; to be authentic and to have worth, regard cannot be priced. This is why at Christmas, Dr Offer argues, we are so reluctant to give cash as a gift – and even when we do (because it is much more efficient), we try to disguise it as book tokens or vouchers, or even sugar the pill by including the cash in a Christmas card.

Cash is faceless and too much like a wage; it turns the economy of regard into the economy of market exchange, which precisely undermines its purpose. If a relationship has a cash value we cease to be monopolists of our regard, and enter the market exchange economy where commodities are priced. Like prostitutes, our love is now up for sale – and the cherished regard is no longer worth having. Indeed, it is the very uncertainty about the 'price' that is put on our relationship and to what degree our gift will be reciprocated that defines the whole economy of regard.

But this quest for regard is not only about satisfying our humanity as social beings; it has its own economic logic. When we interact socially we open up the chance of gaining regard. Indeed, the only way to gain regard is to have social relations. Regard both promotes sociability and is promoted by it.

This is where the economy of regard overlaps with the economy of market exchange. Advances in game theory and even in biology show that co-operation is more efficient than competition. In the animal kingdom, those species that have the capacity to be nice rather than nasty to each other gain an evolutionary advantage; computer tournaments simulating various games strategies show that co-operation between participants produces better results than competitive ploys.

What has raised human society above animal barbarism is the capacity to co-operate; but co-operation depends upon sociability – and sociability is propelled by the economy of regard.

The key social unit in which the economy of regard dominates is the family. Sexual exchange, Dr Offer writes, is a form of gifting that underwrites marriage – in the same way that the gifting of time, commitment and love underwrites the relationship between parents and children and from which both parties benefit. Parental care is a crucial, unmeasured, gifted ingredient in the formation of human capital – and one reciprocated by children when their turn comes to care for their ageing parents.

And these are expensive gifts. Bringing up two children costs the average woman who gives up work more than £200,000, according to one estimate – while one in seven British adults, about six million people, is providing unpaid care to a family member, friend or neighbour. None of these relationships is defined by an exact calculus of economic advantage as supposed by the free market textbooks – but without this functioning of the regard economy society would break down. The public expenditure cost of replacing the gifted care of the elderly, says Dr Offer, would alone exceed the current spending on the NHS.

But gifting and the exchange of regard intrudes well beyond the family. Any good salesman knows that closing a deal depends upon having built up a strong personal relationship of trust with the customer – and successful entrepreneurs have relied upon a solid network of financial backers who have trusted them through the uncertainties of growing a young business.

And even that Santa Claus employer, apparently gifting his workers job security and higher than necessary wages, is getting back higher morale and commitment – and, by lowering job turnover, saving him- or herself the necessity of retraining and then closely monitoring new recruits to see if they can perform as well as is wanted.

The economy of regard is the essential glue of both a well-performing capitalism and the good society.

This is understood, if only subliminally, by every human being. It is why there is growing scepticism at the blind way the government is driving impersonal market relations beyond their proper domain – from privatizing the recruitment of civil servants to running the blood service as a business. Reciprocity, trust and giving without calculation underpin our sociability – so don't get too angry at those credit card bills as you survey the financial ruin of another Christmas. You have been playing your part in the economy of regard; and your lack of certainty about whether it is all going to be reciprocated is part of the human condition – and why those right-wing thinkers and commentators warming to Tony Blair and idolizing Michael Portillo, who insist on the primacy of market relations, are on the wrong side of the argument.

So stand your friends another round of drinks! A happy and prosperous new year in the economy of regard.

Guardian, 27 December 1995

Happiness that Money Truly cannot Buy

Friendship is under assault. Across the industrialized world there is a rise in clinical depression – and the single best protection against it, psychologists find, is the presence of friends and family solidarity.

But we are making fewer friends than we did. The consumer society and too much exposure to market relations, it seems, are part of the process of losing us friendships, weakening bonds of kinship and bringing less happiness.

This would have seemed an unremarkable observation to Marx or Freud. Both averred that the logic of market capitalism was to turn too many relationships into commodities that are bought and sold – thus destroying their worth. The point of friendship is its particularity and non-tradability; it is specific to the two parties to the relationship and cannot be sold on or exchanged. Its very value is the bond created over time – what economists call sunk costs. Even Michael Portillo would not want freely to trade his friendships.

But the late twentieth century lacks critics of capitalism of the stature of a Marx, Freud or Keynes – so that when the current recovery does not generate a feel-good effect the debate about why is essentially sterile. The John Major/Jerry Hanley view is that perceptions are lagging behind reality and voters will soon realize that the economy is doing well. Without a robust anti-capitalist intellectual tradition to draw on, few dare take on such a Panglossian view with any confidence.

Yet it could be that the old critics of capitalism were right – and that the lack of a feel-good factor betrays a more fundamental malaise: that while capitalism may be efficient at generating wealth and change, it remains as destructive of what human beings value most. It is the very march of deregulation and laissez-faire economics about which Conservatives boast that is generating the insecurity and perceived loss of individual control to impersonal economic forces that lie at the heart of the current mood.

This is the central platform for a paper* by Professor Robert Lane of Yale University. He cites work showing how those under forty years of age are three times more likely to become severely depressed than older groups. Other research reports that across nine countries people born after 1945 are ten times more likely to suffer depression than those born fifty years earlier. In Britain between 1985 and 1990, there was a 42 per cent rise in mood disorders among children aged under ten.

The question is why. The rise in depression signifies a wider unease in society that is reflecting itself not just in depressed consumer confidence but in widespread insecurity.

The weakening of interpersonal bonds and sanctions that makes it possible for Lloyd's syndicates to cheat on their Names or cars to be broken into wantonly is also uprooting people's interrelationships. Once those start

* Robert Lane, *The Path Less Chosen: Giving Friendship Priority over Commodities* (Yale University).

to go, their personal esteem falls, which in turn generates inadequate personal relationships.

Professor Lane stresses that lifting consumption, either through raising the growth rate or lowering personal income taxes – the economistic response of pundits and right-wing Tory backbenchers – will not improve well-being. There are rewards from consumption, but they are nothing like as great as economists boast. Human well-being is much more complex than simply sating wants by spending in the high street, Professor Lane argues, and he shows how one index of well-being ranks the principal source of satisfaction as family (especially for men). Financial security follows, and then 'having fun'. Acquisition of goods and services ranks below even one's chance of getting a good job.

But Professor Lane warns against simply blaming the market. It is obvious that before you can commoditize relationships there must be a predominant economic and social organization built around negotiable market contracts, thus extending the capacity to subject human relationship to the iron laws of supply and demand. Yet the existence of market contracts does not mean necessarily that friendships have to be sacrificed; human beings, Professor Lane says, have an infinite capacity to compartmentalize their behaviour and protect their humanity from market rationality.

Moreover, the market itself only survives if parties to contracts are prepared to trust each other – to accept some basic non-market rules of human intercourse. This is why Robert Frank in his book *Passion Within Reason* argues that emotions – jealousy, anger, love – are essential to successful economic interaction; and why face-to-face contact is important. Only thus can we make judgements about the trustworthiness of the person with whom we are doing business. Only by threatening our rage and anger or offering our reward through affection can we reduce that risk.

For example, face-to-face contact has long been one of the secrets of the London financial markets' capacity to create relations of trust – coexisting with some of the fastest-moving and most flexible markets in the world. But if for centuries 'my word is my bond' was one of London's anchors because of the implied reputation for integrity, the notion has suffered a decline in the last twenty years. Think only of the Lloyd's insurance market or the pensions scandal to see how standards have declined – paralleling the rise in personal depression.

The common thread is not the fact of the market economy, but the market economy when it runs to excess – extending the principle deep into society as the new right has done.

Here, economic efficiency is said to be created only by reproducing shadow markets, as in the NHS or BBC; happiness is predicated upon consumption, and the only virtuous activity is material enrichment. Once this culture becomes common, Lloyd's insiders can justify their amoral behaviour towards their Names, and the National Blood Transfusion Service can feel no compunction about regarding itself as a business and blood as a commodity like any other.

But markets, as Lloyd's showed, need human value systems of trust alongside the calculus of market rationality to function well – as does the blood service. Not only that: once markets are allowed to threaten family and financial security the consequences are incalculable. Indeed, social psychologists are now revisiting John Bowlby's ideas that security is the key to human well-being, with only secure families able to offer love to children. If security is in short supply, parents turn to their children for it – inverting the parent-child relationship.

If all this is true, then the lack of a feel-good recovery betrays a more serious malaise. The new structures in the labour market, with the increasing difficulty of securing and holding a full-time job, do not merely raise the saving rate or deter consumption. They are entering the very marrow of human experience – and impacting on our readiness and capacity to build and maintain networks of families and friends, which are the prime source of human satisfaction.

During the 1990s, more than 300,000 people every month joined the ranks of the unemployed – more than 1 per cent of the labour force and many more than in the 1970s. At the same time, one in eight of the unemployed leave the totals every month – finding work or dropping out of the labour market altogether.

The average retirement age has continued shrinking to below 55. Most people are at greater risk of being unemployed – and having their working lives truncated – than at any time since the war. The fall in unemployment in 1994, although welcome, has not basically changed that picture.

The forces generating these changes are well known. Britain's employment protection legislation is weak. The demand on boardrooms to produce high returns is intense – and the easiest way to deliver in a period of low inflation is by stripping out labour costs. The risks of fluctuating demand are no longer absorbed by companies; they are displaced on to their workforces. Risk, actual and perceived, has increased hugely.

But the support systems have been weakened – both those offered by the state and our informal networks of friends and family. Economic recovery will continue in 1995 but the human malaise will intensify; capitalism has been allowed too much freedom and its success has been too unqualified.

In the meantime, drink to your friends and family this Christmas week; even if they irritate you, they are the shields against depression – and, if things carry on as they are, there may be fewer of them around in ten years' time.

Guardian, 27 December 1994

PART IX

Lessons from Elsewhere: Alternative Models of Capitalism

Tory Fantasy of Far Eastern Promise

It was an important week. It set the seal on the Conservative Party's decisive move to the right that began with Major's resignation in July and is now largely complete. The new right embraces easily the most right-wing ideological position since the war; a high-risk gamble, but in the current circumstances the least bad option.

The party – creature and ally of the British state throughout its history – has declared war on the very institution that made it. A new iron has entered Conservatism's soul. The liberal, one-nation wing has joined the Redwood/Portillo right in regarding lower public expenditure not merely as a means of lowering taxes, but of reinventing Britain as an Asian-style success story. The extraordinary growth rates of the 'Asian tiger' economies – Hong Kong, Taiwan, Singapore, South Korea, Thailand, Malaysia – are said to have been built upon a small state with minimal public expenditure, light regulation and low taxation. Britain must follow their example.

The minimal state is not just a preoccupation of those who believe in curbing the state's size for ideological ends: it is seen as the route to prosperity and growth. The redefinition of priorities does not stop there. Britain must reorganize its trade and foreign policy to be less Eurocentric and concentrate on building trade and diplomatic links with these new Asian markets. This requires, as a minimum, a semi-detached relationship with over-regulated Europe. This is the foreign policy position which Malcolm Rifkind announced in Blackpool. A crushing argument is used with doubters: globalization and competition make any other course impossible.

So compelling is the logic of all this that if the European Union makes it difficult for Britain to pursue its new destiny of becoming the Hong Kong of Europe, there are a growing number joining the Maastricht rebels in arguing that Britain must leave the Union. Norman Lamont openly floats this option, and this week released a pamphlet setting out his arguments.

Euroscepticism and the urge to find pre-election tax cuts are integrated into a wider Conservative view of the world; even the one-nation wing finds it difficult to dissent from this. John Redwood loosed the idea in July, the party conference endorsed it and last week one of the great (if slightly used) battle-cruisers of the Conservative left, the Governor of Hong Kong and ex-chairman of the party, Chris Patten, gave it his thoughtful imprimatur. It was no accident that Douglas Hurd, speaking on the same day, also licensed it.

Yet the party may be making a colossal mistake – mainly because the project is so outlandish and so poorly grounded in fact that even the Conservative Party could not sell it to a sceptical electorate. The British may not want or be able to become surrogate Asians – nor is it desirable that they should. The entire concept rests upon an incorrect theory of Asian success; and in the long run, the viability of arguments matters. The means to change our state – damaging cuts in already tight public spending in the run-up to an election – will be impossible to disguise from a British public stubbornly attached to the things the state provides, from public libraries to the NHS. Even Patten, in his speech, acknowledged that the minimal state was not the only reason for Asian success. But the point stood. Patten agreed with the basic proposition – that the small state, low government spending and free markets are necessary and sufficient conditions for growth. Public spending should fall below 40 per cent of national income and stay there.

But no serious inquiry into the origins of Asian growth supports the Conservative thesis. Asian growth has not turned on low government spending, but rather on high investment and saving ratios, nearly twice as large as anywhere else in the world. Cheap and plentiful investment capital is the most important determinant of growth everywhere, not just in Asia. Low government spending did not deliver such high saving and investment rates; almost everywhere, these result from government action – savings are compulsory and governments ensure that the savings are used for industrial and commercial investment. In South Korea, Thailand, Malaysia, Taiwan and even Singapore the government has gone even further – directly starting industrial enterprises while protecting and sponsoring others.

Studies from distinguished social scientists and business analysts, including the LSE's Professor Ronald Dore, Robert Wade at the Institute of Development Studies, Japanologist James Abbelgen and, most recently, Francis Fukuyama report the same phenomena – even if they stress different aspects. Asian capitalism is dynamic in part because it is more longterm in its outlook since it depends less on Anglo-Saxon-style stock markets; in part because of the role of vigorous company networks, often underpinned by families, in securing a steady base load of orders and mutual support for individual firms; in part because an enabling state backs young firms, provides cheap credit, constructs chains of suppliers and stimulates the use of new technology. Even a study by the World Bank conceded that the state had often been central to generating growth – if only through building an educated and trained labour force. Surprisingly, it also concluded that equality stabilized growth.

The intervention has been market-friendly and the governments firmly committed to capitalism. But to equate Asian success with the minimal state is wrong – as anybody familiar with Singapore's Lee Kuan Yew, South Korea's generals or Japan's extensive system of administrative guidance would bear testimony. There is cut-throat competition and pursuit of profit – but the cultural and social context is very different from that imagined by the Conservatives. Charles Hampden Turner, co-author of *The Seven Cultures Of Capitalism*, argues that Asian capitalism (and Japan in particular) shares its approach to competition with the martial arts tradition; the idea is not to knock your opponent out and establish monopoly dominance but to recognize his value in providing competition. If he is in trouble, you stand back to let him recover. This is not the Tory concept of primitive competitive capitalism.

And can those double-digit growth rates continue – dependent as they are on ready access to the US market, vast social dislocation and environmental degradation? During the Cold War, the US was prepared to accept Asia's booming exports as part of the price of supporting those societies against the threat of communism; no longer.

Asian growth rates, although high, have begun to subside. Professor Paul Krugman of the Massachusetts Institute of Technology argues that such growth was the result of 'perspiration rather than inspiration' – it forced people into factories, depleting the labour pool. This could only be done once. As the costs of environmental degradation catch up, the growth rates will slow; more so as it becomes clear that the foundations of growth – suppressing demands for decent living standards and working conditions from newly industrial workforces, often through banning trade unions and military intervention – are neither sustainable nor tolerable. Ralph Dahrendorf stresses this: success has been delivered by a social authoritarianism that is anathema to western liberal democracies.

Yet to a Conservative Party increasingly attracted to social authoritarianism, this is a positive merit. The old right like the idea of further limitation of trade union rights, the regulation of sexual relations to curb single parents, the introduction of corporal and even capital punishment, and the elimination of the 'dependency culture' by allowing the poor to suffer the consequences of being poor. If they can be dressed up as necessary preconditions for economic and social success because they all occur in Asia, ancient prejudices can be given their head. The libertarian instincts of the new right can be abandoned – and a populist authoritarianism can take their place.

This process has been under way for some years, and Michael Howard at the Home Office and Peter Lilley at Social Security are taking it further. Howard's flirtation with repressive authoritarian changes to the criminal justice system is well documented – less so Lilley's changes to the welfare state. Individually, these may seem trifling; but together they represent a substantial change in its role as a comprehensive safety net. Unemployment benefit is to become the job seekers' allowance available only conditionally; sickness benefit has become incapacity benefit, payable only after much tougher tests; housing benefit, the *Guardian* disclosed this week, is to become more minimal without discretion to help individual cases. Britain, running the lowest-cost social security system in the West, including North America, is to tighten it still further.

Health and education services are also under intense pressure which this year's budget negotiations will increase. In health, the private finance initiative, charging and rationing will together end the NHS as a universal system of health provision; in education, the standardization of expenditure as vouchers are introduced means the balkanization of a universal education system. Governmental functions are broken down into Next Steps agencies. The ultimate Conservative fantasy is being enacted before our eyes: the state is being privatized.

This is now being given extra ideological edge by the foredoomed attempt to emulate the Asians. The state, even in Asia, has played a more creative role than Conservatives allow. Cuts in public spending will have a depressive rather than stimulating impact on economic activity. Economic management is a more subtle art than a rolling back of the state and a celebration of price stability; and capitalism is a more subtle system than free market theorists imagine. It needs to be managed, as the Asians have proved.

And there is a larger question of values. Social authoritarianism and purposeful neglect of the living conditions of the majority have no parallel in British cultural and political traditions. The Conservative right invokes a mystic reverence for a 'Britishness' based on the sovereignty of the House of Commons, but Britain pioneered religious tolerance, stood as a first custodian of universal human rights, threw over repression as a means of social and political regulation, and curbed the excesses of capitalism. There is no political or cultural validation for the Conservative path. You cannot find it in the writings of John Stuart Mill – or of Jane Austen.

Britain is not compelled to surrender its commitment to social justice, public endeavour or its own cultural legacy, despite the posturing about globalization (less complete than the right would have us believe). The idea that the country could become an independent global actor, or important in Asia, is political fantasy. This is desperate stuff. It is a political opportunity for the Opposition, but also a source of alarm. The Conservative Party has lost its bearings. Given its historical claim on power this could yet be very dangerous – for both the British state and society.

Guardian, 28 October 1995

Britain Falls Short of the Mark

It is less than three years since John Major mused that, following the Thatcher reforms, sterling was set to overtake the sclerotic German mark and become the strongest currency in Europe. Sterling then stood at DM3; on Friday night it closed at an all-time low, just below DM2.24. Germany may not meet the approval of the British new right, but it does pass the market test.

Yet Mr Major was not alone. *The Economist, Sunday Times* editorials and other cheerleaders for the British free market experiment had written off the German economy. Its over-strong trade unions and tightly regulated economy contrasted unfavourably with British 'flexibility', while high government expenditure and taxation were throttling the private sector.

With welfare spending running at levels half as high again as in Britain, a minimum wage and firms sheltered from the efficiency-inducing pressure of take-over, the German economy was a basket case. Inward investment was flooding to low-cost Britain and soon the capital markets would follow. Anybody who knew anything about economics could see that – couldn't they?

Yet the German economy last year lowered unit costs by 10 per cent, the steepest decline in the postwar period. German export volumes grew by only 8 per cent last year, a source of much despair in the republic – while Britain's 8 per cent growth, already tailing off while Germany's accelerated, was hailed as a miracle. And if Germany is plagued by unemployment, in the west of the country the rate never went as high as in Britain – and is currently falling from 8.1 per cent, compared with our 8.5 per cent.

Let's get real. As German growth picks up to 3 per cent over the next two years, combined with inflation of 2–2.5 per cent, and the budget deficit incurred from reunification falls back to the lowest in Europe, there is only one conclusion. Germany delivers. Here is a capitalist economy that combines price stability, social cohesion and solid growth – even if there are cracks in the seams and much internal self-examination.

What is the secret? It is productivity. The institutional apparatus that the new right deplores is part of the social market economy that delivers high investment, high skills and high productivity – and from which flow high real wages, low nominal wage growth and the revenue base to fund Germany's famed social security system. Output per worker is about a fifth higher than in Britain. This is relational rather than spot-market capitalism – a system that tries to marry the gains from co-operation and consensus with the dynamism of profit-seeking enterprise.

The structure has three interlocking supports. There is the centralized wage-bargaining system in which industry-wide unions negotiate with industry-wide associations to set a wage contract that becomes the industry minimum – defying the arguments of the British Department of Employment that only decentralized wage bargaining with employees in weak or non-existent unions can produce rational settlements. The German model, as the graph shows, produces consistently low wage growth; herein, as much as the independence of the Bundesbank, lies the secret of Germany's low inflation.

Building upon the predictability of low inflation, there is a training and financial system committed to investment in human and physical capital. The dual training system combines vocational courses in schools and technical colleges with on-the-job training – paid for partly by the state and partly by firms. Two million apprentices profit, compared with a quarter of a million in Britain, giving Germany the best-trained workforce in Europe.

In support there is an investment-friendly financial system, furnishing German industry with an avalanche of cheap, low-margin, long-term debt while guaranteeing firms security of ownership. The lower cost of capital and the lower target returns to keep more patient, committed shareholders happy also allow investment levels to stay at 20–25 per cent of GDP – a quarter higher over the cycle than in Britain. Result: higher productivity.

Yet the system faces growing criticism – of which Professor Norbert Walter's debate contribution, from the right of the economic spectrum, is typical. Germany is losing its dynamism, runs the argument. The emphasis on 'relational capitalism' has gone too far, obstructing innovation and flexibility.

The criticisms tend to start with the wage bargaining system – especially after last week's effective 4.5 per cent wage settlement between the metal workers' union, IG Metall, and the engineering employers. The complaints are not only confined to the right.

Claus Schnabel, at the centrist Institute for German Business in Cologne, wants more flexibility in the way industry-wide wage deals are interpreted. New firms are not signing up to industry associations, he says, because they want the freedom to tailor wage deals to individual circumstances. Large firms may be able to afford the settlement, but keep their overall costs down by demanding huge price cuts from their subcontractors – who cannot afford them because they are forced to pay the same industry-wide wage deal.

Germany's *Mittelstand* – the medium-sized business sector – is picking up the bill for social solidarity, but as international competition intensifies, it can no longer afford to pay. What is more, with neighbours such as Poland, Hungary and the Czech Republic – where wages are a tenth of those in Germany – the danger is that firms will simply relocate production in order to lower costs.

Siegmar Mosdorf, a rising economic star in the SPD, is concerned about the lack of innovation, with Germany seemingly incapable of moving from its staple industries of chemicals, engineering and automobiles. The financial system does not supply the amount of British- and American-style venture capital for new start-ups – but there are also signs it wants to back away from its role of providing long-term finance and involving itself closely in company affairs. Deutsche Bank no longer wants to fulfil its historic role of providing a chairman for the steel company Thyssen – and this on its 125th birthday!

But the observer needs to be wary. Every recession since the mid-1960s has been marked by waves of German self-examination and self-doubt. According to University College's German expert, Wendy Carling, angst about the durability of the social market is a key mechanism for its continual modernization.

In any case, German capitalists are not the bunch of softies depicted by their critics. In east Germany, many sectors employ only a fifth of the labour force that they did five years ago, while manufacturing employment in the west has shrunk by 12.5 per cent over the last two years – echoing the severity of job-shedding in Britain in the early 1980s. Labour productivity has surged by 15 per cent over the last two years – an improvement unmatched by deregulated Britain.

And this, as Wolfgang Scheremet of the German Institute for Economic Research in Berlin points out, has been negotiated with Germany's social settlement remaining intact. In fact, it is because it has remained intact that it has been so easy to get union agreement to swingeing job cuts and even, as in the case of Volkswagen, wage cuts. Consensus still delivers more rational outcomes than the exercise of brutal employer power in an atomized labour market.

Nor are the fears of a German capital flight borne out by the figures. In 1993 (the last year for which full figures are available), Germany's total investment was DM550 billion – and only DM1.4 billion was invested in eastern Europe. Of total overseas investment of DM20 billion, three-quarters was directed at the rest of the industrialized world. If anything, eastern Europe is being short-changed.

Despite all the questioning, the Germans remain wedded to their economic model. Bankers will continue to provide long-term finance, but more flexibly; the wage bargaining system will continue, with concessions over how the 1,630 hours per worker worked every year are distributed. The debate is how to modernize and adapt the social market economy; not replace it with Britain's spot-market, low-investment, low-productivity capitalism.

The Germans, for so long a menace to themselves and Europe, have constructed a civilization in which social cohesion and prosperity are inter-dependent. If the model founders before the demands of globalization, there is little hope for the rest of us. Spot-market barbarism will reign.

Guardian, 13 March 1995

Germany Defies Prophets of Doom

Suppose manufacturing productivity in Britain had jumped 20 per cent in two years, unit labour costs had fallen in 1994 for the first time since the war and exports from the poorest fifth of the country were growing at nearly 25 per cent as it reindustrialized at a pace surpassing Asia's miracle econ-omies. The Conservative press and the OECD would be cooing with delight.

Moreover, if inflation was 2 per cent, growth rising on trend, the trade surplus booming and the public-sector borrowing requirement a mere 2 per cent of national output, the evidence would be nearly complete. Here was a well-run economy that was set fair. Ministers would claim vindica-tion for the government's policies of avoiding the sclerotic regulations, strong trade unions and high taxes that plague competitor countries like Ger-many.

Sadly, however, this economy is not Britain; it is Germany. It is, of course, not a completely rosy picture. Unemployment in the western four-fifths of the country is nearly as bad as in Britain, at around 8.2 per cent, but in east Germany it is considerably higher. The dynamism of German exports has come in the country's historically strong areas – chemicals, capital goods and engineering – and there has not been the same success in some of the rapidly growing high-tech sectors. The rate of new business formation and inward investment is also lower than in Britain.

The question is whether these weaknesses portend the collapse of the German model and British-style capitalism points the way to the future. This is the Cabinet's view and, in a less ideologically committed way, of the Treasury, Bank of England and mainstream opinion. Economic success depends on macroeconomic stability and market-orientated supply-side reforms – code for weakened trade unions, minimal welfare, attracting inward investment and low taxes. Trying to copy the German framework is futile.

It is so German that neither the system nor any of its parts are reproducible in the UK. It may have worked well in the past, but in a global marketplace all national economic institutions, however long-termist, have to submit to the same forces that have compelled Britain to take the route it has. Even Tony Blair in his Mais lecture, while admitting German financial institutions might have merits as instruments of long-termism, saw little reason for doing the same thing in Britain.

Yet put at its mildest the consensus is inconsistent and short on evidence. The supposed inability to import 'foreign' institutions and practices proves to be highly selective – so that the Bank of England, shaking its head at the mistaken innocence of commentators who want to introduce German industrial investment banks into Britain to address short-termism, is one of the most fervent advocates of copying the independence of the Bundesbank. If it suits the interests of the Establishment, German institutions are copiable; if not, then they are beyond the pale.

The view that the German system is redundant is hardly supported by the facts – and in this respect the OECD's report on Germany published last week is a landmark. The OECD is instinctively hostile to almost all of the elements in the German model – from its bank-dominated financial system to its tax-financed welfare system. Yet it had to concede that Germany was doing well. Far from Britain triumphing in the battle of the economic models, it was more likely that there would be a convergence around the best of the two, the OECD opined.

The key German attribute is the high level of investment, so that, for example, manufacturing capital per worker is half as high again as in Britain. The Bank/Treasury line is that this is wholly explicable in terms of Germany's macroeconomic stability – and has nothing to do with Germany's financial system or the system of decision-making in German firms.

This is an astonishingly absolutist argument, but it is where you are led if you do not want to challenge the structures of the City and British capitalism – and also believe that decisions taken in free markets are unimprovable. The City is a series of free financial markets, hence the institutions and practices are necessarily the best. If the outcomes are poor, the reasons lie elsewhere – bad government macroeconomic policy. Governments make mistakes; private agents never do.

Yet the OECD devotes a chapter of its report to ownership, control and decision-making in German firms, tacitly recognizing that these structures deserve to be investigated on their own terms rather than seen as creatures of a low-inflation environment. Moreover, it is forced to concede that the way the system works is a source of strength, lowering financing costs, lengthening time horizons and lifting investment. It may rely on the 'continuous participation by banks, business partners and employees in the running of companies', in contrast to the British model, where the shareholder interest is dominant.

The OECD refutes the rather silly arguments in a recent paper from the Centre for Economic Policy Research, *Banks, Finance and Investment*, that German patterns of company financing are not dissimilar to those elsewhere. The OECD shows how the system must be examined in its entirety – linking company decision-making, ownership patterns and the structure of the financial institutions.

The system in which the voting rights in German firms are pooled in the banks' hands so that ownership is stable also ensures that banks get high-quality information; this guarantees high levels of long-term loans – supplemented by government-owned investment banks – and low dividend pay-outs. These, combined with low inflation and the tax system, mean that German firms have some of the cheapest after-tax funds among leading industrialized countries. No one element is responsible for all this; the way the system works is the key.

There has also been a text-book example of the structure at work – in east Germany. Five years ago, the region was a basket case: there were few viable trading enterprises – and west Germany had to assume the burden of financing a new industrial infrastructure for 16 million people. The mobilization of long-term finance, channelled in the main through west German firms taking over bankrupt east German companies and supported by German banks, has been awesome; and now the results are coming through. Growth in 1994 was 9.2 per cent; unemployment is dropping sharply; migration to the west is falling; exports are booming; investment is high. If Britain had faced the same challenges would it have produced such results?

The OECD is forced to concede the system's merits. It advocates rectifying faults such as the lack of venture capital for high-tech business start-ups, but there is no call to privatize the state investment banks or enlarge the role of pension funds and insurance companies as share owners at the expense of banks. Indeed, it says that the continuous monitoring of management by banks and employees goes a long way towards remedying the deficiencies of the stock market system, where the only recourse when management is poor is to sell to hostile predators. It even recognizes that the system of financing and ownership partly explains Germany's lower strike record, low levels of job turnover and higher levels of training.

At bottom Germany is successful because it limits and directs the power of capital, so producing better results than if it were left to its own devices. This is partly a legacy of the national effort at postwar reconstruction; partly because the structure is an 'insiders' system, sanctified by German nationality laws; and partly because the system's success has helped to perpetuate its legitimacy.

It cannot be imported wholesale into Britain, nor should it – but we can try to find ways of doing the same things in British style. Capital does require regulation, and long-termism has to be entrenched within institutions. The OECD believes the two systems will converge, but even that presupposes a degree of change for which few are arguing – and even fewer are prepared.

Guardian, 4 September 1995

Shock that Threatens Downtown America

President Clinton, in his State of the Union address last night, spoke to a Middle America that has never had it so tough. Men's wages, even for those with a college degree, have been falling in real terms for over ten years. (It may be even rougher at the bottom of the pile – but generosity of spirit doesn't come readily when your own living standards are under such constant pressure.) It is this constituency that voted so enthusiastically for Newt Gingrich and the Republican Contract with America fifteen months ago. Taxes, big government and welfare were at the heart of the American malaise, argued the Republicans – and tax cuts seem even more desirable when your own income is falling. Gingrich's trick was to appeal to self-interest and the public interest at the same time.

But even as Washington reverberates to the sound of Democratic President and Republican Congress arguing not over the merits of downsizing government, but rather over the pace of change and to what degree the poor should share the burden, there are subtle signs that the argument is moving on. The Americans are beginning to be alarmed at developments in their famed 'flexible' labour market, and worried that inequality and under-employment may menace not merely the economy, but beyond it the good society and even the American dream.

After all, it was de Tocqueville who argued in the 1830s that it was the 'equality of conditions' that underlay the stability and unity of American society, along with Americans' notions of social and political equality. Now, as American inequality climbs to new heights, sound heads – even on the right – are querying whether de Tocqueville's aphorism still holds. This degree of inequality may be unsustainable.

The American political debate is as yet resounding to the familiar tunes, with multi-millionaire publisher Steve Forbes challenging for the

Republican presidential nomination, climbing the opinion polls in the New Hampshire primary by canvassing a regressive flat-rate 17 per cent income tax for all. But sooner or later reality breaks in on even the most ideological of positions.

Larry Lindsey used to work in the White House advising George Bush, and as an economist of Reaganite persuasions became a governor of the Federal Reserve Board – the US central bank – in 1991. The former Harvard professor holds impeccably conservative views about the merits of balanced budgets, the distorting impact of taxation and the need to shrink government – but his evidence to the House of Representatives last month about the worrying trends in income inequality makes gripping reading.

Mr Lindsey is worried, as a central banker, that too many low-income families are incurring too much credit-card debt. The credit card is the great badge of membership of American society, with the credit-card companies this year planning to market 2.7 billion cards to 250 million Americans – up from 2.1 billion last year. In the old days the credit card was the preserve of middle- and upper-income groups, but demand is rising dramatically from low-income Americans – both to have their badge of membership and to finance credit so as to maintain their standard of living as their incomes fall.

It's not the 'democratization' of credit that worries Lindsey, with the proportion of black and low-income households reporting credit-card debt nearly as high as white middle-income households; it's that the trends are unsustainable. Workers generally are receiving a lower share of national income than they used to; but low-income families' income is falling sharply as hourly wage rates drop in real terms. Nor, with current tax and welfare policies, is there any end to the process in sight. Ultimately falling incomes will collide with rising debt, and servicing the credit-card debt will become impossible – a financial crisis waiting to be triggered by the next round of interest-rate increases which will one day come.

Lindsey dismisses the Gingrichian argument that workers are compensated in part by rising dividends and stock prices through their share holdings in mutual funds (American versions of unit trusts). Eighty per cent of households, says this Republican economist, receive no dividends at all; and 2.5 per cent of households receive three-quarters of all dividend payments. Most Americans live off their declining wage packets, and as the share of wages in national income falls towards 50 per cent from the 66.6 per cent it used to be in 1960, the growth of consumption is faltering as well.

Lindsey is suitably cautious, but his message is unmistakable. In the same way that the quadrupling of oil prices in the early 1970s represented an economic shock, so rising inequality is a form of economic shock today. It threatens financial stability and the sustainability of the US recovery alike.

But it doesn't stop there. American society is rocking from the fall in hourly wage rates for unskilled men and the accompanying disguised un-employment – MIT's Professor Lester Thurow reckons that true unem-ployment is nearer 14 per cent than the official 6 per cent. Hourly wage rates of $5 (£3.30) or less do not offer even subsistence diets and rents; but that is the rate for more than 10 per cent of US jobs. With 2 million extra to join their numbers as the Gingrichian welfare 'reforms' bite, US econ-omists estimate that wages at the bottom will fall by up to another 15 per cent.

But in desperation the badly paid are leaving the labour market alto-gether, stealing and dealing in drugs just to survive. One-third of all Amer-ican blacks between the ages of eighteen and thirty are now either in prison, awaiting trial or on bail. This is close to an urban hell.

In Chicago a group of researchers from the local universities has estab-lished that there are four job-seekers for every job opening in Illinois – and that only 4 per cent of the jobs on offer would allow a welfare recipient with children to provide for basic family needs. In Chicago alone, a city of 3 million, wages are so low and welfare so threadbare that 80,000 individ-uals cannot pay rents even for the worst housing, and with public housing being phased out, there is no option but to live on the street. If reproduced in Britain this would imply 1.5 million living rough.

Yet this is the world that John Redwood, in Washington on Monday to ally his Conservative 2000 think-tank with the Gingrichian Progress and Freedom Foundation, invites us to emulate. There may be powerful forces – international competition, the pressure from the financial system for ever higher returns, new technologies that compel corporate 'downsizing' and 'delayering' – that are generating these trends, but that raises questions. Even if efforts to modify them are condemned to fail, itself a contestable proposition, it is not true that nothing can be done to alleviate the results.

For something must be done. Downtown Chicago is resplendent in its skyscraping affluence and self-confidence; but nearby there is the growing urban wilderness of South Chicago. The gangrene of violence and decay will engulf even the downtown area one day. Conservatives are coming to recognize this, and also that redress will involve extra taxation and collect-ive effort. The social questions of redistribution are about to re-enter Amer-ican politics even at the zenith of the right's success. They will surely cross the Atlantic too.

Guardian, 24 January 1996

Age of Anxiety as Communism Collapses

The collapse of communism and the retreat of Russia to its smallest size since the eighteenth century are events whose implications are still barely understood. An empire and an ideology which dominated the Euro-Asian land mass have disappeared; in their place are fifteen new states with more – witness the events in Chechnya – trying to join.

All simultaneously confront an economic, social and environmental legacy from communism that beggars description. Not only do they not possess the industrial and service-sector capacity of even a banana republic; communism also destroyed their legal systems and political cultures.

The jubilation with which the collapse of communism was greeted has now passed into growing anxiety about the future. Eastern Europe may, with proper access to western Europe's markets, succeed in following the trail blazed by Poland and the Czech Republic, where output is growing and inflation easing – but for the former Soviet Union (FSU) the problems look increasingly intractable. Descent into economic and political anarchy is ever more likely – and western Europe cannot expect to remain immune.

But so grievous is the communist legacy that no other outcome seems possible. Plainly there have been horrendous policy mistakes made by the FSU republics, and the 'shock therapy' suggested by some western advisers was imposed on countries without financial or labour markets, or even legal and social security systems. Inevitably it has produced social and economic distress with little positive to show for it – as John Gray argues in his recent pamphlet for the Social Market Foundation. But criticizing shock therapy is easier than developing a viable alternative economic programme.

For, given the starting point, there was no easy way of turning the republics of the FSU into functioning capitalist economies, complete with democratic institutions and functioning party systems. And, as the leading exponent of 'shock therapy', Jeffrey Sachs, fires back in his Social Market Foundation response to Gray, the idea that economic transformation could be undertaken without any budgetary and monetary disciplines is equal madness. The resultant hyperinflation would have wrecked the entire enterprise.

The Gray/Sachs exchange is eloquent testimony to the desperate economic and political straits in which Russia and the other republics find themselves – and the poverty of options open to them. While Gray correctly indicts Sachs for his ahistorical view of how capitalism came about and his attempt to make Russia conform to some hybrid of Reaganite and Thatcherite free market ideals, Sachs invites Gray to consider the commonality between capitalisms rather than their differences. Both points are valid; and both underscore the plight of the FSU.

Gray is right to argue that a variety of capitalist models could have been offered to the Russians, of which the American variant is most unsuitable and the German Rhineland social market variant more accommodating. He is also right to argue that capitalism is socially produced – partly by government design and partly by historical and cultural legacy.

The notion that free markets and industrialization happen spontaneously is for the birds. Perhaps the only example is the British Industrial Revolution – and even that required trade protection, a single market, political stability, a system of common law and a merchant class made rich by the preceding two centuries of overseas trade and empire. These were exceptional historical circumstances that free market economists have generalized into a universal truth.

The classic example of the laissez-faire delusion in the Russian case is privatization. Here the fact of private ownership *per se* is meant to bring benefits because free market economics teaches that the benefits of private ownership develop spontaneously in markets – for which the only world example, Britain, is a special case. Yet giving public enterprise back to the local workers by way of vouchers may allow the enterprise to be classed as 'private', but without the legal means of the voucher-holders exercising their ownership rights the transfer is but a legal fiction.

The same nomenklatura run the enterprise; there is no discipline on their actions; the capacity of the enterprise to raise funds externally is unchanged. Indeed, privatization can actually make things worse, because the social security system under communism was enterprise-based: health, unemployment pay and even pensions were provided by the enterprise which, once privatized, is no longer under any obligation to continue. Privatization in a legal and institutional vacuum has served to undermine the already scanty social safety-net while taking only the first step on the road to a functioning capitalism. Unless systems of company law, corporate control and capital-raising are developed in tandem, it will make things worse – not better.

Gray's view is that, had the economic transformation process been informed by the social market approach of the Germans, fewer such mistakes would have been made.

While that is reasonable enough, Gray cannot finesse the counter-point made by Sachs that, while social market and Anglo-American capitalism may have many differences, they are united by common phenomena, none of which existed in Russia and all of which had to be created. A successful capitalist economy has to have a stable currency. It must permit freedom of international trade and accept inward investment. There must be private property rights and private ownership, together with some system of corporate control. There must be a social safety-net.

Shock therapy, says Sachs, was not about detailing whether the Russians should choose the social market or Anglo-American means of establishing private property rights or corporate control; it was about saying that a beginning must be made rapidly towards some system, after which it could evolve in ways specific to Russia.

Sachs is most compelling about the imperative of establishing 'hard budget' constraints. Capitalist enterprises must have penalties for making losses; governments cannot spend without limit; central banks cannot print money with no constraint. These arguments hold, whatever capitalist form a country adopts; any other option spells perdition.

But if there is more common ground than either allows, Gray has the better of the wider argument. The march of capitalism, he says, is undermining the West's own institutions – ranging from Gatt to the European Union.

One important piece of glue was the common enemy of the communist bloc. But it has disappeared; and at the same time the rise of unemployment is unravelling the legitimacy of the postwar political settlement and destabilizing the West's democratic institutions. Sachs and his ilk are inviting the FSU to join a world that is itself in flux.

Sachs's thunderous paeans to the successful conclusion of the Uruguay round, the global capital market and the universal acceptance of the western economic model have a hollow ring beside this. Yes, western capitalism has triumphed but, as Eric Hobsbawm argues in his monumental account of the twentieth century *The Age of Extremes*, the gains cannot be regarded as secure. Western democracy, held up as a model to the FSU, is encountering a crisis of leadership and sovereignty. External economic pressures deny governments autonomy; but public opinion, shaped by an increasingly dominant media, demands instant and autonomous responses.

Yet the decline in public authority comes just as it needs to be exercised more imaginatively than ever before – both supranationally and nationally – to make the kind of political interventions for which both Sachs and Gray call. Sachs remains an unflinching apostle of the need for a more aggressive response to the FSU's needs, above all for hard currency to underpin exchange rates and so limit imported inflation.

But that is not forthcoming – paradoxically, for the very reasons Gray and Hobsbawm provide – that with the West in such flux its leaders have lost the legitimacy with their publics to launch any such initiative. Yet the issue is increasingly not social market or Anglo-American capitalism – but containing the unmanageable strains thrown up by communism's demise.

The West's own crisis impinges on the East, whose decline into anarchy will in turn intensify the West's own problems. The world needs a compass better than simple appeals to democracy and markets – but there is none to hand.

Guardian, 2 January 1995

That's the Thing about Paper Tigers: They Burn

Make no mistake. The series of devaluations, stock market crashes, bank collapses and International Monetary Fund rescue packages in Asia constitute the most serious shock to the world economy since the oil price rises of the seventies.

If the Japanese government mishandles its reaction to the gathering crisis in its banking system next week, then contagion could spread across Asia bringing not merely an economic downturn, but recession and financial calamity.

The backwash in Britain in terms of lost jobs, falling share and property prices and Asian inward investors retrenching will be felt by everyone. It will also mark the end of the laissez-faire, balance-the-books approach to running economies that has spread across the world. The conservative intellectual backdrop to New Labour not clawing back the £3 billion undershoot in its public spending plans, or the Japanese government refusing to bail out its banks, will be revealed as threadbare and exploded. Global deregulation of financial markets and the refusal by governments to manage demand will come to be seen as the handmaidens of financial collapse and unemployment. A new debate about governing the global economy and world financial markets will be joined in earnest – and the legacy of the Thatcher/Reagan years will be buried.

Already, enough has happened to force some reappraisal of the international financial system. If Portugal, Sweden and Italy had suffered stock market crashes and had applied for more than $100 billion of IMF aid, accompanied by austerity packages, then most Britons would have taken notice. If, on top, there had been a run on the banks in Holland, a financial crisis in Spain and the German government was facing the collapse of its financial system as one of its leading banks was forced into liquidation, the sense of panic would be palpable.

If we saw that the only route back to prosperity was to export to a United States that would not, and could not, accept our exports as it becomes more protectionist – and that the last buffer to supporting the international order, the IMF, was itself in danger of running short of funds – then the media would be full of doom-laden reports and discussion.

But Asia, where events of such proportions have been occurring almost daily, is far away – even if its fortunes are bound to those in Europe by ever closer trading and financial links. Half the Thai banking system can close; there can be a run on a bank in Hong Kong; the Japanese economy can totter; the IMF can impose swingeing austerity package after package – but it is hard for these events to command the attention they deserve. What they reveal is the shallowness of the international financial order, and the serious consequences of constructing a world in which governments are told not only that they should be powerless, but feel they are powerless. One of the hallmarks of this crisis, and why it is so potentially dangerous, is that Asian governments have been so uncomprehending of the forces at work.

As with all economic crises, the operation of the financial system is at its heart. One of the baleful results of the eighties was that governments heeded the special pleading of the extravagantly well-paid denizens of the world banking community and removed controls on moving their funds internationally and on what assets they might invest in – all without building any comparable global system of regulation and supervision. That has made the financial community very rich but it threatens to make the world poor.

Banking is a simple enough conception; deposits are accepted from a myriad of depositors who never want their cash back simultaneously and who are constantly replenishing themselves. This allows the bank to lend some proportion of that cash to its borrowers at a higher rate of interest than it pays out to the depositors. It is a confidence trick, but one that works as long as the activities the bank has supported with its lending are seen by everyone to be sound. If they are *not* sound, then the bank loses money and it can only pay its depositors back by digging into its own reserves. But those are finite, and once that capital is exhausted it has to cease trading.

What has happened in Asia is that the confidence trick has been unmasked, and the lending that banks have made all over the continent has been exposed as unsound. Thai banks lent to property developers to support vastly overpriced office blocks; Korean banks have supported state industries losing billions; and in the case of Yamaichi Securities, Japan's biggest ever potential bankruptcy, there was unhappy involvement in organized crime. Individually, each collapse could be handled comfortably; the problem is that they are happening simultaneously, so even sound banks are pulled into the mess. With stock markets falling on top, collateral for loans can be destroyed overnight.

Lending contracts as banks pull in their reins, and the economy slows down. If the banks start pulling in their cash from abroad, as the Japanese banks have from Korea, that slows down the economy in question even more. A vicious circle is set up. Banks now set aside some of their precious capital and reserves; that means they can lend less; and that causes prices and economic activity to slow down.

In Asia, where countries such as Korea, Thailand and Indonesia are dependent upon Japanese banks coming up with lending, the contagion spreads. First their losses hurt Japan; that makes Japanese banks less secure; they lend less abroad, so causing further losses overseas – and the whole continental economy implodes like a pricked balloon. Nor does it stop there. The backwash will be felt in Europe and America.

The way to prevent this is never to allow it to happen in the first place. Bankers and financiers always plead that they should not be regulated nor their activities tightly controlled. The world has moved from spasm to spasm as it gives into bankers' demands – as in the twenties – and then cleans up the mess – as in the thirties. Asia looks as though it is about to enter the clean-up phase of the cycle.

But the first requirement is to stop the contagion spreading any further now. All last week, the Japanese government flip-flopped about, first saying it would underwrite its banks, then allowing one to go bust, then saying it would support other banks and finally allowing Yamaichi Securities, complete with some $24 billion of liabilities to go belly up. It was an unedifying spectacle. The Japanese government first promised to respond to the prolonged slow-down in Japan by boosting demand; then it levied taxes; then it cut them – and all the time the banking system is plagued by bad debts and the economy by paucity of demand. What is required, simply, is an unconditional offer of international support for all Japanese banks – and a vast programme of public works to kick-start the economy. It may seem very Keynesian and very Old Labour; but anything less and the world faces the slump of its second biggest economy.

In sum the Asian tigers no longer look very tigerish. When they closely regulated their economies, they prospered; when they became the free market paragons of conservative imagination, they have nose-dived. Events in Asia are but another reminder of capitalism's innate instability. It may be better than any other system we know, but that does not mean we should worship at the shrine of its infallibility.

Observer, 23 November 1997

Sun, Sea, Wine and Loneliness Down Under

It's a continent on the other side of the world where British and American traditions easily commingle. Its cities boast the largest suburbs and its per-capita incomes still place it in the first rank of nations.

It's a generous and easygoing country, where beach life and surfing are integral to the way of life. But globalization and free market individualism have visited contemporary Australia – and the results are increasingly un-happy.

By the standards of economic rationalism – the phrase Australians use to describe neo-conservative Thatcherism – the country should be prosper-ing. Inflation is eliminated, with price levels falling; taxation and public spending are low; welfare spending is aggressively means-tested; and the entire economy has been opened up to international competition, liberal-ization and privatization. Yet, as I discovered last week during a six-day visit, there is little sense of rising prosperity; rather there is growing anxiety about the country's economic and social future.

Talk to Labour politicians and there is the concern you might expect about employment, the hollowing out of the Australian economy and grow-ing inequality. But in social policy a new word is entering the vocabulary of preoccupations that is as unexpected as it is original. Australia is becoming a lonely society, they observe, especially in its sprawling suburbs. Lone-liness is emerging as a hot political issue.

The heart of the problem, as seen by Lindsay Tanner – the shadow federal transport minister and tipped as one of the restless Labour Young Turks most likely to succeed to the party leadership – is the way globaliz-ation and market values have upset the fragile economic and social balance on which successful suburban life is built. When Australia was growing, its great coastal cities could spread effortlessly outwards, creating the famous individual quarter-acre 'block' complete with a pavilioned bungalow in endless grids of streets – variously celebrated by Dame Edna and the script-writers of *Neighbours*. Large employers in city centres and factories in the outer suburbs underpinned employment – and underwrote Australian community and social life.

But a number of savage trends have undermined this fragile social system. The decline in manufacturing employment is more accentuated in Australia, now representing less than 25 per cent of all employment – and even mining and agriculture employ little more than 5 per cent. This is a service economy where intellectual property is more important than large factories, and which has generated no net growth in full-time jobs for nearly a decade. There is the cohort of highly paid workers in the knowledge and information industries – but then there are myriad new, insecure and casualized forms of employment in everything from tourism to education.

But this kind of service-sector employment no longer underwrites suburban community. Instead of the systematic and regular patterns of social interaction that accompany regular paid employment and which are the foundations of community, interaction has become sporadic and intermittent. Worse, for those caught up in low-paid jobs accompanied by spells of unemployment, the new structures reinforce a downwards spiral not so much into poverty but solitude and desperation. In a market society, people take a more hard-headed approach to their relationships, trading them in when they consider them unsuccessful; women, for example, leave their unemployed or poorly paid husbands with rising aggression.

Thus one of the new phenomena in the Australian suburb is the marginalized, divorced middle-aged man, living alone, without the old structures that might have reintegrated him into society. There are few large-scale employers, and the old underpinnings of suburban life – the clubs and societies – have been eroded by the twin effects of erratic patterns of long working hours and the desocializing impact of television. Male suicide rates, except for New Zealand where the same processes are more advanced, are the highest in the world and growing fast. Ten per cent of young Australians commit some form of self-harm. There is an upsurge of bullying, stealing and vandalism in schools. Whatever else, 'economic rationalism' has not promoted much happiness.

The trends undermining community and neighbourhood are pervasive. The search for public spending cuts, for example, has intensified the momentum to charge every user of every service its economic cost – from transport and, in Western Australia, even to some hitherto free beaches. Access to the public goods that lubricate suburban life has become progressively more expensive, bearing down hard on lower-income groups. In short, the cumulative impact of globalization in all its manifestations – from pressure for spending cuts to weakening organized labour – has been an upsurge in social marginalization and sheer loneliness.

In Western Australia, the leader of the state's Labour Party, Geoff Gallop (a friend and confidant of Tony Blair), has made the loneliness and insecurity issue a central feature of his party's political positioning. In the state election last year, he tried to make the reviving of the Australian suburb a major plank of policy, an initiative which helped him subsequently win the party leadership. Innovative ways of supporting sport, childcare and even encouraging research into local community history were all part of a package aimed at boosting people's sense of belonging and capacity to participate in the life of the suburban neighbourhood.

However innovative such programmes, they are stillborn if the underlying economic trends carry on tearing away at the bonds of association and relationship. In response, Labour is moving leftwards at both national and state level, talking about a more active industrial policy, strengthening trade unions and the need to re-imagine the structures of Australian capitalism. As it does so, it has taken a lead in the polls for the first time since it lost the national election eighteen months ago – with the current Howard federal government looking outdated, wedded to a policy programme that might have made sense in the eighties, but not today in a lonelier and uncertain Australia. Australian politics are known to influence New Labour – so the message is clear. It should prepare to move to the left.

Observer, 2 November 1997

PART X

*The State We're In:
Constitutional Struggles and
Economic Revival*

Royal Reform Key to Real Recovery

The morning the royal separation was announced trains were running late on the Bakerloo Line because of signal failures. Surfacing to hail a taxi there was a habitual London sight: a man begging inside the door of a boarded-up shop and another rummaging in an overflowing refuse bin. The taxi soon hit gridlock; there was an IRA bomb scare. This is Britain in December 1992.

Nor is it going to change, even if a so-called recovery is beginning. London Underground's cash limits, set in the Autumn Statement, imply reduced investment and the deferral of modernization plans into the next century, and the combination of social security laws, youth unemployment and housing policy that has produced such homelessness is equally embedded. And who sees an end to IRA terrorism and a settlement in Northern Ireland? London mornings are going to get no better for years.

But amidst this decay there are signs of the new – paradoxically signalled by the fractures in the House of Windsor and the improbability of any upturn being other than inflationary and unsustainable. Economic and constitutional crises are not accidental. They are profoundly linked – and as Britain's pre-democratic state structures creak under the strains of their incapacities so it becomes clearer that they offer neither the instruments nor culture with which the British economy can be reorganized. And that reorganization must be the precursor of any sustained recovery.

But it is in part because Britain's state structures are pre-modern that attempts at governmental economic initiatives have been so disappointing, convincing the Conservative Party that a pro-free enterprise position implies the disengagement of the state from economic intervention.

By international standards this is hardly proven and even by the standards of British history it is not very robust; protection and managed finance characterized the Industrial Revolution and recovery from the 1930s recession – but such episodes are regarded as exceptions rather than the rule.

Thus economic policy under the Conservatives has been essentially destructive in its institutional aims; the object has been to create an atomistic world of competing individuals and firms – and nationally determined wage bargains, regional investment incentives and publicly owned monopoly assets have been broken up, dismantled and privatized.

Yet the appeal to self-regulation, independence and voluntarism upon which this crusade has depended has profound roots. Culturally and constitutionally the Conservatives' attack has been supported by the notion that firms individually and in association are sovereign bodies; that is what they are obliged to be by law and how they define themselves in practice. It is not only City bodies that insist on the right to regulate themselves: British horse racing and newspaper publishers make the same claim. The state is seen everywhere as an intrusion upon the province of independent bodies; independence and freedom are portrayed as unqualified independence together with freedom from the state rather than rights that have accompanying responsibilities.

Thus Mrs Thatcher and Mr Major's calls for freedom and choice have had a resonance unique to Britain; and reinforced by free market economics a potent ideology has emerged absolving us all – and especially the middle class – from anything more than securing the very best deal. The more public institutions have deteriorated from neglect, the more interest 40 per cent of the electorate has had in escaping the public domain, empowered by tax cuts and the acceptability of private schooling and health. The officer class are jumping ship.

Non-intervention, notions of individual sovereignty and economic exit have gone hand in hand, but with wider results that are baleful. The point about production and exchange is that they take place under conditions of structural uncertainty; and this the price mechanism alone cannot mediate.

Thus in financial relationships institutional investors may use their power to secure high dividends that are irrational on wider economic grounds, but which the market alone cannot unravel; and the same is true of other markets. Behaviour has to change, law and institutions must be reformed; but how is that to be achieved amongst autonomous companies and self-governing organizations which resist state initiative as bureaucratic interference and acknowledge no wider responsibility?

What was always an uphill struggle has been abandoned completely, and we are left with unreformed market failure – regionally, industrially and financially. Worse, short-termism is further entrenched because longer-term success is so elusive. Thus employees press for the highest immediate wage claim, investors for the highest dividend, bankers for the most recoverable loan, government for the most effective near-term spending cut, and so the economy slithers into the vortex, unable even to sustain a durable upturn without collapsing into inflation or a difficult-to-finance balance of payments deficit.

At heart the private failure originates in the conception of self-governance and its public obligations; but that in turn is inextricably linked to failure in the public domain. Enter the House of Windsor. No account of British parliamentary democracy, characterized by the discretion of the executive branch of government and above all by notions of sovereignty, is complete without the monarchy. It is the monarchy and the affection in which the royal family has been held that has legitimized the whole quasi-feudal structure; and equally it is the fact of monarchical power that dynamizes the structure and obstructs notions of reform. Her Majesty's ministers continue to assemble in her parliament to do her pleasure; and from that all else flows.

In particular it is the unqualified notion of the relationship between a sovereign House of Commons (a sovereignty borrowed from the monarch) and a subject people that informs notions of what is constituted by good governance. For example, a sovereign body of shareholders meet in an annual parliament to examine the stewardship of directors to whom they have delegated complete discretion to maximize their profits. No other responsibility is admitted; and no other authority needed. Shareholders are monarchs of all they own.

The model is breaking down. When managers had secured some in-dependence from their owners' demands the system functioned less relent-lessly; but now that the stewardship of company assets is permanently on sale in the stock market via take-over, managers are bound to short-term profit maximization again and there is growing restlessness about the implications for investment, production and employment.

Notions of self-regulation too are breaking down; whether in the sale of life assurance products, newspaper reporting or redress against the police the public want better than a resort to self-regulating bodies run by the offend-ing interests themselves. To rebuild private constitutions of governance re-quires a reconstruction of the public domain. As long as the House of Windsor sanctified the British system there could be no movement. Yet now it seems the enchantment is cracking, with the royal family unable to bear the load of modernity any more than nineteenth-century trust law can accommodate the demands of modern pension funds.

Prince Charles and Lady Di could not make their marriage work in part because it had to be impossibly perfect to correct all the other fault lines in the system. If a medieval constitution allowed too much centralization, the corruption of the honours system and the emergence of a one-party state, at least there was the saint-like princess and honourable prince to excuse it with their grace and popularity. No more. The royal family's travails gravely weaken the feudal state of its dignifying elements just as the urge to democratize it grows more pressing. All around the evidence that the status quo must give is growing. Ideas of independence, the common interest and social obligation need to be reinvented; and this will open the way to solving problems as disparate as Northern Ireland and a disintegrating rail system.

To unravel the Irish issue requires a redefinition of Britishness; a func-tioning rail system requires the acceptance of taxation and subsidy to further common ends. That requires a new constitutional settlement which, in turn, requires a redefinition of the royal family's relationship with the state. The change must come; without it our lot will be bombs, division and disintegration.

Guardian, 14 December 1992

Moment of Truth for the Rentier State

Britain's one-party state and ailing economy may seem disparate universes – but they are profoundly linked. The same culture and value system so hostile to production is fostered and nurtured by conservative governing structures, whose priorities are financial and administrative. Britain's rentier state begets a rentier economy and financial system; improvement in the latter requires reform of the former.

The moment of truth may be arriving more quickly than anyone can guess. It is not merely that the packing of every public institution in the land – from district health authorities to the parole board – with Conservative Party nominees is making the scope for abuse of Britain's antiquated system of governance obvious, but that the lack of productive capacity threatens the sustainability of the approaching upturn.

As economy and polity alike stagnate in a Sargasso Sea of amoral drift, the links between the degraded public domain and a decaying productive sector will become more obvious.

The first straws in the wind are a new interest in production and manufacturing, together with official acknowledgement that Britain should not, after more than two years of recession, be suffering from such a severe structural trade deficit. Importantly, the Governor of the Bank of England recognized last week that the situation could not continue indefinitely and worried whether, as a result, Britain would even be able to grow at its trend rate of growth. Had Britain a more robust productive sector, he implied, then it could support a higher pound, more stable prices and more employment, absolving the authorities of the agonizing decision they will soon face of slowing down an already barely recovering economy because a balance of payments and sterling crisis is looming – and so more inflation.

The contrary view, strongly held in the Cabinet and City alike, is that the British economy is in for a good run. Even pessimists have to concede that years of recession have left the economy producing anything up to

£45 billion less than if it had grown at even a disappointing rate of long-run growth; and just catching up this 'output gap' implies growth.

Equally, with inflation worldwide the lowest for a generation, any rise in British inflation following devaluation will soon fall back and – with the pound – competitive profits, exports and investment are all set to rise while the Chancellor is compelled to keep consumption depressed with higher taxes. Two or three years of relatively good performance, with inflation only blipping higher, are nearly guaranteed.

It's a seductive argument, and it is true that the 'output gap' – probably nearer £20 billion than £45 billion – will be closed, so giving the illusion of growth for anything up to eighteen months. But beyond that the Governor's instincts are nearer the mark than the optimists', who have to believe the Thatcher reforms worked and were only obscured by disastrous membership of the ERM.

Supporting the case for caution is Peter Warburton, at Flemings Research, who reports that six out of the fastest-growing categories of consumer spending in the last three months of 1992 – cars, household fruit and vegetables, wines, brown goods, footwear and holidays abroad – have import contents at or above 50 per cent. As consumption swings up, it is likely to suck in a disproportionate increase in imports, notwithstanding devaluation.

Gerard Lyons, at DKB International, calculates just how weak Britain's trade position now is. Exports in 1992 covered 61 per cent of consumer goods imports, 96 per cent of intermediate goods and 102 per cent of capital goods imports, he says – and that at the tail-end of a long recession. In 1980, exports covered 60, 170 and 151 per cent of imports from the same categories – a calamitous fall-away.

Despite wholesale privatization, the virtual extinction of the closed shop, the growth of huge inequality of incomes as incentives, the collapse of trade union membership and managers winning the 'right to manage', there is not the productive capacity at hand to capitalize on the opportunity presented by devaluation and upturn. Ten out of the last thirteen years have not seen even sufficient investment to replace capital scrapping in the manufacturing sector. The reason is that Britain's anti-production or 'rentier' culture and the values that underlie it remain firmly in place, paradoxically inflamed by the very reforms that were meant to exorcize it.

It is all-pervasive. Partly as a hangover from the Empire; partly as a result of state structures constructed to encourage administration and the exercise of sovereign legislative power; and partly as a result of the dominant political party drawing so much electoral support from the south-east. The British upper middle class is wedded to values that are distant from the complex and demanding world of production. They remain dividend- and rent-seekers rather than risk-takers; wedded to property speculation rather than entrepreneurship, and attracted to the fee-charging professions and Civil Service rather than competitive business.

Building non-hierarchical teams, applying technology, recognizing obligations to a wider community and taking a long view are wholly foreign.

The world view goes very deep. It is reinforced daily by 'business' news that emphasizes bids, deals and short-term profit performance; it expresses itself as a national preoccupation with inflation rather than unemployment; and the pre-eminence of the City of London in Britain's business life ensures that the country's commercial elite trusts free markets not only as an ideology but also as a way of making fabulous salaries. If Britain is to build a populous *Mittelstand* of small and medium-sized enterprises as well as reinvigorating its current top 200 companies, this value system must be challenged.

For, however clever a technical proposal, or well researched a proposal for institutional change to stimulate production and the accompanying culture, it will run into the brick wall of 'rentierism'. In the latest edition of *Renewal*, for example, Karel Williams, of the University of Central Lancashire, and his co-authors call for a new 'productionism' and propose a reorganization of corporate taxation so that the more companies add value compared with some norm the more tax is rebated, while at the same time there should be regulatory limits to the proportion of profits that can be distributed as dividends. The idea is to bias the tax system to favour production and investment.

It's a good and workable proposal, but in British terms its advocacy and introduction is an uphill struggle; any government that tried to launch it would be lambasted. It is the same story on reconstituting the financial or training system. Britain's landlord-rentier culture stands as the sworn enemy of any such initiative.

Financial institutions will insist that their priority is to operate as stewards for growing dividends, and they cannot be expected to acquire the skills that allow them actively to judge management decision-making of the companies which they finance. Banks look for property collateral; investors for secure earnings growth – it is for others to make and produce.

Companies tend to be run as the personal fiefdoms of the chief executive, with corporate strategy seen as an act of will imposed from above. Again the value system lying behind this is that of the rentier; assets must be redirected and worked harder to yield greater financial returns, not created and grown to accumulate wealth through returns on physical and human investment.

All this is validated in the public domain by Britain's landlord state; centralized in London, collecting its taxes but never proactively engaging in wealth generation itself. Above all there is the Conservative Party, grounded in a rentier electorate in the south-east, transmuting English land-lordism into a political philosophy.

So, reconstructing the state and reorganizing the electoral system are essential components in the creation of a production culture. And at just the moment when concerns are rising and the linkages emerging between the economic and political, the Labour Party has had the good fortune to find the Plant Commission favouring electoral reform – the last but essential component in any constitutional overhaul.

It will be bitterly resisted, the argument being that to surrender first past the post is to surrender Labour's chance of forming a majority government and having its turn at the controls of the landlord state and a chance to impose technical and socialist solutions on Britain's problems.

It is a defensible position, but ultimately conservative. Temporary tenure of the rentier state leaves the landlord value system intact, just as it did in 1951, 1970 and 1979 – and the technical and institutional reforms are quickly reversed.

Labour and the opposition parties should be after bigger game; the creation of a production culture and the state structures to support it.

The signs are that the message is striking home and that the public, locked in a drifting economy, may at last be ready to listen.

Guardian, 5 April 1993

Time to Sever the Thin Blue Line

It all connects. The long dominance of the Conservative Party in British politics, the character of the British constitution, the highly political nature of British business and the debilitating structure of the economy are not independent phenomena.

They are interlocked, and the significance of last week's ministerial resignations and the prospect of the crisis continuing this week is that the chickens are coming home to roost.

Mr Major's problem is that the only satisfactory response is to attack the basis of the Conservative Party's supremacy in British politics – the lack of rules in areas ranging from party funding to honours and appointments to quangos. Already some members of the Nolan committee have signalled that they want to extend their remit to the issue of party funding. And so they must – that is the fuel that makes the system run. Small wonder that the right is uneasy; it sees where this might lead.

Establishing a proper distance between those who occupy the public and private spheres will require a recasting of the relationship between the Conservative Party and British business; and this is the fulcrum around which both the British economy and polity turn. It is not only that the Conservative Party, with an ageing and dwindling membership, relies on business contributions from home and abroad to outspend the opposition parties; it is that an influential part of British business – especially in the City – is anxious to support the Conservative cause to the last. If there is to be a more arm's-length and transparent relationship, the whole nexus of party contributions, honours, contracts, private access to decision-makers, discretionary regulation, partisan implementation of competition and merger policy etc. that takes place at the moment will be disturbed. But that is only the exposed tip of a much more menacing iceberg.

It is often argued that Britain has less overt corruption than other European countries, and so it has – but that is largely because the system allows the right a hegemonic position without having to engage in underhand activity. The British social and political system so efficiently entrenches the Conservative elite through a system of informal networks that corruption on a Mediterranean scale never needs to be deployed.

Nothing is left to chance. The Financial Times survey of 1,000 schools at the weekend reported that the top fifty schools ranked by A level results are all private; only twenty of the top 200 are state schools. Private schools educate one child in fifteen but account for one in four of British university students – and disproportionately more at Oxford and Cambridge. Spending more than twice per student than their state rivals, they are secure conduits to the higher echelons of economy and society.

As centres of educational excellence they are a national resource; and many parents are purchasers only because of the failings of the state system. But that is not the point. The system is the bearer of the gene which reproduces a Conservative elite – notwithstanding the significant minority of its products who (thankfully) declare independence from its values. Private education can only justify the scale of its influence in Britain by its appeal to private choice and liberty; important values they may be, but necessarily the role of the commonweal, equality and social solidarity receive less emphasis. How else to justify their pre-eminence?

Thus is the basis laid for the well-trodden avenue to the key sources of power, ranging from the City to the media. Anybody who believes that a meritocracy rules in British business, and that membership of the right social and political caste is not fundamental, needs to observe the facts. Jeremy Paxman and Anthony Sampson* have detailed the grip that the

---

* J. Paxman, *Friends in High Places* (Harmondsworth: Penguin, 1991); A. Sampson, *The Essential Anatomy of Britain: Democracy in Crisis* (London: Hodder & Stoughton, 1993).

privately educated, Conservative elite has on the British system; for non-members there is a glass ceiling – and too many of those who break through are even more anxious to show their devotion to the tribal gods of Conservatism.

This interconnection of the class system and the party needs two more elements before the hegemony is complete. The first is Britain's state structures. It is not only that their protection of the hereditary principle helps to fuse class and power; it is also that the British state is fundamentally uneasy about disturbing the twin gods of self-regulation and shareholder sovereignty. The state lacks the institutional equipment, competence or intellectual confidence to challenge them; it has always, in a sense, been a semi-privatized affair which the government's recent reforms have carried to their logical conclusion.

These twin gods serve the important political purpose of allowing the business elite to protect a very particular definition of its own interests. The dominance of financial values above all others in British business life; the lack of any body of law that sets out the responsibilities of owners and directors beyond profit maximization and the prevention of malfeasance; the all-too-ready willingness to regard workforces as troublesome and disposable commodities – this is a particular business culture indeed. It allows those at the top the 'freedom' to wheel and deal, and amass fortunes; but as an instrument of long-run economic success it has shown its weaknesses. Yet it is this system that 230 of the top 1,000 companies contribute to the Conservative Party to preserve.

The significance of the events of the last fortnight and the Scott inquiry alike is that the British state, complete with its tortured monarchy, no longer has the legitimacy to bear the load of endorsing Conservative hegemony in all its ramifications. The more the private networks are exposed, the more obviously inadequate the old reflex responses. Neither inquiries by Sir Robin Butler nor simple declarations by MPs of their interests are sufficient to clear the air. A clean-up requires a new conception of the polity – and of the wider economic and social system with which it is intertwined.

There is a growing recognition that the contract between the governors and the governed needs to be recast, but that will only succeed if at the same time British business becomes less anxious to protect every aspect of the status quo – and so drop its role as paymasters to only one party. The fears of sequestration and nationalization that prompted such loyalties have gone; the question is rather which kind of capitalism should business operate within – and about this it can and should respect the democratic process. But that in turn will require a less politicized social system in which the dominant elements of British social and educational life are no longer Conservative preserves.

Instead of the winner-take-all economy and polity, the aim should be a stakeholder economy and polity in which all have an interest. Nor need this be cloud-cuckoo-land. The politicized British business community is now 70 per cent owned by the great pension funds, insurance companies and unit trusts which are doing no more than investing the savings of the majority of the British public. Many readers of this column will already, via their pension or insurance policy, own shares in the great contributors to the Conservative Party, like United Biscuits, Glaxo, Rolls-Royce, Whitbread and P&O. Your view was never invited – but you find your investments supporting a political party. It could be different.

This is but part, however, of the wider problem of the disconnection between ownership and management of companies – and the lack of any clearly delineated system of corporate governance. It is this that is at the roots of the short-term financial returns demanded of British business; but it also allows British business to be so politically partisan – because *de facto* the lines of accountability are so very weak.

Yet we are unlikely to think creatively about how companies are owned and governed if there is no attempt to think about how the state is governed. As the crisis over sleaze continues, the concern that pressure groups like Charter 88 have over the constitution and its links with the wider social and economic system are shown more obviously to be at the heart of the British condition. The good news is that it is out in the open; the bad news is that the problem is so systemic.

But there is one remedy open to any reader: write to whoever runs your pension, unit trust or endowment policy and say that you don't want the companies in which your savings are invested to support a political party. If enough of you did so, it might even make a difference.

Guardian, 31 October 1994

A Mad Way to Run a Country

As an exercise in hamfisted, second-rate government the events of the last week take some beating. Ministers have lost control of a potentially containable situation with disastrous results. The reasons they have lost control betray the deep-seated structural malfunctions of British government that now urgently require to be addressed.

There are well-advertised excuses. Technology and science, it is said, are breaking such terrifyingly unpredictable ground that it is silly to hold ministers to account for developments whose malevolent by-products were not anticipated at the time decisions were taken. There are new levels of risk with which we simply have to live. Nor is Britain alone in suffering the depredations of poor regulation and venal producer interests. The way the French allowed Aids-infected blood to be used unchecked for years or the Spanish failed to prevent lethally infected olive oil from entering the food chain show that BSE is but another example of a general trend.

Yet while both arguments have force, neither counters the case for constitutional reform; rather they reinforce it. Increased danger is an occasion to strengthen civil society's defences rather than do nothing. From the earliest moments in 1980 when ministers decided to take minimal action to inhibit the spread of BSE while keeping the quality of their advice secret, to the unwillingness last week even to pre-notify the European Commission of developments, we have watched Britain's discretionary, secretive system of executive government at work. Or rather not at work.

The residual informal checks and balances in the system – the doctrine of ministerial responsibility, the role of the Civil Service as an independent custodian of the public interest and even the tradition of MPs having an obligation to Parliament that transcended party interest – have all been gradually whittled away since the middle of the century. What is left is the brutal exercise of executive power legitimized by quinquennial first-past-the-post elections and the shrinking, now rather dog-eared grace of the House of Windsor. This is too thin a basis upon which to organize the contract between governors and governed when the nature of legislative and executive decisions is becoming more complex.

Yet what makes the constitutional arrangements especially menacing is their current ideological marriage with a corrupted view of free market economics. The best free marketeers are as suspicious of the way beef producers and British agriculture gain such privileged treatment from the Ministry of Agriculture as any liberal. Competition should rule and subsidies be reduced.

Yet in the eyes of ministers the promotion of 'market forces' has become coterminous with the simple promotion of British business's interests as British business defines them. Regulation is 'burdensome' only if it obstructs a vested business interest from doing what it wants. Opposition to monopoly does not extend to more aggressive policing of takeovers even if they reduce competition. Government intervention is bad unless it can boost private profits.

The awesome power of the British state has thus been deployed to service vested and partisan interests – whether it be allowing regional electricity companies to be snapped up in takeovers, or offering sweeteners of billions to the consortium bidding for the Eurotunnel link. The approach to Britain's beef producers is the same phenomenon.

Indeed the treatment of Britain's cattle herds over the last forty-five years accurately reflects the state's now chronic reluctance to protect the public interest, especially if it involves regulation or public expenditure. The aggressive and rapid responses to the outbreaks of foot and mouth disease in 1967/8 and 1981, even though the disease was not communicable to human beings, stand in sorry contrast to the tale of prevarication and unwillingness to act of the last ten years.

In 1967 alone 211,825 cattle were slaughtered with compensation at today's prices of some £350 million, while the record of the debates in the Commons of the much more limited outbreak in 1981 reveals a Conservative Party that still believed in public purpose, regulation and the common interest. Fifteen years of new-right demagoguery and those instincts have been debauched and corroded. Douglas Hogg, arguing in Cabinet earlier this week for the slaughter of cattle over thirty months old, would have had more allies in 1981; now he has to rely on the clamour outside, extending yesterday to the National Farmers Union, to make a case that should have had more general ministerial support.

Yet while ministers, as in the Scott inquiry, can protest that every decision in the long catalogue of errors was in itself defensible, each is framed by the same weakness: scientific research hamstrung by government cuts; regulation inhibited by lack of manpower to verify that rules were being obeyed. And over the past few weeks a now demoralized Civil Service, whose public-service ethic has declined, apparently less capable of forging a proper line – and persuading ministers to adhere to it.

Executive discretion, *pace* Lord Acton, absolutely corrupts those who come into contact with it. A British government jealous of its sovereignty and terrified of its Eurosceptical backbenchers was never likely to notify the European Commission of its intentions. Britain now confronts a worldwide ban on its beef exports, while it finds itself negotiating for potential compensation for any cattle slaughter from the EU – having maximized hostility to its position. This is diplomatic incompetence of a high order – almost matching its handling of consumer confidence.

The British executive branch of government requires more active scrutiny of its decisions by a legislature that is not in thrall to it; that can only come from an elected second chamber. There must be a Freedom of Information Act so that officials know that their advice will be publicly scrutinized. The intermediate agencies of the state – whether they are the Health and Safety Executive, scientific advisory boards or regulatory agencies – need to be properly funded and independent rather than poverty-stricken ciphers of central government.

Constitutional reform is meant to be the concern of only the metropolitan chattering classes. It is not a doorstep issue, it is said. Conservative politicians rage that it will lead to ruin. Not so. Rather it is the way Britain is governed that is leading to ruin – and for some of our fellow citizens the agonizing experience of living through their own physical collapse. The case for reform is proven. What is required is politicians with the nerve and commitment to sell it – and then execute the change.

Guardian, 27 March 1996

Snow White Ideology and the 30 Million Dwarfs

It has been a very 1990s Christmas. More people than ever have spent Christmas abroad; more people than ever have found traditional Christmas excess beyond their means. The divisions opening up in our society are never starker than at this time of year; bleak beggars in the London subway while in Harrods £1,000 hampers are selling out.

This inequality is no accident. Run the economy with sufficient slack to create a reserve army of unemployed, reduce taxation for the better-off while curbing welfare provision, and the results are as predictable as clockwork. Nor can any welfare system known to man fail to creak under the strain; once the numbers eligible for state benefit rank around 20 per cent of the population, as in Britain, the cost of providing universal assistance becomes explosive.

But not to provide assistance to all is equally costly. Making welfare discretionary, targeted on the 'deserving' to make it 'cost-effective', is to make it discretionary charity. Worse, the value system that justifies this, stressing individualism and the duty to opt out, hardens hearts and promotes a pervasive Hobbesian brutishness. It absolves those who have from involving themselves in the fate of those who have not, and ultimately that destroys haves and have-nots alike. In a fundamental sense it is decivilizing.

For the great initiatives that have marked the rise of western civilization have been inclusive. Whether building drainage and water supply systems, inoculating against disease or launching mass education the effectiveness of each initiative has revolved around its capacity to embrace all. The Victorians may have begun building drainage systems in those parts of the city that could afford them because to do more implied taxation: but the middle class soon found that to protect themselves against cholera they had to build drainage systems for all. The same is true today for family breakdown, crime and education; we all suffer from the consequences of societal disintegration but the enemies of the civil can admit no social response.

For social responses require collective action, social institutions and large transfers of resources from those who are advantaged to the disadvantaged

– precisely the policy mix excluded by the current framework which aims to make us responsible as individuals. From housing to pensions we must provide for ourselves rather than support institutions of mutual insurance and collective action.

The new individualism is presented as a moral crusade, but for most people there is a more urgent consequence. Average British wage-earners simply do not have the income to make individual provision for their families and the hazards life brings. For example, to service an average £50,000 mortgage requires £3,960 a year; to own, run and insure a four-door saloon car requires £4,400 a year.

Average earnings are £18,300 a year: allow for £4,730 tax and national insurance and there is not much left over after buying food, heat, light and clothes. For luxuries like holidays or new furniture there has to be another income in the average household – which is why most families in Britain are simply not viable unless there are two earners.

Yet the world of individual provision thrust down our throats by the new right requires more onerous payments on top. For example, to acquire a pension of £12,000 a year in 2020 in today's terms (two-thirds of average earnings) requires £3,120 year in payments to a personal pension plan (and that assumes investment returns of 8.5 per cent). Average school fees are £4,960 a year. A standard Bupa health insurance premium for a couple in their 30s is £360 a year. Can the average earner aspire to any of this? Even if taxation were substantially reduced these items are beyond most people.

For Britain's income distribution is incredibly skewed, as revealed by the famous imaginary parade of dwarfs and giants. Suppose the British could parade through Hyde Park for an hour, their height corresponding to the average income. It is only after 37 minutes, compute Stephen Jenkins and Frank Cowell in a University College of Swansea Discussion Paper, that we would see the first average-height person, with the first quarter of an hour taken up by dwarfs below 3 ft tall. We would have to wait three minutes before the end before we see the first over 11 ft. In the last seconds we see the real giants with one or two of the tallest over 100 yd high.

Thus, for the overwhelming majority, universal education, health and social insurance paid for by a redistributive tax system are vital components of living well; yet it is precisely these institutions that have been assaulted over the past fifteen years. But the Conservative politicians who have authored these reforms are not malevolent; they require public support for what they have done and are planning. Michael Portillo, the ideological Chief Secretary to the Treasury, genuinely looks forward to a world in which taxation and public service alike are very much reduced and private provision and personal responsibility enhanced: it is a combined moral and economic position. That two-thirds of the country do not have the wherewithal to afford the private provision he plans troubles him little.

What is puzzling is how British democracy has thrown up a party committed to an ideology directly against the interests of the mass of voters that wins elections as comfortably as it does. The explanations are familiar – distrust of the opposition, the collapse of socialism as an animating political force, the Conservative media, the sense that the Conservative Party is non-political and defender of middle England, rising real incomes in the 1980s etc. – all partly true but they obscure the most salient political point.

The Conservative Party's constituency is rooted in the world of the last third of the income parade; many Conservatives simply do not comprehend the actual options of ordinary men and women because they do not represent them. It is no accident that the decline in One Nation Toryism has mirrored the party's increasing reliance on its southern base, with 215 seats below a line from the Severn to the Wash. John Redwood, Michael Portillo and Peter Lilley (the trio of right-wing 'bastards') represent the classic Tory home counties constituencies of Wokingham, Enfield Southgate and St Albans respectively on a majority of votes cast, and they have wives whose earnings make them income parade giants. Their personal lifestyles, those of their acquaintances and of a critical mass of their constituents are a world away from the lives lived by most Britons. The gap between them and the country is hardly surprising.

There is an increasing polarization of political support. The number of marginal constituencies has been steadily declining, as Martin Linton and Mary Georghiou show in a well-argued pamphlet; in the 1960s there were over 150 true marginals, now there are under 100.* Eighty-five per cent of the electorate, 37 million people, live in constituencies in which their vote is unlikely to make any difference and where in consequence the parties are unlikely to make much of an effort. Democratic politics becomes less and less responsive to real needs and concerns – territory in which new right ideologues can flourish.

But Labour has a parallel problem. It may poll more votes in the south-east outside London than any other region in the country, but it holds only three seats and its retreat in the counties is well documented. Linton and Georghiou say that it had more than 40 per cent of the vote in Bedfordshire, Norfolk, Oxfordshire and Gloucestershire in the 1951 election; now its vote is derisory.

Its over-representation in the north makes its reflex action a defence of structures it knows are vital to its constituencies' well-being but one that helps give Labour the character of being always resistant to change. The 1945 Labour victory was built on national support impossible to reproduce today and makes winning a true mandate for change politically out of reach.

* *Labour's Road to Electoral Reform* (London: Labour Campaign for Electoral Reform, 1993).

Unblocking British debate thus requires an unblocking of the political system, and in particular the way the country votes. A more proportional voting system that genuinely enfranchised more of the electorate would surely change the character of both parties and oblige them to compete for votes across the whole of the income parade.

The structure of our welfare and political systems is thus profoundly interrelated, as is the demotion of full employment as a policy aim. If we want policies that reflect what we are, we first need a political system that forces politicians to engage with us as we are and not what they hope we will become.

Guardian, 28 December 1993

It is Broke, and it Needs Fixing

There is no getting away from it. The argument about the constitution that is now being joined in earnest is not about dull technicalities. It is at heart a complaint about the kind of country we have become – and a statement about what kind of country we want to be. It is politics of the highest order.

To a Conservative apologist for the status quo, this is barely comprehensible. If there are problems about contemporary Britain, they can be ascribed variously to moral decay, liberal values, regulations – particularly if they come from Brussels – lack of patriotic fervour and, above all, an inbuilt capacity to whinge. The British constitution represents the acme of political arrangements, as the prime minister argued last Wednesday, entrenching freedoms and personifying Britishness; its essential contours are largely unimprovable even if there are some minor reforms to be made at the margin.

John Major's speech, aimed at setting out his constitutional stall and to be followed, we are promised, by further pronouncements from his ministers, is a classic statement of the Conservative position. It is at once plausible and an exercise in deception – both of himself and the public. There is, for example, a truth in arguing that the constitution has gained legitimacy and stability over the centuries, and there are some hard questions to be answered about devolution of power to Scotland and Wales – notably the over-representation of Scottish MPs at Westminster once Scotland has its own Parliament – that the devolutionists have scandalously not confronted.

But beyond that, Major enters a realm of high speciousness and political

fantasy. He must know the absurdity of claiming that the boundaries between executive, legislature and judiciary are policed by mutual restraint,
that power has not been centralized, that the House of Commons allows
the 'people' to control the executive and the House of Lords is not politically biased. The political aim is not to enlighten or be straight; rather it is
to frighten voters about the constitutional aims of the Opposition parties.

But the substantive point stands. After a near-century of constitutional
innovation that began with the Reform Act of 1832 and ended with the
extension of the franchise to women on the same basis as men in 1928,
Britain has had nearly seventy years of constitutional stagnation. There were
failed attempts to reform the House of Lords in 1968 and to establish devolution in Scotland and Wales in 1979. The select committee system
was established by the incoming Thatcher government better to organize
parliamentary scrutiny of government, but with increasingly disappointing
results; with some honourable exceptions the committees offer only tepid
criticism of the government – reflecting the fact that the majority of their
members are from the governing party. Yet constitutional Conservatives in-
vite us to believe that the system arrived at in the 1920s must be defended
with our lives; that any attempt to meddle with it would, in Major's words,
'unstitch our way of life' and threaten 'the institutions that make us one
nation'.

Yet resisting reform is as much of a political statement, as Karl Popper
once famously argued, as reform. It is palpable nonsense to argue that British constitutional arrangements are so perfectly honed that any reform must
perforce be damaging. We all know, whether we are members of a trade
union or a bridge club, that the rules by which an institution is organized
are fundamental to its character, culture and mode of operation. How an
organization is run depends on its constitution, and that in turn will determine its character. And whether it is the constitution of county cricket or
the role of non-executive directors in British companies, civil society boasts
hundreds of examples where the constitutional question is alive – and
central to developing either the sport or corporate life in the face of new
trends and problems.

But if there has been no inhibition in investigating how the rules of the
game might better change to respond to new realities in our economy and
society, when it comes to the full pomp of the British state, it seems the
same vigour and vitality has to stop. Nothing can be changed. There are no
problems to be solved; and, according to Major, any experiments 'would
undermine our stability and introduce new uncertainties for no good
purpose'.

This complacency must be pricked. Any healthy polity must continually
update its political system. The power of the British executive branch of
government is too great, is growing greater and needs to be curbed. Bills

are poorly drafted. Scrutiny is token. There is little or no recognition of citizens' rights, so Parliament regularly enacts legislation that offers no basic redress – whether it be to fathers under the Child Support Agency or the privatized utilities and their customers against the ruling of the new regulatory bodies. In the past few weeks it has empowered the unaccountable security services to act as a new state secret police force and now plans to damn asylum-seekers to pauperization without blinking. The House of Commons is the supine plaything of the majority party; its rules and practices are arcane. Above all, the members that fill its benches only partially reflect the balance of political opinion in the country at large.

The second chamber's interventions are erratic, and the fact that its representation is permanently loaded in favour of the Conservatives is a standing offence to any conception of democratic government. It serves as a wholly ineffective check and balance, relying on occasions when its life peers can muster sufficient votes, energy and willingness to outgun the dead weight of Conservative hereditary peers. It is an all too visible reminder that, in Britain, birth continues to matter more than ability.

But this is not where matters end. The political system has a complex interrelationship with the wider economic and social system. Politics is not, after all, a game that is played independently of the economic and social order – it is shaped by it and in turn helps to shape it. The centralization of power in Britain and the lack of autonomy offered to cities, towns and villages in deliberating over their own affairs has a prime role in weakening the country's civic culture. Participation in local decision-making is a mug's game; there is little scope to shape spending and local institutions so that they serve local needs and ambitions. The men and women in Whitehall take those decisions for you or appoint those in the multiplying numbers of quangos who will act for them – and never more so than under Conservative governments.

But this in turn affects the stock of the country's social capital – or put another way, its reserves of trust and commitment. All human interaction needs to be underwritten by a recognition of mutuality of obligation, otherwise economy and society have no constraint on those who cheat – ready to renege on any commitment because another appears to be immediately profitable. A successful market economy depends on the twin engines of competition and co-operation, flexibility and commitment – but the capacity to co-operate and commit originates in a willingness to reciprocate others' good actions; and that is helped if people can work in situations where they learn that altruism, co-operation and commitment pay dividends.

This is complex. Trust is created in part from family and religious experience – but is fostered or hindered by the extent to which public institutions, those that lie beyond simple buying and selling in markets, allow people to learn the value of co-operative and collective action. If local public institutions disallow this possibility, then an important creator of social capital is weakened – and with it the possibility of the good society and economy. All over the country there are town halls, parks, reservoirs, schools and colleges that are the legacy of previous generations' willingness and capacity to do good public acts locally; under the current political arrangements, it is much harder. Herein lies one of the sources of political disaffection that expresses itself in the growth of single-issue politics, the DIY culture and falling voter turnouts.

And last, there is the genuine revival of local nationalisms. The Welsh and Scottish strains are well known, but one of the by-products of Euro 96 has been the reappearance of the St George's flag. The English too are beginning to reaffirm their nationhood. None of this needs to be threatening; indeed here is a source of healthy vitality that properly expressed could be a source of rejuvenation – not merely in Scotland and Wales, but in England. But it requires political expression, hence the case for Scottish and Welsh parliaments. And with devolution in place, the English could begin to disentangle what is British – and what English.

It is plain that the current system needs to be overhauled – and Conservative resistance, while covering itself in the guise of high principle, is wholly self-interested. It is no accident that the Conservative Party's long domination of British politics has coincided with a protracted period of constitutional stagnation; it is the main beneficiary of the way things are – from the first-past-the-post voting system to the notion of Britishness of which it has made itself the great champion. It is, after all, the Conservative rather than Labour party conference that culminates in a lusty rendering of 'Land of Hope and Glory', and waving of the Union Jack.

Labour's constitutional programme is thus a challenge that threatens Conservative hegemony more purely than any other policy programme it has ever espoused. It needs not only to win the argument, but once in power to organize the sequence of legislative change very carefully. After all, as the Constitution Unit has calculated, constitutional bills – taken as they are on the floor of the House of Commons – are extraordinarily expensive in parliamentary time. Maastricht took 185 hours; the Scotland and Wales Acts together in 1978, 270 hours; and House of Lords reform in 1968 was broken off after 85 futile hours. Given that there are 400 hours of legislative time in a parliamentary year, constitutional reform could engulf Labour's five-year term.

Tony Blair needs to avoid this at all costs. By holding a referendum before introducing devolution legislation, he not only correctly entrenches the changes democratically but opens up the way to speeding the devolution bills through the Commons – a stroke on two fronts that was long overdue. Moreover, he has a powerful argument, citing the precedent of the Conservatives' local government reorganization in 1985, that given the popular mandate he would be within his rights for some clauses to be discussed by standing committee – and so save yet more crucial parliamentary time.

The more open question is whether devolution should precede rather than follow the more important discussion over the structure and voting system of Parliament; it may be true that Scottish politics compels action, but it is putting the cart before the horse. It also opens the debate up at its weakest point, for there is no doubt that, in equity, Scotland's over-representation in London should be reduced – something which Labour refuses stubbornly to countenance.

The high ground remains the strongest and best political territory. The system must change to conform to basic democratic principles and reconnect Parliament and people. Centralized power must be curbed. Britain's tradition of civic culture needs to be reborn. There need to be firmer lines of accountability in public life. The risk is not in changing; rather it lies in doing nothing – and Blair's convictions on this issue present Conservative Britain with its deadliest threat yet. For this is an argument it stands to lose.

Observer, 30 June 1996

A Princess, a Funeral and a Nation's Sadness

If it was a long walk for the two young princes, it was longer by far for the Prince of Wales. At the end of the most extraordinary week in recent British history he had to maintain his dignity before a crowd of millions in the most tragic of circumstances – every step enhancing Princess Diana's claim on the nation's affections even as it weakened his own. She will haunt him for the rest of his life, just as she will live on in the hearts of her sons.

But all three must wonder whether the consecration of their lives to a mission – upholding the monarchy – is any longer worth the sacrifice for a people whose own desire for them to carry on supporting an obsolescent and dying institution is waning before their eyes.

For although the day was the burial of a princess amidst all the pomp of royal pageant, it was paradoxically a uniquely democratic event, and as such a mortal threat to the conception of monarchy. It was not merely that Elton John was allowed into the sacred business of the burial of the mother of Britain's next but one king, or that so many concessions over the character of the funeral were shaped by pressure from below; the Palace seriously misjudged not just the public mood but its own capacity to stay aloof from it.

The momentum has simply been unstoppable, with tens of millions of Britons insisting on their right to participate – a demand of citizens rather than subjects. In 1997 people expect their individual right to grieve to be respected and the family that purports to represent the nation to be seen publicly to share in the collective mourning at the highest possible pitch. The people's wishes are now sovereign; the Crown must follow where the people lead.

The pressure for the Royal Family to be as demonstrative as those laying their wreaths may seem unreasonable and even inhumane; after all, grief is no less for being privately rather than publicly expressed and the close family in any bereavement should surely be allowed to find their own way to deal with such an unexpected loss.

But Princess Diana is and was a collective national property in a way that only her death has exposed. The scale of the collective response and the feeling shared by her millions of mourners who feel they knew her personally is tribute to a new culture of intimacy, enabled by today's all-encompassing media and fostered by a new democratic spirit.

The famous and celebrated are known more closely than ever before. But this intimacy, we now discover, is not one-way traffic and has its own explosive dynamic. The idea has taken root that the people have the right to know intimate personal details of those in public life. Princess Diana was a prime exponent and prisoner of this culture and, to the extent that her death was caused by paparazzi in search of intimate photographs, ultimately its victim.

Accompanying this culture of intimacy is a new confidence among ordinary citizens that their opinions are worth as much as those of anybody else; today they gave their verdict on the Queen's speech with the self-confidence and aplomb of television veterans. The deference to those higher in the social scale, along with a stoical acceptance of the status quo that used to be a hallmark of British life, have disappeared completely.

This is in part because the media have removed the mystique of those in high places; in part because a generation of comprehensive education, with its deep attachment to egalitarian values, has implanted a belief that everybody is empowered to an extent that the elite – almost exclusively educated privately in schools where egalitarianism is non-existent – has yet to grasp; in part because of the way women and their emphasis on the personal are occupying a more central place in our national culture; and in part because in these reflexive, uncertain times all values are in a state of flux. The elite itself is no longer certain that its values are worth defending to the last – from a refusal to show affection in public to the royal protocol surrounding flags at half-mast.

Charles and his sons are in the eye of this hurricane of demands for intimacy and its accompanying democratic demand for voice – but they cannot respond without undercutting the very principle of monarchy.

Kings can be neither democrats nor the objects of intense personal scrutiny without giving up what it has always meant to be a king in Britain, which is why the Queen sounded so awkward in emphasizing her role as grandmother as well as monarch. It is why neither retreat to aloof dignity nor a full adoption of Princess Diana's affectionate, human approach to winning legitimacy works as a way forward for the monarchy. Thus its passing, at least in its current form, is foretold.

Indeed Diana herself, who at one time wanted to capture this new mood and put it to the service of the monarchy, towards the end of her life realized the attempt was beyond the capacity of the Windsors. The pass had been sold and she predicted that Charles's appetite for kingship was fading, as was the likelihood he would ever make it to the throne. She can hardly have guessed that she herself would play so important a role in creating what is approaching a revolution in British life – although in describing herself as the 'ultimate rebel' she may have suspected more than she let on.

However, intimacy and the need to express voice cannot alone explain the response and the intensity of emotion that the funeral aroused. For Diana met the need of a lonely, secular society for solidarity and warmth – and for secular saints. The British of the egalitarian postwar years, creating a welfare state in which all had a stake, could unreservedly cheer Elizabeth II at her coronation as their collective embodiment – but the past twenty years of rising inequality, decaying public institutions and celebration of private activity in private free markets have created a new society that is more individualistic, more insecure, less anchored in its values and more alone.

Happiness is no longer gained from the service and duty that is at the core of the Queen's world view; it has to advance individual well-being in a world in which we all make it up for ourselves – hence the growth of quackery, crackpot cults, alternative lifestyles and, now we find, the sudden and irrational conferral of near-sainthood upon Princess Diana.

But canonization would not have come Diana's way if she was not felt to be worthy, and here there is a truth that conservative commentators wish to play down or ignore. Diana would not be thought good if the causes she had espoused had been privatization, workfare and the charity ball; her instincts, amazingly for one with her background and education, took her unerringly to the liberal wing of the spectrum of supportable causes. Homelessness, Aids and landmines are all issues with which the Conservative mind is instinctively uneasy – and an important reason why the responses of William Hague and the Conservative Party to the past week have been so feeble. They don't see the point of Diana's campaigning; and the criticism levelled by her against them for their hopelessness on the landmine issue was well deserved.

Britain may be a less rooted and more individualistic society than it was but, it turns out, it is more liberal, kind and egalitarian than the metropolitan media and political establishment allow. Blair's victory last May was testament to that and to the gathering demand for wholesale change; last week is but confirmation of what we should have known.

All this is important for the future. This is not a society which can any longer sustain a constitutional role for the monarch; the committee Charles has appointed to consider the future of the monarchy will have to grasp the nettle. Charles himself, with any plans for marriage to his long-time lover Camilla Parker-Bowles now doomed, and seen by many as the architect of Diana's tragic death, is too compromised a figure to make kingship work even if he wanted to. He must decide whether he will allow the crown to pass directly to his son when his mother dies; and if so the Prime Minister must decide in turn whether to support such a move or whether the role of monarch as constitutional head of state must go.

The institution can stagger on but amid so much other constitutional change – notably the elimination of the hereditary principle in the House of Lords, an important buttress to hereditary monarchy – it is clear the end is approaching. Indeed the Royal Family itself may will it, so Britain becomes the first republic brought into being from above rather than by revolution from below.

The role of the media in a society increasingly preoccupied by the intimate and personal also has to be re-examined. The balance Britain has struck in law between its scant protection for intrusion into the private and personal, its over-protection of reputation through draconian libel laws and stress on secrecy and non-disclosure of information no longer corresponds to the core values of British society nor the pressure points the media are generating.

A new balance has to be struck, with libel laws being relaxed and new rights to information being established – but with the press reciprocally accepting limits, in particular to the way highly personal pictures are obtained and published. To hope that the issue will go away is no longer possible; the incorporation of the European Convention on Human Rights into English law will provide a body of law that a privacy-conscious public will want to use – and after this week's reaction to the paparazzi the press would be advised to be proactive rather than seen as reluctant partners in responding to demands for more responsibility. The argument that nothing can be done to challenge the status quo because all laws can be evaded in a globalizing world is a council of despair – and not true. Newspapers, like any British citizen within British jurisdiction, must observe British law or suffer the consequences. Globalization is irrelevant.

But Diana's standing was inseparable from her beauty and grace – something which she herself recognized in her ceaseless attention to her fitness, clothes and make-up. She deployed her beauty to support her mastery of her other attributes – to empathize, to feel, to confess and to nurture.

It is a sign of the times that such values, more easily expressed by women than men, are now so dominant in our culture that they have evoked such a thunderous response. The feminist revolution, to which she was the improbable midwife, has come of age.

Monarchy and society alike have been profoundly touched by her life and by her untimely death. We are different from what we were. Whether we will grasp the opportunity to be better is in our own, now lonelier, hands.

Observer, 7 September 1997

PART XI

The Times they are Changing?
New Labour's First Year

A New Era? Definitely

Democracy works. The country, in thrall for so long to a Conservatism that no longer reflected its culture and values – if it ever did – has acted decisively. Voting tactically to hit as hard as they could, the British have buried Toryism for a decade at least, perhaps even longer. The new House of Commons reflects a liberal Britain submerged for too long – inclusive, fair-minded, outward-looking and deeply democratic – and which shows every sign of sticking. Mr Blair and his Cabinet have been given room for manoeuvre and an endorsement the scale of which was beyond their expectations. They now owe it to their electorate to seize the intellectual and political initiative and exercise power as creatively and imaginatively as possible. They have well and truly won; Conservative ghosts can be exorcized.

A defeat of the magnitude the Conservatives have suffered is not just a psephological curiosity. It betrays deep-set trends, and in the Conservatives' case some that have been evident for years. The Tories had not won a parliamentary by-election since January 1989; they had lost a succession of local authority and European elections. The win in 1992 was an aberration, an upward blip in a long-run downward trend. Party membership is dwindling and ageing. The ready access to foreign money to fund the party has turned into a Mephistophelean bargain – excusing the party the necessity of having a strong local organization and ultimately wrecking its political base. Cheques from Hong Kong millionaires do not a political party make.

The weakness in the party's position thus predates ERM membership and runs much deeper; it began in 1988, when the combination of the poll tax and the cuts in the top rate of tax to 40 per cent signalled that the Tories really meant what they said when denying the existence of society, insisting that the rich must have limitless incentives and the poor suffer endless privations. Support was plummeting throughout 1989 and early 1990 as the poll tax riots showed that the British would not accept the degree of unfairness the tax implied. And although John Major's first act on becoming prime minister was to set about scrapping the tax, victory in 1992 deluded him and his party that inequality and unfairness, along with the economic and social conditions that produce them, were not fundamental threats to their political position. Instead the political argument got displaced on to Europe, with results we all know.

But scepticism has not proved a vote-winner. Despite the efforts of the *Mail*, *Telegraph* and *Times*, there was no discernible swing to Eurosceptic candidates; rather it was tactical voting that had far more effect. The electorate may be suspicious of some aspects of European integration, notably the single currency, but that emotion was trumped by another: hatred of the Tories. And that in turn was prompted by another sentiment, remarkably little reported upon – the detestation of the inequality, insecurity and unfairness of the society the Tories have built. That was why there was a landslide on Thursday.

The task of Conservative reconstruction is made much more difficult by seismic changes in the cultural landscape. It has been the party of the Union Jack, allying to itself the symbols of authority – received pronunciation, high social status and even personal deportment – that come with economic and social success. No more. The crowd welcoming Mr Blair to Downing Street waved the flag as enthusiastically as at any Tory party conference, and the British showed on Thursday that they have no truck with the portfolio of attitudes that so frequently comes with the British upper class – homophobia, dislike of Germans, turning a blind eye to sleaze. Tory candidates tried variously to capitalize on these emotions in Exeter (don't vote for a homosexual), Edgbaston (don't vote for a kraut) and Tatton (stand by our man, at least he's one of us); they were all roundly defeated. Moments like those on Thursday night and Friday morning sent collective shivers of pride and humility down millions of spines. We, the people, had acted as we really thought and felt – and against cant and bigotry. It was, simply, magnificent. Liberal Britain was back – and how!

The Labour Cabinet has an immense opportunity to redefine the terms of political debate and recapture the language of political exchange. The frenetic Euroscepticism characterizing the last few years has weak political roots, as the Referendum and UK Independence parties found to their cost. It was rather the complex interaction between a small parliamentary majority and the atavistic instincts of some right-of-centre press proprietors and editors that gave the issue such high political salience – and which has now passed.

But if the constraints are fewer than seemed imaginable a few days ago, there are cautions none the less. Mr Blair won his landslide with a lower proportion of the vote than that with which Mr Wilson lost in 1970; it was the Lib Dem vote taking forty-six Conservative seats and lowering the Conservative vote in over 100 more that secured him his landslide. It was Mr Ashdown's abandonment of equidistance, making it easier for Labour voters to support Lib Dem candidates in the West Country and south-east that was fundamental – along with Mr Blair signalling with pre-election constitutional talks with the Lib Dems that New Labour really was not a tribal party any longer. New Labour in power needs to focus on governing well, and on being unrelenting in maintaining the political coalition it has created.

But if that means standing by the promises that old bogeys are for ever banished, it also means being brave about launching out on a non-Conservative agenda. And here the auguries are already better than seemed likely just days ago. Jack Straw is emerging not as a Michael Howard clone but as a Home Secretary who might genuinely combine rehabilitation and toughness on the causes of crime along with being tough on crime. Robin Cook has set out the terms of an imaginative foreign policy that is genuinely radical and internationalist, and above all constructively engaged towards Europe. Mr Brown will introduce a windfall profits tax that will finance the best-funded attack on long-term unemployment made in Britain. The environment is going to have a higher priority in both Mr Cook's and Mr Prescott's thinking than it has had before. Chris Smith at Heritage will breathe some life into British arts policy, while Frank Field's appointment at Social Security heralds a genuine shake-up. Devolution for both Scotland and Wales heralds the first steps in a vast programme of constitutional change.

The wider question is whether Mr Brown can find the resources to back these initiatives with higher taxation, and whether the party can bring itself to move the basis of British capitalism in a stakeholder direction – two policies that can be relied upon to be greeted with hysteria by the right. But Labour should have wised up after the campaign; hysteria from its political opponents does not mean either that they are right or that they command widespread support. It needs to remember and succour the 62 per cent that voted for change; here is an electoral constituency that, although it has existed for the last decade, has not before been expressed in the composition of the House of Commons. Now it has, and it must be kept together. The early signs are that Mr Blair and his team have every intention of doing just that. We really are witnessing an extraordinary and transformatory moment in British politics. The wilderness years are over.

Observer, 4 May 1997

Break the Locks on Labour's War Chest

The first Labour Budget for eighteen years was riskier than its author let on – even if it did reveal a welcome new set of priorities. True, Britain's public finances now look rock-solid. But that is not the issue.

The money for the welfare-to-work programme, health service and re-building schools is too small-scale, even if a step in the right direction. To make any significant impact on social exclusion and the dilapidated infrastructure, Gordon Brown will find himself relying, like his predecessors, largely on the private sector doing what the state will not or cannot.

It is a gamble. A gamble that the economy will generate jobs and investment in the high-interest-rate, high-exchange-rate phase of the economic cycle. A gamble that the private finance initiative, stalled for years, will finally take off. And a gamble that the public will endure more years of indifferent public provision.

If the gamble fails and the private sector responds less than energetically, the private affluence and public squalor inherited from the Tory years, and the alarming inequalities in British society, will scarcely be dented. And all this while the state is in the strongest financial position since the war to take a different, more proactive stance if it chose.

The government's stance is partly a matter of conviction, partly a tribute to the ascendancy of neo-conservative theories about economy and society, and partly about the success in the US of a range of policies which New Labour is openly copying.

Both Mr Blair and Mr Brown are impressed by the American experience over the last five years – and at one level they are right. The intense squeeze on the US public sector and steady reduction in the budget deficit have been accompanied by a fall in long-term interest rates, low inflation and an investment boom.

The question is whether this pattern will be reproduced in Britain with its own history, institutions, values and incentives – and whether, even if it were, the British are prepared to pay the price of widening social inequality and weakened social provision.

The government's emerging strategy is to get as close to the US model as possible while taking limited measures to ameliorate the social costs within the bounds of fiscal 'prudence' and a conservative consensus it hesitates to challenge. Perhaps it has judged both the public mood and economic options brilliantly. But it could have seriously underestimated the hunger for better public services and overestimated the capacity of the private sector to deliver; if so, the battle ahead will be over whether it uses its considerable scope to spend and borrow – or sticks to its guns.

The first difficulty is that the American boom has more complex roots than simple incantations to deficit reduction and flexible labour markets suggest. The US has enjoyed a long period of low interest rates along with a cheap dollar; by contrast Britain is embarking on its experiment with rising short-term interest rates and a seriously overvalued pound.

Moreover, the US has a critical mass of indigenous industry whereas, apart from pharmaceuticals and some branches of aerospace, Britain's industrial base is decaying.

In his public statements after the Budget, Mr Brown showed he wanted a lower exchange rate. His difficulty is that he has no policy instrument, having eschewed tax rises on incomes and consumption and the introduction of credit restraints, to achieve his aim – even as the need for action grows. Britain's rising consumption and property prices will be carried into a full-blooded boom by the £30 billion of spending power unleashed in building society demutualizations – rather as the two great waves of financial deregulation lifted consumption in the early 1970s and mid-1980s. An 8 per cent interest rate is close to a certainty and senior Bank of England officials do not exclude 10 per cent – signalling an intense economic squeeze.

But Mr Brown has given one major boost to saving and investment: the abolition of dividend tax credits. As people respond by increasing their pension contributions to compensate for the lost tax credits, savings will rise; there will also be a new accent on long-term capital growth rather than short-term dividend gains by institutional investors. It is easily the boldest stroke in the Budget and its impact will be rippling through the financial system long after Mr Brown has moved on.

The welfare-to-work programme, like the government's plans for health and education, is hampered by its poverty. Although the £3 billion plan seems generous at first sight, it is spread over five years. The annual £80 million for the long-term unemployed means only 40,000 can receive the £75-a-week subsidy at any time, and as the successful schemes – like those of the Wise Group in Glasgow – have cost six or seven times as much, the impact on long-term unemployment promises to be minuscule. The assistance for 18- to 24-year-olds is more generous but £700 million to £800 million a year only just exceeds in real terms what Lord Young attempted for the Tories in the mid-1980s.

Given that two-thirds of those currently on employment and training programmes go back to unemployment, while the record of voluntary organizations in employment generation is poor, hopes for lasting success depend on the vigour of the wider recovery. As the Employment Policy Institute warned last week, the government would be unwise to bank on the scheme becoming self-financing or raising the long-run growth rate.

The planned spending on education and health also requires more examination. The £1.3 billion for school building from the windfall profits tax is again to be spread over five years. The £1 billion for education and £1.2 billion for the health service next year are allocations from the contingency reserve that would have been made anyway – and still leave spending lagging behind the projected growth of gross domestic product.

Interestingly the Financial Statement accompanying the Budget gives 2.25 per cent as the maximum for annual public spending growth in a range of simulations. If this genuinely represents the government's thinking, the warnings of the Institute of Fiscal Studies (IFS) that current spending plans cannot be met without a substantial restructuring of the welfare state must be taken seriously.

Britain will not be able to afford simultaneously a growing NHS, rising education spending and an effective system of social security. Something must give. Either the public sector will become more second-rate; or large parts of pension provision and social insurance will be turned over to private, individual insurance; or the government will spend more. It could certainly choose the latter course: the IFS and Goldman Sachs in their pre-Budget briefing took the view that the public finances were on a sustainable footing anyway – and that was before the Budget disclosure that tax receipts would be £5.8 billion higher next year because of faster growth, and before Mr Brown raised another £4.1 billion with new taxes.

In short, New Labour has a war chest of at least £10 billion to spend *each year* – and still leave the public finances on an ultra-sound footing. If it further widened the tax base, there would be up to £5 billion more. Inequality could be narrowed; educational opportunity transformed; inner-city and ghetto estates reconstructed; and the welfare-to-work programme given real teeth.

Previous Labour governments have not had the luxury of such choices; financial panic has forced them into fiscal conservatism and retrenchment. New Labour cannot hide behind such fears. It is rich enough to shed its conservative clothes if it chooses and become a modern social democratic party espousing a genuinely social democratic programme. The question is whether it wants to make that choice.

Observer, 6 July 1997

Labour must Stop Ducking the Issue of Inequality

Britain has become a shockingly unequal society: the top 10 per cent enjoy an income equal to the whole of the bottom 50 per cent. As a country we have the highest proportion of children living in poverty in western Europe. The link between poverty and poor health, family breakdown and indifferent life chances is inescapable. Poverty – grinding, unavoidable, debasing – is the daily reality for a growing number of Britons.

Yet, so far at least, this has had little impact on the political debate. The Conservatives are largely indifferent: the poor don't vote and, if they do, don't vote Tory. In their lexicon, poverty is the down payment a society makes for its success; to attempt any systematic programme of poverty alleviation is by definition self-defeating. It creates dependency, undermines the work ethic, and places an insupportable and unfair tax burden on the better-off. In any case, the notion of a poverty trap is illusory because those in poverty do not stay there long. Those who do are the feckless who refuse to help themselves.

It is telling that, despite its majority, the Labour Party has assumed a similar position. Its manifesto does not talk of redistribution of income, nor of significantly improving the welfare state as a commonly held system of social insurance. Indeed there are pledges on not raising income tax rates and on meeting the Conservatives' tight targets for public spending for the first two years. The only two instruments with which the government has permitted itself to attack inequality – at least early in its administration – are the minimum wage and the welfare-to-work programme. These are important policies, but alone their contribution to alleviating poverty must be limited.

One of the difficulties is that the argument about inequality has been defined exclusively in moral terms. Roy Hattersley believes it the moral duty of the better-off and the Labour Party to extend support to the worse-off; he is opposed by a coalition, extending from Frank Field to David Willetts, which believes that such support undermines the moral obligation of the poor to help themselves. In political terms, such powerful competing moral claims cancel each other out, leaving the better-off in a stronger position. Redistribution, if not backed by political power, needs better arguments than these.

A more solid argument is that inequality is a burden for the rich. Unequal economies and societies are unstable. They make constructing the common system of values and beliefs which underpin any functioning social order much harder – as can be witnessed by living in contemporary Britain. The top 10 per cent can buy themselves such high-quality private education and health care that they cease to have an interest in the education and health care the state provides; they resent the taxes they have to pay for services they will not use. One of the underpinnings of the welfare state – that it is perceived as a structure for everyone – is thus eroded; it becomes a second-best system from which the better-off escape. The boldness which allows them to argue that this escape is a moral obligation for them and the poor helps legitimize their self-interest.

In a sense, New Labour is already a prisoner of the political economy that inequality has created. The famous promise not to raise income tax rates has its roots in the way low taxation is seen by middle England – as an essential component of the way it now lives, and its independence from what the state provides. But in the next breath middle England deplores the inequality it sees all around, and certainly deplores the economic instability which inequality breeds. The violence in the British economic cycle is in part because the pattern of demand is so unsteady – rising sharply in economic upturns as the disadvantaged are pulled into employment, and falling sharply in downturns as marginal workers are sacked and their spending power drops as they rely on income support. This weakens investment and the long-term growth of GDP – and ultimately the position of the better-off.

That is not all. Professor Jonathan Bradshaw's recent work for the Social Policy Research Unit shows 32 per cent of British children live in poverty – and that the growth has been explosive in the last ten years. A cycle of deprivation is at work that will stunt the lives of millions – incubating crime and poor health. To live in an unequal society thus sullies everyone; we become complicit in a system in which fellow citizens are condemned to conditions we would not wish for ourselves, while we accept economic instability and a debased public domain as the inevitable concomitants. We are all worse off.

Yet rather than accept the argument for more equality, New Labour feels compelled to argue for more equality of opportunity – a concept they believe more embracing and acceptable to middle England. Equality of outcome is off-limits in today's political climate; the best hope is to argue for a meritocracy of opportunity – to work, learn and train.

This is fine as far as it goes, but still begs the larger political question. Equality of opportunity requires public structures and public funds, and that in turn requires public spending and taxation; it is redistributive of opportunity – and that is as much a challenge to the vested interests that benefit from the current order as straightforward income redistribution. But Labour's initiatives are hardly robust; there is no longer a duty on employers to provide training as envisaged in the pre-election policy papers, merely a 'right' of young people to ask for training, contingent upon employers having the funds. The welfare-to-work programme is modest in scope, and its reliance on compulsion validates the Tory defence of inequality: that an individual is responsible for his or her unemployment and has made a moral choice in favour of idleness.

Labour must decide where it stands on inequality – and recognize that its alleviation requires the mobilization of resources supported by brave and powerful political arguments. Smuggling in policies does not help; they leave even modest initiatives at the mercy of forces that need to be challenged directly. In eighteen months' time the freeze on public spending will be lifted, leaving Labour with a large financial war chest it can use to improve benefits, health and education. If it wants to change the parameters of debate, it must act. The question is whether it will.

Observer, 3 August 1997

Scotland has to Seize the Day –
for All our Sakes

Scotland must come good – and not just for its own sake. An emphatic double 'yes' in the referendum will unlock the gate that has for so long barred the road to more general constitutional change – for devolution in Scotland will trigger much-needed reform throughout Britain. The urgency of the task has suddenly become apparent. All through the extraordinary scenes following Princess Diana's death the public's impatience with the values and structures of Britain was plain; constitutional modernization is becoming an imperative.

In short, the relationship of Scotland, Northern Ireland and Wales with England needs to be recast if it is to survive. The notion that they can stay forged together as a United Kingdom under one central crown and sovereign parliament – with a centralized bureaucracy and minimal local decision-making – is no longer sustainable.

It is no accident that the votes in Scotland and Wales are taking place as peace talks begin in Northern Ireland, with Sinn Fein at the table, offering the strongest chance since partition of an enduring settlement to a Northern Ireland with devolved political power. Nor is it coincidence that the hardest questions for a century are being asked about the monarchy. The British are feeling their way towards a new constitutional settlement – and if the Scots funk their key role in the process this week, they will let down not only themselves, but the whole country.

The case for Scotland having its own parliament is in any case overwhelming. The national parliament in Westminster does not have the legislative time to pass the many second-order laws needed to address particular Scottish concerns. The Scottish Office needs permanent scrutiny of its actions. Decision-making needs to be brought closer to the Scottish people. There are knock-on consequences for the Scottish economy and society. As political power returns to Scotland, so financial and business power will follow – reversing the long process by which takeover and merger have emasculated Scotland's business community. Equally, the trust and social capital that are an essential component of a market economy need to be constantly replenished, and one of the best means of instilling the values of co-operation and collaboration is through working together in local public initiatives. Scotland will find devolution a means to such rejuvenation.

The counter-arguments are weak or misguided. This is not the first step to dissolving the union with England; last week's mourning for Diana, by uniting the country in grief, showed also that the union between Scotland and England is fundamentally strong at the emotional, and therefore most potent, level. Opponents have also been doing their best to demonize the tax-varying powers, but in truth they are modest and no more than is necessary to instil a healthy sense of fiscal realism. As for the over-representation of Scottish MPs at Westminster, Labour's white paper concedes it can no longer be justified, lancing the issue at a stroke.

Agitation for home rule driven by nationalist sentiment in Scotland and Wales has not yet found a powerful echo in England beyond a generic English nationalism tending to define itself with reference to Europe. However, London has been invited to join the party and, if devolution is successful in the capital, it will be copied in other English cities and regions.

The completion of that process is thus the answer to the West Lothian conundrum that Scottish MPs at post-devolution Westminster will be able to interfere in English issues, while English MPs will be denied the same influence in Scotland. If Britain becomes a federation of regions and states, each with its own parliament, superintended by the federal parliament in Westminster, then all MPs will have an equivalent role.

Such a devolved state would also address the suffocation of Britain's current civic culture, weakened through lack of autonomy for cities, towns and villages. The voluntary sector, which plays a vital role in mobilizing communities to respond to local problems, has too often been denied the support that it needs for security and stability. The local and regional communities need to win back their self-respect and potential for benevolent action.

Home rule, therefore, should hold few fears either for Scotland or the UK. The Scots have always suffered from a certain political and cultural schizophrenia: a resilient national consciousness has struggled with the fear of exclusion from the larger polity. On such anxieties the opponents of devolution have repeatedly played. The same dreary tunes will be heard this week. But Scots should not be afraid. It should not take street demonstrations for the feelings of ordinary people to be made known; they should flow spontaneously into the political system. That means developing new institutions from the grass-roots up. On Thursday Scotland has the chance to begin a process of profound importance for the British state. It must seize the day.

Observer, 7 September 1997

Blair is Forcing us to Make the Hardest Choice

The approval ratings reach new peaks. Formal political opposition is non-existent. Within the Labour Party, few with ambition dare say anything 'off-message'. Every Cabinet member is aware of his or her disposability. Mr Blair is in more control of his government, party and country than even Lady Thatcher at her zenith. It is remarkable, but also, in a democracy, profoundly dangerous. No politician has the monopoly of wisdom to warrant such a monopoly of power.

Yet his dominance is in part deserved. The folklore is that Britain is a very conservative country, but the reality has always been more complex. There is a long-standing progressive liberal tradition, reflected in the past in the fight for political enfranchisement, social improvement and individual happiness – and which was never stilled even at the height of the Conservative revolution. Indeed, the paradoxical result was to make that tradition – with its compassion and enlightened social intervention – seem more, and not less, important.

Blair has seized the new moment with masterliness. The most important part of his conference speech talked of rebinding the liberal and labourist traditions that had split at the beginning of the century – of uniting Keynes, Beveridge, Tawney and Bevan under one political banner. The split in the progressive tradition, as he remarked, is the overriding reason why Britain has been largely governed from the right since 1918.

Hence his overtures to the Lib Dems and his willingness to press on with a modernization of political institutions whose structures, especially the voting system, have so favoured the Tory cause. He understands well the devastating political and cultural impact of putting the Tories out of office for two full parliamentary terms, something which has not happened since 1918. Apart from anything else, it would seal Britain's membership of the European Union – and offer real prospects of European leadership.

In aiming so high he is surely right, but what has propelled him to his astounding poll rating is that he has redefined the objectives of the left – while simultaneously talking the Thatcherite language of individualism, hard choices, the primacy of free and flexible markets, and extreme economic orthodoxy. This is sometimes presented as matching compassion with ambition, and as the third way between the European and American models.

In fact it is neither. Mr Blair is no Tory, in the sense of instinctively favouring social deference, the legitimacy of inheritance, delight in punishment and celebration of pre-modern institutions. He is as much opposed to these as any other Labour leader. But Toryism is but one strand in right-of-centre thought, distinct from the economic and social conservatism to which Blair is wedded – something the right-wing think-tanks and Tory press have understood. This is the deadly ambiguity: Blair is reuniting Keynes, Beveridge, Tawney and Bevan – but only to challenge the essence of what they stood for.

It is important not to overvenerate these great progressive thinkers. Times have moved on, as Labour modernizers stress. Older verities – mutual responsibilities, and that the best form of income support is paid employment – certainly need to be revived.

Early in his leadership, Blair saw himself as doing just that while confronting fossilized British progressive thought with the new realities. No more. His conference speech highlighted the degree to which he has given up on the progressive liberal tradition. He has set his face against the redistribution of income, the social causes of crime, the regulation of markets and the use of the state directly to re-engineer failing economic and social institutions. Instead, he invites his party to enter a world of Samuel Smiles's self-help, Old Testament covenanting, the acceptance of duty and governmental minimalism. He celebrates 'flexible' labour markets in which capital is strong and labour weak.

This discarding of the liberal tradition in the name of 'hard choices' that will reduce public provision and displace risk on to the weak and disadvantaged is not only unnecessary – it is intellectually and politically misguided. Proactive fiscal and monetary policy, Keynesian-style, *is* harder with globalizing financial markets – but it is still possible; moreover Keynes was right to point to a dynamic mismatch between savings and investment flows as the cause of instability in market economies. Disengagement and non-intervention are not a recipe for capitalist success.

Equally, Beveridge's social insurance system may create incentives for dependency and fraud that need addressing. None the less, the most efficient means of insuring for old age and illness remains regarding everyone as insurees. Inequality may be harder to resist in an individualistic culture, but that does not make it any more socially and economically acceptable or efficient. Taxes may be irksome, but rationing or privatization will not conquer social problems.

Moreover, the financial background against which the 'hard choices' are made is uniquely favourable. The OECD projects that Britain will repay its national debt by 2025, alone in Europe. British taxation is among the lowest in Europe as a proportion of GDP. Social security spending is the lowest of all. The country, bluntly, is rich.

The true hard choices are thus to resist the Conservative clamour for an absurd weakening of the public infrastructure, unwanted reduction in welfare help and the unnecessary promotion of private insurance.

In confronting his party with wrong choices that compel it to renounce what it should stand for, Blair will destroy its capacity to represent the British progressive tradition. Education and welfare-to-work are not alternatives to comprehensive social insurance and progressive taxation – they should work hand in hand. Those of us who still believe that Keynes, Beveridge, Tawney and Bevan have something to offer – albeit in a contemporary guise – are also facing hard choices. The growing realization is that we may soon not be able to look to the Labour Party to represent what we believe.

Observer, 5 October 1997

Blair's Big Tent is Now Blowing in the Wind

Big-tent politics allows broad coalitions but tents are not meant to be permanent. We are living through political times which cannot last and which may end in a surprisingly early nemesis. The last week's events over Europe are but the first storm warning.

Blair's government is in danger of forgetting the first law of politics. Square off your enemies but secure your political base by looking after your friends. Without that you are directionless and politically barren.

It is becoming clear that we are witnessing a remarkable act of political transvestism. The leaders of New Labour wish to change it into a party with a genuinely conservative programme. In the absence of any powerful groups arguing for the left's goals of full employment, social justice, equality and the assertion of the public interest, New Labour's development of policy has followed an ever more vigorous conservative trajectory. The crisis over spinning is closely connected to the need to manage the political fall-out.

It must be conceded that on welfare-to-work, or on constitutional change, Labour is meeting its manifesto commitments – a vestigial radicalism dating from its days in opposition. It is only when you look more closely at how policy has developed in government that the degree of the swing to conservatism becomes apparent. Almost no decision since May defines new political ground.

Privatization, for example, continues apace. No-win, no-fee reforms to legal aid mean litigants will have to turn to private insurance before starting potentially ruinously expensive lawsuits; justice is being privatized, with insurance companies' judgements of how a case might develop now more important than those of the courts.

Nor does privatization stop there. The Commonwealth Development Corporation is to be privatized, setting a precedent for sales of 49 per cent of the equity in Channel 4 and the Civil Aviation Authority – all under consideration. When the inventory of public assets is complete we can expect more sales, with the government no more believing in public ownership to secure the public interest than its predecessors. Some sales may be justified, some may not – but the principle defining the difference is not clear.

The rationale for all this is that British public accounting rules make no distinction between current and capital spending, so that the sale of an asset counts as a receipt that will lower current public spending. It is as if it made sense to sell your house to finance your gambling debts. This is classic fiscal short-termism, which the government promised to review but has so far done nothing about.

Thus the already dubious argument for asking students to borrow £1,000 to finance their tuition fees – a fairer mechanism would have been a graduate tax but that contained the dread word 'taxation' – is overturned by the Treasury's refusal to allow any of the revenue to be used for extra university spending.

And so it goes on. There are islands of progress, such as health. Significant new resources have been won and important strides made in public health with the plans for an independent Food Standards Agency. Even the libertarian right accepts that the NHS has to be sustained and that regulation of the food chain must be wrested from the producer interests in the Ministry of Agriculture.

In the main, the story is building on the outgoing administration's thinking. Number 10 seems as wedded to privatization, contracting out and the market principle as John Major. Proposals to strengthen trade union rights are being watered down and flexible labour markets are celebrated. There is intense pressure on the Low Pay Commission to come up with the lowest possible minimum wage with as many exemptions as feasible. Meanwhile there will be no substantive changes to company law, corporate governance or takeover practice.

On European Monetary Union the government considered an early referendum but cavilled before the might of the tabloid and right-of-centre press. There are important reasons for scepticism about the euro, not least the degree to which the British and European economic cycles are out of synch, but a self-avowedly pro-European government should never have found itself in the position of even spinning that it would not join the euro during this Parliament. The government is now in the same box as Major –

sandwiched between a sceptic press and the pro-Europeans and damned to lose control of the political initiative.

The government is in this position because it lacks an idea of what it wants to do with power, whose interests it is serving and what kind of economy and society it wants to build. It makes minimalist statements, or trails them well in advance to manage the reaction because it fears what that reaction might be, not least from its own side.

Into the gap stepped the spinners, telling what their masters intend but in such a way that there can be important course corrections if the process starts to go wrong – just as tomorrow we could well learn that the door is still open to our joining the euro this Parliament, whatever was said last weekend.

The spinning is thus an integral part of the current political story. But it is also destructive. On top of the powerful rivalries in Cabinet is a near-paranoia about who is spinning what to whom, and an anxiety to pre-empt any negative spin with spin of your own. If the political direction were clearer, it would matter less because that would be the bigger political story – and there would be a genuine reason for senior ministers to make common cause.

This is a tinder-box waiting to ignite. The core political base is too narrow; the political objectives are too conservative for a left-of-centre party; the underlying economic rationale for such conservatism is too weak; and the attempt to centralize control of the party too nakedly self-serving. We cannot tell how nemesis will arrive; all you can say is that unless Mr Blair decides to tackle these problems at their root – which he could yet do – a potential political tragedy awaits.

Observer, 26 October 1997

Didn't he Do Well? Well . . . Did he?

Labour, for so long the party whose social heart led to it being labelled as the party of economic mismanagement, is suddenly the party of sound money, fiscal rectitude and economic competence.

But it hasn't lost its heart, say its defenders. It has redefined it. Its new watchwords are individual opportunity and duty, supplanting the old emphasis on solidarity, collectivism and rights and reflecting the new public mood.

And if it is not storming the commanding heights of the economy or even gently reforming some of the institutions of British capitalism, it is doing something more subtle; storming the commanding heights of the state through its programme of constitutional reform. It has met its manifesto commitments, created the conditions for peace in Ireland, sustained its coalition and embarked on a trajectory that is neither old left nor new right. The 'Third Way' is being defined before our eyes, and the electorate like what they see.

But the price, say critics and friends alike, is the loss of any ambition to change the economy and society for the better. Its shedding of socialist ideology and commitments has now gone so far that it cannot even make the modest claim to be a social democratic party. The Third Way only disguises its emergence as a party of the right. The Adam Smith Institute celebrate it as a genuine conservative party; for others, as David Marquand has argued, it has become a British-style Christian Democratic party. It may not be a new Tory party, but there is common agreement that New Labour is a defender of the capitalist status quo rather than its reformer, and a critic of the poor, with their reliance on state hand-outs. Even its radical constitutional programme can be portrayed as no more than could be expected of a bourgeois party committed to modernization and devolved government.

This may strike some as unfair, but the continuity of policy – and even its intensification – with that of the outgoing Major administration is undeniable. The commitment to meet the same spending targets for the first two years of this Parliament is one of the most conspicuous legacies, but the full list makes even more telling reading. Whether on law and order, commitment to lowering corporate taxation, the refusal to enlarge trade union rights, on extending the principle of privatization (notably prisons), on the private financing of public-sector investment, on the retention of selective grammar schools and city technology colleges, on introducing student fees and on preserving the purchaser-provider split in the NHS, New Labour has persevered with Conservative policies.

Indeed in some matters, as David Selbourne has written, Labour has gone further than the Conservatives. Private businesses have been invited to help run twenty-five education action zones; and the new Register of National Assets has been compiled in preparation for the privatization of core areas of government.

And yet, and yet. The unexpected windfall of undershooting the spending targets last year was not spent on lowering inheritance or capital gains tax, as it would have been under the Tories; it was used to help hard-pressed health and education.

Moreover at the margin Labour wants to use its power to benefit the majority rather than the minority, and while Selbourne may scoff at overusing 'people' before every noun – from the 'People's' Lottery to the

'People's' Budget – this is not just spin-doctor-driven populism. A host of micro-decisions away from the public eye, ranging from Jack Straw's policy of community rather than prison punishment for minor offences to Clare Short's interventions over British aid, betray a party whose instincts are more humane than their predecessors'.

And if, to follow Marquand, Labour is becoming a Christian Democratic party aimed at enlarging individual opportunity and – to cite Selbourne – has rediscovered the importance of duty in strengthening Britain's civic order, these are no mean changes. The economism of the Conservatives has given way to a new emphasis on binding society together. There are weaknesses in this approach, notably that it forces individuals to adjust to markets with no parallel attempt to shape markets to meet individual needs, but it is a different economic and political trajectory from simple conservativism.

Yet while Labour has a stronger sense of the need to sustain social capital and the civic order than the Conservatives, it has made so many concessions to the right that its efforts are grievously hampered. Selbourne focuses on how the continued influence of private security firms in the criminal justice system undermines a core notion of citizenship and the common weal; after all, the upholding of law and implementation of justice is the ultimate public good to be undertaken by the state.

To accept that this should be privatized in the name of economic efficiency is to permit a poverty of the public domain that no party in a democracy should accept. Down this road lies civil decay and a new public barbarism.

Moreover, there is a basic flaw in the contention that promoting opportunity and duty can construct a society in which everyone can be a winner. It may have the immeasurable political advantage of excusing the party from any reform of the privileges and operating practices of British business, finance and professions and thus allow the generous incomes of the middle class to go untouched. But to leave the structures of the economy well alone, while lionizing the businesspeople responsible for running it, is to make a number of corrosive assumptions.

The British economy is not a high-investment, high-productivity economy, and this can no longer be blamed on collectivism and Old Labour. Nor is the operation of modern capitalism essentially benevolent. It generates vicious inequality, with job insecurity at the bottom and outrageous incomes at the top. The paradox is that capitalism is simultaneously destructive and creative; the task of a government of the centre and centre-left is surely to minimize its destructiveness and maximize its creativeness.

Yet so enthusiastic is New Labour in its embrace of the market that no such subtlety can exist in its thinking. There is a well-defined strategy to manage the media, the political cycle and the internal processes of the

Labour Party; and there is a generalized attachment to the 'nice' values of human rights, opportunity and duty. But the party lacks any governing ideology underpinned by a distinctive and coherent model of the way economy and society work. The 'Third Way' is supposedly neither free market capitalism nor old socialism, but the advantage of both those models is that they rested on a clear set of guiding principles. Without such principles New Labour risks being no more than a group of well-intentioned men and women making it up as they go along.

Herein lies a tension that is as yet subterranean but which must ultimately surface with damaging, perhaps fatal, results. For there is a choice about the 'Third Way'. It could amount to a philosophy of social liberalism, in which the structures and inequalities of British market capitalism are taken as a given but where the state tries to alleviate the worst effects without challenging or hurting the interests of the advantaged. Or it could become a modern version of social democracy in which there is more determined redistribution from rich to poor, along with a recognition that the institutions of market capitalism can and should be creatively reformed – the broad aim of the so-called stakeholders.

Blair falls broadly into the first camp; Brown into the second. So far their collaboration has been creative, with Blair heading off Brownite initiatives that might offend middle England, while Blair has had to concede that some of Brown's covert redistribution in his last Budget, along with his determination to make welfare-to-work effective, has had positive effects.

But in benign economic conditions the core arguments can be fudged. As it becomes obvious that social exclusion and inequality are deeply embedded in the economy, and that British business is endemically short-termist and averse to investment, the social democrats in New Labour will demand action that the social liberals will contest.

Yet the social liberal wing will not be on strong ground if the programme on social exclusion is palpably not delivering results and the welfare-to-work programme is running out of steam. Blair will want to side with the social liberals, but the underlying and unaddressed weaknesses of the British economy will fatally undermine his case both with the party and the country – and be the cause of his downfall.

This is far away yet, but the British economy has trapped every postwar government in the end. Blair will need to be more clear-eyed about Britain's economic failings than his immediate circle allow him to accept. And more determined about acting than so far his rhetoric has indicated he will be. But even if he does eventually fall because of his economic and social conservatism, he will have bequeathed one inalienable achievement. He will have overhauled and democratized the ramshackle British constitution. For that alone he was worth electing.

Observer, 26 April 1998

Afterword

After the last eleven sections it should now be clear that the problems of Britain's rather special form of capitalism are traceable not only to its unique political and economic institutions, but also to the way those institutions are sustained by an accompanying value system. When the City argues, for example, that 'ownership does not matter', it does not mean it is indifferent to public or private ownership. The City means that it should not matter whether assets in Britain are owned by the British *privately* or by foreigners *privately*. What matters is that the assets are operated 'efficiently', in other words maximizing shareholder value. It is this doctrine that permits the privatized electricity distribution system, for example, to be sold almost entirely to American utilities for the highest price, thus maximizing City fees, on the grounds that the assets have to be held in Britain to discharge their economic function and can hardly be shipped abroad. But as a by-product of privatization, American companies are now responsible for the greater part of the distribution of electricity in Britain. The pricing and investment policies of a central public good like electricity are thus determined by American managers responsible to American shareholders. The tax yield becomes dependent on their wider company structure and approach to the payment of taxes. The assumption is that these interests will necessarily be compatible with those of British consumers because 'economic efficiency' has only one expression and there can be no clash of interests – the kind of claim communists used to make about 'actually existing socialism'. But that there are such clashes of interest is self-evident.

However, not only are these problems not addressed, they are ignored: once it is accepted that 'ownership does not matter', these issues can be written out of the script. A value has been translated into a policy and entrenches the legitimacy and interests of a very particular set of City institutions, takeover practices and even regulatory structures. British regulators, after all, are not supposed to make judgements about ownership; they are mandated simply to monitor the results of the assets under management however they are owned. For them too, ownership does not matter unless it is monopoly ownership; and here intervention is feeble.

Ownership of course does matter, as do the corporate and legal codes under which ownership rights and responsibilities are exercised and policed. In a capitalist economy, the terms on which private property rights are held and exercised are the fountainhead around which a particular market system turns. Their impact radiates through labour markets and the capital markets alike, and spills over into consumer markets. All are linked, and underpinned by a common value system. The dominant values and assumptions of British capitalism and British business include: neutrality over ownership; the imperative of maximizing shareholder value; the economic necessity of the right to sack workers freely; and the right to minimize tax payments by structuring a company to be tax-efficient if necessary through fictitious if legal corporate structures. These values in turn shape the institutions and legal architecture, which feed back in turn into the wider culture. And the economic world is, in its turn, nurtured by social structures and values which are closely linked to the political system and its core values. This is why I have felt that constitutional questions are integral to any wider programme of economic and social renewal. From the point of view of the individual citizen, the acquisition of economic, social and political rights is self-reinforcing and indivisible; the rights to unemployment benefit, high-quality education and public information are not separate but interlinked. And in terms of values, the same holds: obligation-less property rights will produce a business culture with a cynical attitude towards taxation, consumers and workers – and that is much easier if the lines of democratic accountability are weak, so that political authority has little inbuilt constraint. The political constitution becomes the model for corporate constitutions. It all connects.

It is because of this interconnectedness of institutions and values that I regard the stakeholding idea as so important. It is a trump card to use with neo-conservatives, because it compels them to argue for the merits of British capitalism, not in contrast to some unobtainable and unachievable socialist blueprint, but against an idea of capitalism which plainly has more attractions than their own. It immediately makes the agenda more subtle, initiating a debate about a choice of capitalisms, highlighting the degree to which social cohesion and economic efficiency are interdependent, and asking to what degree they could and should be traded off against each other. Instantly the argument is cast in non-conservative terms. Framing contemporary political and economic debates around the notion of stakeholding stresses the values of trust, inclusion, commitment and social cohesion – and demands that neo-conservative notions of the primacy of choice, flexibility, short-term profit-maximization and fatalism about inequality have at least to be qualified, if not discarded. The left could again set the terms of ideological debate.

The right, aware of the political advantage that flows from intellectual dominance, has been very much faster to see the threat and opportunities of the idea of stakeholding than the left. When Mr Blair invoked stakeholding in his Singapore speech in January 1996, the intensity of the reaction and scale of criticism took both him and the then shadow Cabinet by surprise. But in truth it would have been surprising had the reaction been subdued. At last New Labour offered a political economy to accompany the values in which it said it believed; there were now the outlines of a concrete economic and political programme that could be analysed and criticized. But this was too early for New Labour. It felt that the political coalition it was assembling was too fragile to bear the weight of hostile criticism. Its own view of how it intended its values to translate into policy was in its infancy. It feared that some of the criticism might be correct, in which case stakeholding was not the direction in which it wanted to go. The idea was swiftly buried.

Conservative criticism came at the level of high principle and low politics. Stakeholding, it alleged, was failed tripartite corporatism in new clothes. It would imply abandoning the flexibilities of British capitalism for the sclerotic structures of failing Germany. It was a backdoor means for re-introducing union power. Corporate decision-making, currently focused on maximizing shareholder value, would become compromised and muddled in trying to incorporate other diverse interests into company strategies. Conservatives argued that firms should be profit-maximizers, and if stakeholding helped to improve profits, it would be adopted naturally; if not, there was no point in introducing it compulsorily. Whatever else, important commercial freedoms should not be reduced by central fiat in the name of economic and social engineering. Stakeholding was about compelling people to behave in ways they would not freely choose, and as such was descended from a long left-wing lineage of meddling with markets. The British economy was doing well as it was; it did not need any more intervention.

Each of these points could have been rebutted with some ease. Stakeholding is a universe apart from corporatism. It is about implanting codes and cultures within firms and the intermediate institutions in the warp and woof of economy and society, in an attempt to make government-led corporatist initiatives less necessary, because the problems they seek to redress have already been resolved. As for the union bogey, while it is true that employees and unions are seen in a stakeholder context as having rights and interests that should be inbuilt into corporate decision-making, they have obligations as well. In other words, the unions which would be represented in corporate councils would have a very different identity, conception of self-interest and array of responsibilities than the old-fashioned unions of the 1970s. Nor is it reasonable to argue that legislation to establish a body of stakeholder company law is somehow inadmissible because it restricts corporate freedoms, and thus offends some principle of non-intervention in corporate affairs. Companies cannot be beyond the purview of democratic law-making while everybody else is not. At its limits, this is a profoundly anti-democratic doctrine, with the inbuilt asymmetry that the propertied should be above any legislative framework setting out rights and responsibilities, but the disadvantaged should be within it. In any case, companies do have to take the interests of other stakeholders into account, whether they are suppliers, employers or customers. The gains, for example, from any rise in productivity have to be distributed. Company boards have to decide if it is wages or dividends that should benefit, and in what proportion. What is required is some formal recognition of these facts. Making the shareholder interest overriding is an important cause of the short-termism and high financial targets set for British investment projects, with the knock-on consequences for the increasingly insecure terms and conditions under which British employees work.

As for the charge that German stakeholding shows that all stakeholding is misguided; it falls on two counts. First, the German economy is not a write-off. Over the decade its long-run growth rate will have exceeded Britain's. It has suffered from the terms of German reunification, deflation in Europe in the run-up to the launch of the euro in 1999, and the overvaluation of the mark. It is a tribute to the robustness of its underlying structures that it has managed to weather such shocks and still grow. Its labour market and service sector may be over-regulated, so that growth has not translated into rapid rates of job generation, but that does not mean the entire model is failing. Indeed, at present with unemployment falling sharply, production and exports rising strongly, it looks in good health. All this reinforces the response to the second objection; stakeholding does not have to take the German form. There are some institutions in Germany, notably the education and financial systems, that work admirably; others do not. To advocate stakeholding does not mean that Britain has to reproduce the German model in every respect; it means that as we design a British variant, respecting British institutions and culture, there are lessons to be learnt about what does and does not work in other countries.

The Labour leadership could have made these points, but it chose not to. Equally, attacks from the old left dramatized exactly how stakeholding represented a departure from the old right/left exchanges and heralded the politics of the 'Third Way' which New Labour has been seeking to define, which made New Labour's reluctance even more puzzling. The left's concerns mirrored those on the right. To embrace stakeholding meant, it argued, the formal abandonment of any residual ambition to create an economy and society built on socialist principles. Values like inclusion and individual opportunity may be fair enough as part of a wider economic and social programme, but if singled out as the core of the left's values, this would imply a downgrading of the left's long-standing commitment to redistribution of income and wealth and thus to the reduction of inequality. Is it reasonable to focus on trying to bring the incomes of the bottom 30 per cent closer to the average, while leaving intact the disparities of income and wealth at the top? Is inclusion possible without simultaneously attacking inequality? Worse than this, as far as the left are concerned, promoting inclusion would actually weaken the drive to diminish inequality. For example, if the welfare state was designed to attract the middle class as 'stakeholders', that could mean accepting grammar schools and selection in the education system or tiered treatment in the health service. Stakeholding also seemed to rest on soft values like partnership and co-operation, while not recognizing that there are genuine conflicts between interest groups in a capitalist economy. In particular it risked emasculating trade unions while offering them little in return. In short, stakeholding was a sell-out.

All these were and are arguments that New Labour needs to have with its left. But again it chose not to have them, or at least it judged it expedient to introduce its policies bit by bit, rather than within the overarching philosophy of stakeholding. In the same way that the party retreated before the right, so it has temporized with its left. The preference has been to talk in terms of values that underpin policy, rather than to establish a political economy which informs and binds its actions into a coherent whole. This has the political attraction of allowing critics of the left and right alike nothing to get their teeth into. Policies like welfare-to-work are presented in terms of their values: the right placated by the stress on the moral worth of work, the left assuaged by the stress on promoting full employment. As long as there is no wider economic and political framework in which the policy can be located, the critics' guns are spiked. This strategy allows individual policies to be pitched across the ideological spectrum as political and economic exigencies dictate, without risking the charge of inconsistency. Values are much more elastic in political argument than a firm political economy.

The difficulty, however, is that while this allows a pragmatism in policy-making that can be welcome, it prevents the big arguments from being had and being won; and that in turn makes it impossible to establish a central vision and the political coalition to back it. This helps justify the charge that New Labour is a media creation dependent upon the feedback from focus groups to determine each and every policy initiative. This will work in the short run, as it has spectacularly. In the medium term, it can only imply political implosion and ultimate failure. Parties require a strong political base in civil society if they are to sustain themselves. That base can only be constructed if individuals and interest groups know what the party stands for, and the type of society it aims to build.

The left, and the interest groups it represents, together with the liberal centre, need to be persuaded that stakeholding is the only current, practical way of pursuing progressive politics. Focusing on social inclusion and exclusion are not substitutes for promoting redistributive taxation and developing the welfare state. They are, however, one of the most important dimensions of inequality, and the policy cluster aimed at tackling them cannot solely rest on income redistribution. Action is needed on housing, social networks, education, health, diet, sporting and leisure structures and much else besides; minimizing exclusion is not just about redistribution through the welfare system, whose perverse incentives sometimes worsen the situations it was designed to ameliorate.

However, some of the left's concerns are justified. For example, the New Labour suggestion that individual opportunity can be promoted through education, training, greater incentives and subsidies to employers while all else is little changed is not a viable proposition. The concentrations of work-less households fall in areas where there are few private-sector employers. In any case, firms in rich and poor areas alike accept little or no social responsibility for hiring the unemployed, whatever the incentives. Unless the business culture changes, and unless the government can act simul-taneously to marshal the demand for labour where supply exists in such large quantities, promoting 'individual opportunity' will bring scant re-turn. This requires well-directed public expenditure to support a cluster of policies aimed at reviving a depressed private sector and thus raising the demand for labour; everything from improving the operation of the local financial system to encouraging young entrepreneurs. In the last resort, the public sector itself may need to act as an employer, expanding spending in areas like education, health and childcare for which there is proven demand and thus a proven track record of job generation. The task is to lever depressed local and regional economies into a virtuous circle of higher investment, demand, employment and wage rates.

More subtle still is the need to change the business culture, and the opted-out overclass from which it springs. This is, in part, about recasting corporate law, and thus the legal obligations of companies to their stake-holders. It is also about tackling the great institutional drivers of British class attitudes – notably the private school system – which sustain the belief of the propertied that they have no obligations to the whole. It is also why sustaining a welfare state in which all classes have a stake is so important; here at least is one generator of values that upholds a public purpose and the commonweal.

But such an across-the-board, holistic approach is precisely what con-stitutes stakeholding, and what differentiates it from the 'Third Way', as New Labour characterizes its policies. Some of the language is shared, certainly, and some of the policy programme too, but stakeholding de-mands universality in the application of its values. If obligations are to be clearly associated with rights, then that applies to firms and pension funds as much as the long-term unemployed and single parents. If the aim is to promote trust relationships, then the propertied and moneyed cannot evade their part in the process. If social exclusion is to be tackled, it cannot be imagined that this does not imply income redistribution along with em-bedding of values to support it. Individual opportunity cannot be pro-moted when the institutions that provide opportunities are left unchallenged and unreformed. Economic, social and political rights are mutually re-inforcing; which is why constitutional reform is indissolubly linked to any wider reform programme trying to recast rights and responsibilities.

In my view, stakeholding represents the political economy that New Labour lacks to support its value and vision of the 'Third Way'. It is not problem-free. A stakeholder world cannot be allowed to implode into cronyism. Equally, it cannot operate within an over-legalistic and per-manently contested system of top-down legislated rights. The model has to be constructed around accountability and transparency, and operated by managers and workers alike who accept that they make common cause and have a mutuality of obligation; although even that is a difficult concept, because mutuality has to be carefully defined when power relationships are so unequal. But to map the problems does not mean they cannot be solved, especially when the status quo is not without its own problems and structural costs. The acceptance that there may be difficulties in building stakeholding is not an argument for accepting the status quo.

Perhaps the greatest challenge to stakeholding is the manner in which globalization and the power of the financial markets may inhibit one country's efforts to construct a particular capitalism with particular values. Here my view is uncompromising. Too much financial and economic power has gone offshore, and it is no more reasonable to permit power to be organized around market individualism internationally than it is at home. Nor is the development of the international financial markets somehow a force of nature; they are human creations and resulted from choices that nation states have made about how they should organize their financial systems. If we judge that international financial markets are too volatile, powerful and unaccountable then we must act, and that requires collabor-ation at European and global levels. Although I was a critic of British mem-bership of the ERM at DM2.95, and again of the way the EMU project was designed, my criticism was technical rather than structural. The pound was fixed too high; EMU was arranged too quickly and the bias was too deflationary. However, it is only through a joint European response that any individual European country can hope to gain sufficient protection to develop policies particular to it, rather than surrender to the rule of finan-cial markets and the multinationals. It is true that in a single-currency area the members lose the right to adjust their exchange rate and interest rate. In truth they have little autonomy now. What they gain is exchange rate stability, more control of fiscal policy, and the chance to develop national policies that reflect national choices within the overall umbrella of monetary union. Stakeholding is one more expression of European social market capitalism; it will only succeed within an overall European framework constructed to defend the European model.

At the time of writing everything is to play for. The government has launched a radical programme of constitutional reform, and it is more pro-European than its predecessor. Its welfare-to-work programme is an important signal of its intent. It is clear about the values it wants to promote – inclusion, trust, individual opportunity, autonomy and reciprocal obligation. It could, if it chose, pick up the ideas and themes of the articles here and build them into a distinctive political economy that moulds the best of the social democratic tradition of this century into a new credo for the next. Here's hoping.

INDEX